THE CASUALTIES

OF PETERLOO

The Casualties of Peterloo

M. L. Bush

Carnegie Publishing Ltd

The Casualties of Peterloo
M. L. Bush

First published in 2005
by Carnegie Publishing Ltd,
in association with
The Manchester Centre for Regional History

This edition published in 2019
by Carnegie Publishing Ltd,
in association with
Manchester Metropolitan University

Carnegie Publishing
Carnegie House
Chatsworth Road
Lancaster LA1 4SL
www.carnegiepublishing.com

Copyright © M. L. Bush, 2005, 2019

ISBN: 978-1-85936-236-5

All rights reserved
No part of this publication may be reproduced, stored in a retrieval system, or transmitted in any form or by any means mechanical, electronic, photocopying or otherwise, without the prior permission of the publisher.

Typeset and designed by Carnegie Publishing
Printed in the UK by Hobbs the Printers Ltd

Contents

Tables and maps	vi
Preface	vii
Abbreviations	xv

1.	Analysis of casualty	1
	16 August 1819	1
	The surviving casualty lists	4
	A true mirror of the crowd at Peterloo?	13
	Residence of casualties	17
	Occupation of casualties	24
	Casualties of Irish extraction	28
	The judgment on Peterloo	29
	Treatment of the women	30
	Treatment of the men	33
	Treatment of youth and age	35
	Motives for attack	37
	A massacre?	41
	The perpetrators	50
	Payment of compensation	55
	Notes to Chapter I	57

II.	The Peterloo casualty lists	63

	Index	161

Tables and maps

Tables

1	Causes of injury	3
2	Casualty rates per procession – in descending order	11
3	Casualty rates per head of population – in descending order	22–3
4	Male and female casualties	31
5	Male and female injuries with specified cause	34
6	Injuries to the old (50 years of age and over)	36
7	Injuries to the young (21 years of age or under)	36
8	Injuries with specified cause	44
9	Peterloo death list	45
10	Relief dispensed to male and female casualties	55

Maps

1	The epicentres of support	17
2	Manchester 1819, marked with the residences of Peterloo casualties	20–1
3	St Peter's Field, 16 August 1819 and its surrounding streets	51

Preface

This book is intended to present and analyse eight surviving casualty lists, each of them detailing the injuries sustained in Manchester on 16 August 1819 when a huge crowd gathered, peacefully and without weapons, on St Peter's Field to discuss parliamentary reform and, on the orders of the magistrates, were attacked by soldiers with sabres and bayonets, and by police with truncheons and staves. The outcome was at least 654 casualties, eighteen of whom died of their injuries. These lists were drawn up at the time or shortly afterwards: some to excuse the attack; some to emphasise its brutality; some to apportion relief to the victims. Together, these lists offer fascinating information about the victims and their attackers. In recording the names, sex, age, address and occupations of the casualties, they provide detailed evidence about who was there. In revealing the nature of the injuries sustained, and how they were inflicted, they offer a fresh insight into what actually happened and who was at fault. The event was central to the slow achievement of parliamentary democracy in Britain, as well as indicative of the commitment to this cause of working people in the North West. For this reason the contents and message of the casualty lists have a vital significance which reaches far beyond the Manchester region and must appeal to all with an interest in early nineteenth-century British popular politics. Furthermore, the detailed information the lists offer on a large number of ordinary persons renders them a very useful quarry for family historians seeking detailed personal information in a period when the census records have survived only as statistical overviews and therefore offer no alternative.

The casualty lists were first appreciated by G. M. Trevelyan who urged their publication as long ago as 1922, but without effect. Eventually, they were examined by Malcolm and Walter Bee in a trenchant essay entitled 'The Casualties of Peterloo', published in *Manchester Region History Review*, iii (1989). The purpose of this book is to put Trevelyan's recommendations into practice and, by careful analysis of the lists, to build on the foundations laid by the Bees.

Thanks are due to the University of Manchester John Rylands Library in Deansgate; the Local Studies Unit of the Manchester Central Library; Chetham's Library, Manchester; and the Working-class Movement Library, Salford, all of which have fine collections of original material on Peterloo. A number of scholars have helped me in this work. In response I offer thanks to R. W. Jones and Gina Bridgeland of the Gott Library of Dissent and Radicalism in Brighouse,

Yorkshire; to Michael Powell of Chetham's Library; to Tony Taylor of Sheffeld Hallam University; and to Terry Wyke, Alan Kidd and Douglas Farnie of Manchester Metropolitan University. In addition, I offer a special thanks to Malcolm and Walter Bee whose analysis of the same casualty lists prepared the way for this study. The work was carried out under the auspices of the Manchester Centre for Regional History and its director, Melanie Tebbutt. I am grateful for its support and encouragement. The book is dedicated to the residents of the city of Manchester, my former home for forty-one years.

Wanstead,
London,
February, 2004.

Preface to Second Edition

The comments and acknowledgments made in the preface to the First Edition still stand fourteen years on, as do the findings of the study itself, which Douglas Farnie, pre-eminent historian of the Lancashire cotton industry, generously described as 'a small masterpiece of impeccable learning'. However, in the light of further research and cogitation, several revisions and corrections have become necessary: hence, a second edition.

In the study of Peterloo, a strong urge has prevailed to tell the story, even though Donald Read accomplished this task in 1958 with compelling clarity and convincing scholarship. Since then, at least five narrative histories have appeared of the same event (see below, p. 57, note 4), none of them, however, adding much, apart from some fascinating detail, to Read's original account. This concentration on providing a narrative has led historians to neglect somewhat the task of analysing the surviving evidence, allowing several important questions to go unanswered. Moreover, much of the analysis carried out so far has been driven by the need to pass judgment upon the event. Is it aptly termed a massacre? Or, as Read suggested, should this term be placed in inverted commas to imply a possible overstatement? While accepting Peterloo as an atrocity, historians and journalists nonetheless continue to downplay the significance of the casualty figures, partly by suggesting that the major source of injury was inflicted by the crowd upon itself as it fled the field, and partly by comparing Peterloo with other popular disturbances that, likewise, involved death and injury in their suppression. In making these comparisons, the tendency is not to compare like with like but to relate a mass demonstration, which sought to make its protest peacefully, within the law and without resort to arms, to popular protests which were, by nature, uprisings and which, without scruple, were prepared to used force to obtain their way by riot or rebellion. To compare, for example, the Gordon Riots of 1780, or the Bristol Riots of 1831, with Peterloo, and to suggest that, in the latter, the protesters were leniently treated because the amount of damage inflicted upon life and limb was much less than in the former, is false reasoning. The treatment of the peaceable crowd at Peterloo was equivalent to a massacre because an unarmed gathering of men, women and children who in no way intended violence, came under brutal physical attack, sustaining terrible injuries, from a troop of 1500 soldiers, equipped with cavalry, sabres, pistols, field cannon and bayonetted muskets, aided by a police force of around 500 men, armed with truncheons and staves.

Because of their concentration upon narrative and their focus on judgment, historians have, arguably, allowed certain important aspects of Peterloo to suffer neglect. One is the attitude of the crowd, an expression of large-scale support for Radical Reform in a region where, twenty years earlier, loyalism had reigned supreme and the violence committed had come from loyalist mobs assembled to proceed against the cause of reform either by burning Paine in effigy or by taking action against the property and persons of prominent local reformers. With loyalist activists now dwarfed by the numbers of workers prepared to support Radical Reform, local authority could easily perceive that it had no choice but to assert itself by other means. Peterloo could be seen as a desperate attempt on the part of the loyalist interest to make a come-back. How and why this conversion of loyalism to reform came about remains a mystery, but one that requires a thorough exploration.

Another neglected but important feature of the reformist crowd relates to its occupational character. To what extent were those in attendance factory operatives servicing powered machinery? A striking feature of the casualty evidence is the large proportion of persons, injured on the day, who would have worked not in the large mills but from home or in small workshops and on handoperated machinery (see below, pp 25–7). This impression, however, was drawn from a limited data base of known casualties which, amounting to 660 individuals, constituted only one tenth of the assembled crowd. The evidence of attendance, on the other hand, could be much extended by including not only those known to be present but also those who, because of their residence and reformist affiliations, were likely to have been there on the day. This would allow the addition, for example, of the 280 heads of households who signed a letter of requisition to the boroughreeve and constables of Manchester concerning a parliamentary reform meeting on 16 August 1819 (*Manchester Observer*, 7 Aug. 1819). A much larger cache of relevant names, moreover, could be collected by assuming the presence at Peterloo of men and women from the north-west region who publicly declared themselves for Radical Reform in the early 1820s. From the north-westerly supporters of Richard Carlile, a London journalist present at Peterloo and much appreciated by Mancunians for his denunciation of the massacre, 1700 names could be added to the tally of those in attendance at the meeting (see Michael Laccohee Bush, *The Friends and Following of Richard Carlile* (Diss, 2016), Table A, pp.165–6). There also could be added another mass of names, from the same region and for the same short period, who declared themselves followers of Henry Hunt or William Cobbett. In other words, the number of named persons who were, in all likelihood, present at Peterloo could be increased enormously. With research specifically conducted on these named individuals, our knowledge of the character of the crowd, as to residence, gender, age and occupation, could be spectacularly improved, creating a sample far superior to the one we currently have, which is, predominantly, a compilation of the injured and those who stood witness at the ensuing trials.

Further light could be thrown on Peterloo and its suppression by regarding it not in isolation but as the culmination of a succession of large-scale reformist meetings that extended back to 1816 and achieved a remarkable concentration in the North West between January and August 1819. Encouraged by Cartwright, Wolseley and Hunt, people demonstrated, vigorously but not violently, in favour of universal suffrage. At these meetings, the protesters declared their own identity and purpose by means of ritualised procedures that were quite distinctive from those associated with loyalism. The latter tended to be socially cohesive – for example, processions to beat the bounds or to carry the rush cart, or to celebrate a royal event, or in connection with Orangemen parades or those associated with the Odd Fellows – whereas the former were characteristically working-class and bent on achieving a socially divisive programme of political change. Peterloo played a significant part in this development in the sense of representing an attempt to draw different communities into a regional union, thus preparing the way for the possibility of a fusion between different regions to achieve a national movement for parliamentary reform. With all this in prospect, the action taken by the Manchester and Salford magistracy at Peterloo, and which the government evidently condoned, was incited by the need to snuff out a progression of organised remonstrance that, although peaceable, was apparently threatening to get completely out of hand.

It is well-known that the eye-witness evidence for Peterloo is considerable; and of late a Peterloo Witness Project has sought to identify and quantify the full extent of it, coming up with over 300 items (see Robert Poole (ed.), *Return to Peterloo* (Manchester, 2014), p.133). But a serious problem lies in the quality of this evidence. The reports of spies in Home Office files are obviously suspect since they were not only uncorroborated but produced in return for a system of payment conditional upon the extreme nature of the material. Yet frequently they have been employed as if they were reliable evidence. Moreover, virtually all eye-witness evidence is flawed by partisanship through the prejudicial need of witnesses to support either the loyalist or the reformist cause. In fact, the two versions of Peterloo that emerge from the eye-witness record only agree in one respect: that is, on the enormous size of the crowd, with the loyalists stressing the fact to justify the action taken against it; and with the reformists doing likewise to show that their cause commanded considerable support. Otherwise, the two versions are consistently contradictory: for example, on important issues such as whether or not the crowd was armed and prepared for physical violence; and whether or not the presiding magistrates, and the troops and police at their command, conducted themselves responsibly and efficiently on the day. Two scenarios arise from such evidence, one, of a battle from which loyalists emerge victorious over a lawless mob; the other, of a slaughter of the innocent in which law-abiding reformism is crushed by lawless tyranny. Clearly, while of great importance, eye-witness accounts are fraught with difficulty, obliging the historian to avoid taking their message at face value, and to proceed, comparatively and sensitively, to sift out telling details as to motivation, procedure, composition and outlook.

While the procedure of demonstration has been well researched, with plenty of information unearthed on the use of flags and their mottoes, addresses and their contents, and on the appearance of the crowd in terms of dress and conduct, less accomplished is the research done into the motivation of those in attendance. To what extent, given the crowd's support for parliamentary reform by universal suffrage, was the demonstration simply a political one, an impression formed in recent years by a tendency to react against E. P. Thompson's attempt to characterise Peterloo as a 'class war' (see his *The Making of the English Working Class* (Pelican, 1968), pp. 752–3). Ostensibly, the protest had a political grievance to the fore in demanding a house of commons elected by universal suffrage. But that does not rule out the presence of social complaint; and it might well be argued that the proposed political reforms were a device to improve the condition of the productive part of society not only in relation to the government, through transforming the tax system to make it progressive rather than regressive, and therefore less oppressive of the poor, but also in relation to the nonproductive part of society and its imposition of high rents, low wages and social contempt.

The debate continues unresolved on the impact of Peterloo. Weighing against the claim that it was a major step in the development of British democracy is the enormous delay of ninety-nine years to implement its central demand for universal suffrage. Moreover, did Peterloo matter all that much as an historical event? It is far from certain. Could it, for example, be said to have made parliamentary reform inevitable or even to have inspired later movements, such as Chartism, to press for one man one vote? After all, for the demonstrators, Peterloo marked a humiliating defeat. It seemed to indicate that peaceful demonstrations, no matter how large, achieve nothing by way of reform. Shelley might intone: 'Ye are many, they are few', but what difference would that make if the people did not 'Rise like lions after slumber'? The lesson of Peterloo appeared rather to propose: for the sake of success proceed by other means. But this lesson was consistently ignored, suggesting that Peterloo had a formative impact only through an inability of the British people to learn from its mistakes. Its contribution to reform can therefore be easily overstated; but it should not be completely denied. If it was not to show the way, Peterloo played some part in the process of parliamentary reform by revealing, and by luridly illustrating, that, in spite of the checks and balances of its mixed constitution (with the hereditary principle complemented by the elective principle) and in spite of its social cohesiveness (resulting from a respect for degree engendered by social mobility, and from the deference of the poor upheld by the charity and paternalism of the rich), and in spite of the country's ancient liberties, supposedly the envy of the world, old-regime Britain was, nonetheless, yet another tyranny. This exposure was compounded by the measures the government felt obliged to take to ensure that Peterloo did not reoccur: that is, by passing, shortly afterwards, the Six Acts and by maintaining a standing army, stationed in garrisons attached to the larger towns, to curb unrest, and by creating a professional police force to preserve order, a device quickly branded as a second standing army and therefore another instrument of despotism. A well as branding loyalism with tyranny, the other main effect of Peterloo was to place women, for the first time, as activists on the political stage (see M. L. Bush, 'The Women at Peterloo', *History*, 89 (2004), pp. 231–2).

The striking features of Peterloo were not only that a huge crowd gathered on the day in peaceable and legitimate array to support a sophisticated programme of parliamentary reform (designed to make government directly answerable to the people and therefore more likely to respond to its complaints), and for doing so was butchered by the military, but also that the ensuing massacre was authorised by the magistrates of Manchester and carried out by prosperous Mancunians serving as volunteer cavalrymen and volunteer constables. Whereas the crowd were working people, beset by poverty as they clung to old artisan ways undermined by the development of a factory system of production, their attackers were an affluent group of property owners, clergymen in civil office, publicans, pawnbrokers, small manufacturers and shopkeepers who were either unaffected or favoured by the economic changes of the time. What one group of Mancunians deliberately did to another group of Mancunians, as well as to others, was quite outrageous, causing a magistrate in 1972 to describe Peterloo as 'an incident about which the city could feel little pride'. No wonder its commemoration in the city over the last two centuries has been somewhat muted. Nonetheless, it certainly does not deserve to be forgotten. For these reasons, the recent plans of the Manchester City Council to give it better recognition, on the occasion of its bicentenary, are to be welcomed and warmly applauded. If only to remind us of the need for civility, it surely must be remembered.

As with the First Edition, the Second Edition owes much to the sponsorship and financial assistance of the History Department at Manchester Metropolitan University, for which the author is deeply grateful.

M. L. Bush,
Wanstead,
February, 2019

Abbreviations

Bamford, *Passages*	Samuel Bamford, *Passages in the Life of a Radical*, two vols. (London, 1844).
Baines' *Lancashire Directory*	Edward Baines, *History, Directory and Gazetteer of the County Palatine of Lancashire* (Liverpool, 1824), two vols.
Bee	Malcolm and Walter Bee, 'The Casualties of Peterloo', *Manchester Region History Review*, III (1989).
Bruton	F. A. Bruton (ed.), *Three Accounts of Peterloo by Eyewitnesses* (Manchester University Historical Series, 1921).
Gauntlet	Richard Carlile (ed.), *Gauntlet: a Sound Republican London Weekly Newspaper* (10 February 1833 – 30 March 1834).
MCC Report	Metropolitan and Central Committee Appointed for the Relief of the Manchester Sufferers, *Report with an Appendix Containing the Names of the Sufferers and the Nature and Extent of their Injuries. Also an Account of the Distribution of the Funds and other Documents* (London, printed for William Hone, 1820).
Newgate Magazine	*Newgate Monthly Magazine or Calendar of Men, Things and Opinions* (1 September 1824 – 1 August 1826, printed and published by Richard Carlile).
Peterloo Massacre	*Peterloo Massacre ... edited by an Observer* (Manchester, printed by James Wroe, 1819).
Report, Lees Inquest	Joseph Augustus Dowling (ed.), *The Whole Proceedings before the Coroner's Inquest at Oldham etc. on the Body of John Lees, who Died of Sabre Wounds at Manchester, 16th August 1819* (London, printed by William Hone, 1820).
Report, Hunt's Trial	*The Trial of Henry Hunt, John Knight, Joseph Johnson, John Thacker Saxton, Samuel Bamford, Joseph Healey, James Moorhouse, Robert Jones, George Swift and Robert Wilde for an Alleged Conspiracy to Overturn the Government etc. by Threats and Force of Arms* (London, printed by Thomas Dolby, 1820).

Report, Redford v. Birley Trial	*Report of the Proceedings of the Trial in King's Bench between Thomas Redford, plaintiff and Hugh Hornby Birley, Alexander Oliver, Richard Withington and Edward Meagher, Defendants, for an Assault on 16th August 1819. Taken from the Shorthand Notes of Mr Farqharson* (Manchester, C. Wheeler and Son, 1822).
Rylands	University of Manchester John Rylands Library, Deansgate.

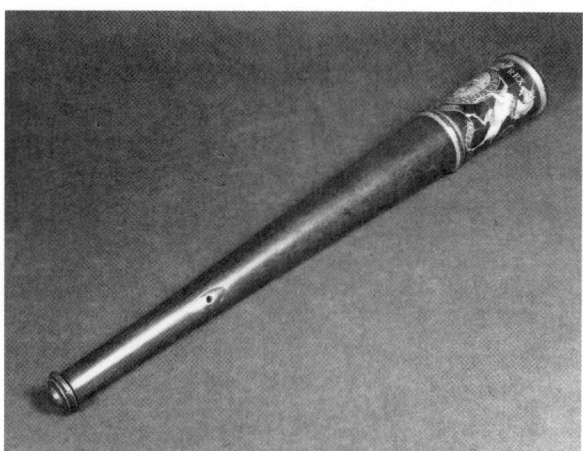

Truncheon as used by the constables to club people as they fled from the field.
MANCHESTER LIBRARY AND INFORMATION SERVICE: MANCHESTER ARCHIVES AND LOCAL STUDIES

1 Analysis of casualty

16 August 1819

On a perfect summer's day in August 1819 – as a faint breeze cooled the heat of the noonday sun and gently lifted the flags to display their mottoes and emblems – a huge crowd, mainly of working people, gathered peaceably on St Peter's Field in Manchester to discuss parliamentary reform under the chairmanship of Henry Hunt, Esq., the leading advocate of universal suffrage. The people present came from not only Manchester but also the surrounding manufacturing districts: notably those centred upon Salford, Bury, Bolton, Failsworth, Chadderton, Middleton, Rochdale, Oldham, Royton, Saddleworth, Ashton and Stockport. While some were drawn to the meeting by Hunt's magnetic personality and ready wit, most attended in the belief that the political reforms he proposed would – essentially by making government policy more responsive to the interests of the people – relieve them of the terrible poverty currently oppressing their families and communities which, although broadly attributed to unemployment, low wages and the high price of consumables, they principally blamed upon a corrupt political system and the favours it showered on those that controlled it, especially by permitting them to go undertaxed and over-rewarded with sinecures and pensions taken from public funds.

Conspicuously present at the meeting were women, the breeze dishevelling their long hair as they enthusiastically doffed their hats to cheer. They attended not only as individuals but also as members of all-female contingents, dressed distinctively in white and bearing their own flags. Although women comprised a small portion of the crowd, the manner in which they organised themselves made them particularly noticeable.[1]* Responsible for it was the recent creation of female reform societies in the North West. Formed in June and July 1819, they were the first established in Britain. They soon adopted a ritualistic procedure in which, at reform meetings, their members would occupy the speakers' platform and then present to the chairman a flag or cap of liberty accompanied by an address from the women that was read out, usually by a man, to the assembled crowd.

The intention at Peterloo was to reenact this ritual. For the purpose, several women, including Mary Fildes, chairperson of the Manchester Female Reform

---

* The notes for this chapter appear from page 57.

Society, mounted the platform with flags and prepared statements. Before it could take place, however, the crowd, on the instructions of the magistrates, was savagely dispersed, the work of cavalrymen charging with drawn and recently sharpened sabres, backed up by the truncheons of the constabulary and by the bayonets of the infantry. The outcome was the injury of at least 654 persons and the seizure and destruction of nearly all the reformers' flags and caps of liberty. The terrible aftermath was vividly captured by a reporter on the *Manchester Observer*, who on the day 'saw six coaches, three carts and three litters loaded with the wounded' on the way to Manchester Infirmary; and by *The Star* whose correspondent reported that on the following day:

> All the roads leading from Manchester to Ashton, Stockport, Cheadle, Bury, Bolton are covered with wounded stragglers, who have not yet been able to reach their houses after the events of Monday ... There are 17 wounded persons along the Stockport Road; 13–14 on the Ashton Road; at least 20 on the Oldham Road; 7or 8 on the Rochdale Road, besides several others on the roads to Liverpool.

The reporter from the *Manchester Observer* had noted that the vehicles taking the wounded to hospital in Manchester had included 'some of the girls dressed in white who were on the hustings'.[2] Among the casualties women figured prominently, most of them wounded by sabres, bayonets, truncheons and horses' hooves rather than simply injured in the crush of the crowd. (See Tables 1 and 5)

At the time of Peterloo, women had suddenly acquired a disturbing public face, the result of their recent intervention in the field of political reform. It was viciously portrayed in contemporary cartoons and newspaper accounts of reform meetings which presented them as sluts and drunkards who had forsaken their femininity and neglected their families. The aim of these female reformers was deeply suspect: no less than a radical topsy-turvydom that would reverse the traditional code of gender to place woman on top. With female reformers seen in this extreme way, the authorities at Peterloo felt threatened by a double revolution: one which would place the propertyless in charge; a second which would end male rule. As they saw it, the social distinctions that held society together were in danger of destruction as working men assumed the role of gentlemen and women behaved like men. The brutal treatment of the crowd at Peterloo stemmed from such primeval fears. For men of property everything was at stake – not only their possessions but also their masculinity. In these critical circumstances, stern action was necessary. To safeguard the current regime, male reformers, it was felt, deserved a violent lesson; and female reformers had to be taught that, if they behaved like men, they would be treated as such, with all gallantry gone and no quarter shown.

Table 1. Causes of injury

Injuries sustained	Male	Sex unknown	Female	Total no. of injuries
Unspecified cause	56	2	18	76
By sabre [a]	188	1	31	220
By truncheon	42 + 5 [b]		21 + 2 [c]	70
By bayonet or butt	15 [d]		1	16
By shot	8		1	9
Shot or sabred	28		5	33
Trampled by horse	110 + 26 [e]		46 + 6 [f]	188
Crushed by crowd	92 + 4 + 26 [g]	1	57 + 6 + 2 [h]	188
Injured by horse or crowd [k]	52 [i]		12 [j]	
Truncheoned or crushed by crowd	9		4	
Misc. injuries [l]	2		1	3
Number of injuries inflicted [m]	602	4	196	802

Notes

[a] Including the baby William Farren who was dropped and injured when his mother was sabred. 91 of the males and 13 of the females in this category sustained other injuries as well, inflicted by weapons or horse or crowd pressure.

[b] Including 17 males who were also sabred. See note [k] to explain the figures added.

[c] Including 1 female who was also sabred. See note [k] to explain the figures added.

[d] Including 3 males who also received other weapon wounds.

[e] Including 35 males also injured by weapons. See note [k] to explain the figures added.

[f] Including 8 females also injured by weapons. See note [k] to explain the figures added.

[g] Including 42 males also injured by weapons or horse. See note [k] to explain the figures added.

[h] Including 21 females also injured by weapons or horse. See note [k] to explain the figures added.

[i] Including 28 males also injured by weapons.

[j] Including 1 female injured by weapon.

[k] For purposes of calculation the injuries in this ambiguous category are shared between 'trampled by horse' and 'crushed by crowd'. The same goes for the injuries in the 'truncheoned or crushed by crowd category' which are divided between 'by truncheon' and 'crushed by crowd'.

[l] 1 male 'cut by an artillery man'; 1 male killed by mob on 18 Aug.; 1 female kicked by a constable.

[m] Because the injured often sustained a number of injuries, their number was much less than the number of injuries inflicted. Of the 654 known to have suffered injury, 482 were men and 168 were women, with four of unknown sex.

The surviving casualty lists

The principal evidence for the injured at Peterloo lies in the casualty lists compiled at the time or not long afterwards. Of the eight surviving lists, six were completed by January 1820, a seventh by 1831 and the final one by 1844. Between them they furnish detailed information on the number of casualties, along with the names, addresses, occupations and ages of the injured, the nature of the injury and of its infliction. G. M. Trevelyan trumpeted the significance of the casualty lists as long ago as 1922. Writing in *History*, he recommended that 'some learned society' should publish the most detailed list, on the grounds that 'it is an historical document of great importance'.[3] But nothing was done.

The spate of books published on Peterloo over the last sixty years certainly used the lists, but essentially as illustrative material and without subjecting them to analysis.[4] The latter was first attempted by Malcolm and Walter Bee in a brief, rigorous, precise, statistical essay, published in 1989, the findings of which amply justified Trevelyan's premiss that, if studied carefully, the casualty lists would demonstrate incontrovertibly the brutality of the attack upon the crowd. Producing a casualty figure of 630, the Bees showed that the injured far exceeded previous estimates, set at about 400. They also showed that police and soldiers caused a majority of the injuries, whereas it was previously thought that most came of being crushed in the crowd.[5] Yet the aim of their analysis was not really to prove whether or not a massacre had occurred, but rather to extrapolate

Drawn and etched by the Manchester reformer James Wroe. It shows the initial attack upon the crowd by the Manchester Yeomanry, with other cavalry in the distance preparing to charge. To the right is the speakers' platform with Mary Fildes holding a banner surmounted by a cap of liberty. Alongside is Orator Hunt. The houses to the right are on Windmill Street; those to the left are on Mount Street. Clearly visible are the top hats worn by the male reformers, the white dresses worn by the women reformers. To the left of the platform the banners of the reform unions are displayed.
MANCHESTER LIBRARY AND INFORMATION SERVICE: MANCHESTER ARCHIVES AND LOCAL STUDIES

from the casualty lists information on the size and composition of the assembled crowd.

The surviving lists fall into three categories. Those in the first category relate to contemporary calculations of injury based on admissions to Manchester Infirmary. They include a list of persons treated at Manchester Infirmary on 16 and 17 August.[6] Published in *Wheeler's Manchester Chronicle* for 21 August, this list contained 29 names, along with place of residence and a brief discription of the injury. The incompleteness of this list was revealed in a closing reference to a further 40 outpatients. Seemingly commissioned by the Manchester magistrates, this list's purpose was to demonstrate that the troops and police had conducted themselves with moderation: by revealing that serious casualties were few and far between, that sabre wounds were infrequent and that most injuries were inflicted by the trampling of horses and the crush of the crowd. In other words, it proposed that the injuries suffered at Peterloo were due to unfortunate accident, not brutal deliberation, and that, rather than the fault of the weapons wielded by soldiers and police, they were largely inflicted by reformers upon their own kind. An exculpatory note attached to the printed list declared:

> Of the 40 [outpatients] who applied during Monday and Tuesday and were dressed, by far the greatest part were hurt by falls, by being ridden over and crushed. There appears to be very few instances of sabre wounds among this class of patients.

That this list of names was far from complete was confirmed in the Infirmary Register Book which recorded that, following the 29 treated on the Monday, two of whom died, a further 34 were treated on the Tuesday, one of whom died. By 25 August it was known that 70 casualties had received treatment at the Infirmary. The chief magistrate at Peterloo, William Hulton, admitted as much to Lord Sidmouth, the Home Secretary, yet saw it as 'proof of the extreme forbearance of the military'.[7] This figure fell far short of those hospitalised: as the *Manchester Observer* reported on 30 August another sixty had been treated at Salford Infirmary.

Provoked by these blatant attempts at cover-up, and especially stung by a letter from Hulton to the *Manchester Courier*, which sought yet again to minimise the number of casualties, the lawyer Charles Pearson, a friend of Henry Hunt and fellow reformer, set out to show that the Peterloo casualties admitted to Manchester Infirmary were grossly unrepresentative of those injured. Aided by Sir Charles Wolseley, Pearson in late August conducted a thorough five-day investigation which produced the names of 209 casualties. Although further names were still coming in, he closed the list on 30 August, sending it to Reverend William Hay, the Salford magistrate who, three days after Peterloo, had hurried to London to inform the Cabinet of what had happened and to show that the Manchester magistrates were not to blame.[8] Pearson arranged for its publication in *The Times* on 3 September.

Pearson's list simply identified the casualties by name and categorised them according to injury and sex. It showed who was wounded by sabre or shot; who was trampled by cavalry; and who was truncheoned by the special constables or crushed by the crowd. In each category men and women were listed separately; and severe cases were marked with a bracketed 'b' after the name to indicate that they had been badly injured. The aim, then, was to show that the crowd was dispersed with great brutality. Yet the list failed to make this point as effectively as it might, mainly because one of its categories contained, without differentiation, both victims of the truncheon and persons simply injured by the crowd, while another category ran together people injured by horse or crowd.[9] In conducting the investigation, he and Wolseley were especially moved by a visit to a village, a community of 50 houses, where a Quaker surgeon showed them 42 persons injured at Peterloo, ten of them by the sabre. Pearson vaguely located the village as in the neighbourhood of Manchester, but three days later Wolseley, in a letter to *The Globe*, identified it as near Oldham. They visited the village on 29 August, drawing up their list the following day. There can be no doubt, then, that the list included the casualties of this village who therefore must have comprised almost a quarter of its names. In the light of this evidence, Pearson reckoned that not fewer than 500 were wounded on the day and condemned the crowd's treatment as 'a carnage'.[10] He failed to provide information on residence, but this is supplied, for all but 56 of his 209 names, by other surviving casualty lists. Moreover, 42 of the 56 named on his list without a known residence must have come from the above-mentioned village near Oldham, although it is not possible to work out who they actually were or which village it was.

Falling into a second category were casualty lists that the radical journalist, James Wroe was mainly responsible for. Like Pearson, he aimed to show that Peterloo represented a massacre of the innocent, not a commendable exercise in crowd control. He compiled two lists, one published in a weekly journal entitled *Peterloo Massacre*. Appearing in two parts, one on the 14th and the other on 21 December 1819, this list named 392 casualties.[11] His second list, printed in the *Manchester Observer* for 22 and 29 January 1820, named 567 casualties: somewhat fewer than the 614 declared in his published total.[12]

Wroe offered his two lists to the public as alphabetical accounts of 'persons killed, wounded and maimed'. Improving on Pearson's list, they supplied, for many of the casualties, a place of habitation and frequently an exact address. The two lists differ from each other in the following respects: the *Peterloo Massacre* list gave a brief account of the injuries sustained but included only the seriously injured and those who had died of their injuries, thus omitting about 200 casualties; whereas, the list from the *Manchester Observer* included the slightly, as well as the seriously, injured, but made no mention of the dead, and also failed to specify the character or cause of the injury.[13] How Wroe came by his evidence remains unclear. Some of it, however, must have arrived in response to the request he placed in the *Manchester Observer* for 13 November 1819, inviting people to tell the paper how they had suffered at Peterloo; and further information was drawn, in all likelihood, from the findings of the Manchester Relief Committee, a body set up to administer financial support for Peterloo victims.[14]

Falling within the same category was a list published in 1831 by Henry Hunt in his journal *Henry Hunt's Addresses to Radical Reformers*. He produced it in response to a recent remark from William Hulton that the injuries suffered at Peterloo were inconsiderable and that the only death to occur was of a woman claiming to be the Goddess of Reason. This list was mostly a copy of Wroe's *Peterloo Massacre* list. However, it added the names and addresses of a further 15 casualties, making a total of 407 (not the 439 claimed by Hunt). As Hunt acknowledged, the list only included the badly wounded. In addition, he suggested that two hundred further casualties were known to have occurred; and over and above the known casualties were 'those who concealed their wounds and had them cured by their own surgeons'.[15]

Also belonging to the same category is the only surviving local casualty list, the work of Samuel Bamford and published in the conclusion to chapter 36 of his autobiography *Passages in the Life of a Radical* (1844). Its declared purpose was to reveal the injuries suffered by those who 'went with the Middleton party'. Of the 16 people listed, 12 come from around Middleton, with 2 from Rochdale and 2 from Blackley. Bamford assumed that Ellen Evans and Ellen Walker, both from Blackley, were different women when, in fact, they were the same person, making a total of 4, not 5, female victims. He also added up wrongly the male casualties: there are 12 men listed, not 11. Because two of his names (Thomas Kershaw and James Weir) appear in no other list, and because the details he provided of Ann Collinge's injury cannot be found elswhere, Bamford's list is useful. Nonetheless, it is not a complete tally of the known victims from Middleton or from Rochdale and Blackley, for other lists supply the names of 7 additional Middletonians, plus 1 for Rochdale and 1 for Blackley.[16]

A final category of casualty lists relates to the dispensation of relief. Two lists of this nature have survived, both the work of the Metropolitan and Central Relief Committee, a body established in London in October 1819 to administer the funds subscribed nationally for Peterloo victims.[17] The first list, in manuscript, appears to be a revision made to a list now lost and originally drawn up by the Manchester Relief Committee, a body founded within a few days of the event. It records the relief dispensed by the Manchester Relief Committee, as well as some dispensed by the Rochdale Relief Committee, on the left-hand side of the page and, on the right, further payments, presumably from the Metropolitan and Central Relief committee, which were often described as 'final'. The second surviving list in this category was published, along with a report, by the Metropolitan and Central Relief Committee, and provides an elaboration, in tabulated form, of the manuscript list.[18] The purpose of both lists was to record the allocation of money raised for the victims of Peterloo. The compilers of both lists were under severe constraints to be accurate, having no wish either to compensate the undeserving or to be found guilty of making false claims.

The Manchester Relief Committee operated from the Church Street warehouse of Archibald Prentice, a local businessman and Radical Reformer. By 11 October 1819 it had uncovered over 400 casualties, the result of 'a careful and rigid inquiry' lasting several weeks. One of its members, John Edward Taylor, revealed that as many as 579 cases had been considered, with 421 of them authenticated 'by strictest personal investigation'. Of the latter, 161 had sustained sabre wounds which were sufficiently severe as to stop their victims from working; and 104 were women wounded by weapons. So far, he claimed, ten deaths had resulted from the injuries sustained; and two of the wounded had gone insane, causing one of them, a woman, to cut her own throat.[19] In the course of October the Manchester Relief Committee compiled a list – now lost – of these authenticated cases, with names, addresses and details relating to age, occupation, children and the nature of the injury, all of which was taken into account when distributing relief. By November this list contained the names of 410 victims and the committee had dispensed relief to over one hundred of them.[20] It was handed to the Metropolitan and Central Relief Committee when, on 5 November, the latter sent a deputation to Manchester to dispense the money it had so far collected. The deputation comprised Joshua Rayner and R. W. Hall, with G. W. Service acting as secretary.[21] Proceeding with great thoroughness, it visited five hundred homes, checking the evidence from the Manchester Relief Committee. This proved a trying task, mainly because several victims identified by the Manchester Relief Committee had changed address and were therefore difficult to locate: so much so that the deputation had to extend its stay by three weeks in the attempt to track them down.[22]

In all, the deputation spent six weeks in the North West, checking the evidence of casualty and dispensing relief. The outcome was a manuscript list which named 333 injured and another 9 persons who had suffered imprisonment. In this period application for relief came from people who for fear of reprisal had previously concealed their injuries, furnishing information on an extra 200 casualties. Before returning to London, the deputation was to relieve 60 of this number, leaving the remaining 140 cases for the Manchester Relief Committee to expedite.[23]

Based on the findings of its deputation to Manchester, the Metropolitan and Central Relief Committee published its own list in January 1820. It identified 420 casualties. Essentially, this list contained all but 4 of the casualties named in the manuscript list plus a further 90, 60 of whom were the additional applications that the deputation had managed to process.[24] In view of its willingness to omit 140 names, the Metropolitan and Central Relief Committee seemed primarily moved by the need to be seen administering relief with due propriety rather than by the need to depict a massacre. Consequently, the list has to be regarded as the most reliable of all the surviving lists, in spite of its incompleteness. As for the names it omitted, they were, in all probability, included in Wroe's *Manchester Observer* lists for January 1820, but without information on age, number of children, occupation or injury. When published, the Metropolitan and Central Relief Committee's list was accompanied by a report which, in summarising the evidence, spotlighted two features that appeared to demonstrate gross misconduct by the cavalry: of the 420 known casualties 113 were women and 130 had suffered 'severe sabre wounds'.[25]

Put together, the eight lists provide a tally of 654 casualties – a number far in excess of Read's estimate of 'about 400' and well above the figure of 600 that reformers such as Archibald Prentice cited at the time in order to stress the enormity of the attack. They also reveal a death toll of 18 (see Table 9) instead of the normally accepted 11.[26]

However, even this revised total must leave many casualties unaccounted for. This is because of two distinctive features evident in the surviving lists. First, the lists contain a very high proportion of people who lived in and around Manchester. Of the 596 names with some sort of address, 364 came from Manchester and its immediate vicinity and 282 from the narrow confines of the manor of Manchester: that is the township bounded by the rivers Irwell, Irk and Medlock. We know, however, that large numbers of reformers came to St Peter's Field from the Ashton-under-Lyne area, yet only 30 casualties were recorded as resident in that area; likewise, for the large party from the Rochdale area, with only 4 recorded casualties. A much more substantial number, 90 casualties in all, are known to have come with the massive party from Oldham; but almost half of that casualty figure were residents of one small village, whereas the procession from Oldham to Manchester had included people not only from around Oldham itself but also from Royton, Crompton, Saddleworth, Lees and Mossley. The likelihood, then, is that local relief records had existed and were either lost or have been only partially incorporated in the surviving casualty lists. The latter appeared to be the fate of the records kept by the Rochdale Relief Committee which were cited in the first list drawn up by the Metropolitan and Central Relief Committee but only with reference to 4 casualties resident in the Royton area. The casualty rate for the Rochdale area is incredibly low when compared with other centres of Peterloo support (see Table 2). This discrepancy is only explicable in terms of lost evidence.

Also casting doubt on the capacity of the surviving lists to provide a complete tally of casualties is that, in the evidence they offer, the seriously injured amount to twice the number of the slightly injured. Common sense, however, would suggest just the opposite, proposing that the slightly injured should easily exceed the badly injured. A range of evidence reveals how people kept quiet about their injuries in order to avoid dismissal at work, denial of poor relief, discrimination

Table 2. Casualty rates per procession, in descending order

Starting point	Size of procession	Number of casualties	Casualty rate
Stockport	1500 [a]	50	1:30
Oldham	6000 [b]	90	1:67
Ashton	2000 [c]	30	1:67
Middleton	3000 [d]	21	1:143
Bury	3000 [e]	13	1:231
Rochdale	3000	4	1:750 [a]

Notes

[a] Estimates vary from 1100 (Moorhouse, see *Report*, Trial of Hunt, p. 130) to 1400–1500 (Philips, *Exposure*, pp. 20–1), to 4000–5000 (Entwisle, see *Report*, Redford v. Birley, p. 452). Entwisle, in all likelihood, ran together as one the parties from Stockport and Ashton. This was easily done as they entered Manchester at roughly the same time and followed the same route (London Road–Piccadilly–Mosley Street) to St Peter's Field.

[b] This procession was a composition of separate contingents, each organised by the Reform Societies of Royton, Crompton, Chadderton, Saddleworth with Mossley and Lees, Oldham and Failsworth, so it must have been very substantial and was undoubtedly the largest to arrive. Estimates vary from 600–800 (Brierly, see *Report*, Redford v. Birley, p. 48), to 5000–6000 (Harrison, see ibid., pp. 27–8), to 6000–8000 (Hibbert, see ibid., p. 172). The lowest figure cited appeared to be a count of the numbers of men marching in ranks, whereas each procession was accompanied and magnified by large numbers of 'stragglers' who sometimes joined the ranks but mostly walked alongside. See Travis in *Report*, Trial of Hunt, p. 55. The size of the party must have differed between what it was when starting out at Oldham and what it was when finishing the journey at Manchester, thanks to having been joined en route by a party from Failsworth (Harrison, *Report*, Redford v. Birley, p. 35).

[c] Estimates vary from 2000 (Mills, see *Report*, Trial of Hunt, p. 77) to 4000–5000 (Hulton, *Report*, Trial of Hunt, pp. 100–1). Hulton, however, was probably committing the same mistake as Entwisle (see n. a) in failing to distinguish from each other the parties from Ashton and Stockport.

[d] Estimates vary from 6000 (see Samuel Bamford, *Passages*, I, p. 200) to 2000–3000 (Morris, see *Report*, Trial of Hunt, p. 52). The Bamford figure includes the contingent from Rochdale which Morris claimed was roughly the same size as the Middleton contingent (ibid., p. 52), rendering 3000 a reasonable estimate.

[e] Estimates made were from 3000 to 4000 (Rothwell, see *Report*, Trial of Hunt, p. 248; Heath, see *Report*, Redford v. Birley, p. 327).

by benefit societies, or imprisonment. This point was made by the deputation of the Metropolitan and Central Relief Committee. To explain a large number of late applications, it commented: 'these poor people had very sufficient causes for their apprehensions'. The same point was made by John Edward Taylor who, speaking for the Manchester Relief Committee, claimed that the numbers wounded at Peterloo were much greater than those reported 'because many persons have endeavoured ... to conceal the circumstance of their having been at the meeting'. The wisdom of concealment was made evident in the cases of persecution that the casualty lists cited.[27] Thus James Chapman, a labourer resident in Salford who, wounded by a cavalryman and crushed by the crowd, was unable to work for ten weeks, claimed to have been refused relief by the parish officials of Pendleton because of his presence at the meeting. Jonathan Clarke, a hatter of Reddish, near Stockport, with seven children, one newly born, was unable to pay the rent after a sabre wound inflicted at Peterloo had put him out of work. Branding him a reformer, his landlord had seized his goods and chattels in lieu of the rent unpaid, selling them for the miserable sum of £2 4s. 0d. After being trampled upon by cavalry, Joseph Hepstonstall, of Stockport, was refused relief by his sick club simply because his injuries had been incurred at an illegal meeting. James Lees of Delph, a weaver of twenty-five, was admitted to Manchester Infirmary with two severe sabre wounds to the head; but then, for refusing to confess to the chief surgeon that 'he had had enough of Manchester meetings', he was denied treatment and expelled from the hospital. Betty O'Neale, a seventy-nine-year-old of Salford, who, having been badly trampled by the crowd, was carried off the field unconscious, refused to apply to the infirmary for treatment thinking that to do so would publicly identify her as a reformer and lead to her imprisonment. Simply, then, as a result of admitting one's attendance at the meeting, relief and treatment could be denied. What is more, jobs could be lost. William Marsh of Chorlton Row had six children, three of them working in Birley's factory. Sabred on the field and unable to work for six weeks because of his wound, he found that Hugh Birley, commander of the troop of Manchester Yeomanry that had first charged the crowd, had given all three children the sack on account of their father's presence at the meeting. It made good sense, not only for magistrates but also for their victims, to conceal information on wounds and injuries; and, arguably, when injuries were relatively slight, they could be that more easily hidden.

A final shortcoming of the surviving lists lies in their compilers' inherent hostility towards the military. Prepared to admit the names of injured Special Constables, they excluded the names of injured soldiers. Thus ten constables appear in the lists (i.e. John Ashworth, Robert Campbell, James Chesworth, Robert Darbyshire, William Evans, Henry Froggatt, William Harrison, Samuel McFadden, a certain Mr Petty and John Routledge), eight of them injured by cavalry and two by the crowd, but, apart from John Hulme, no mention is made of the 67 soldiers allegedly struck by sticks and stones, nor of the 20 injured horses.[28] No matter, the strong likelihood of lost, omitted and undeclared casualties means that the tally of wounded and injured at Peterloo must have exceeded 700 persons.

A true mirror of the crowd at Peterloo?

How useful is this casualty evidence? The Bees accepted it as a valid sample of those present at Peterloo. According to them, one could confidently extrapolate from the lists the proportion of women to men at the meeting; the proportion of children to adults; the proportions of participants from Manchester and other North West townships; the occupations from which they were chiefly drawn; and the crowd's age profile. The same casualty evidence, they thought, could also be used to estimate realistically the overall size of the crowd.[29]

But several doubts arise. For instance, the Bees assumed that, because the women comprised one-third of the victims, they therefore must have formed one-third of the crowd. But they overlooked the fact that a higher proportion of women to men sustained injury. Various calculations were made by men present at the meeting of the numbers of women present. All reveal the Bees estimate to be a gross over-estimation. The eye-witness, Robert Mutrie, put the proportion of women to men as forming one-tenth of the incoming parties and less than one-twentieth of the crowd on the field itself. Hunt reckoned that, in a crowd of 150,000, women numbered about 20,000, so between one-seventh and one-eighth. Contemporary estimates of the proportion of women attending individual contingents make the same point. For the Bury contingent, it was put at one-eighth; for the contingents from Oldham, Royton and the High Moors, one-sixth; for the contingents from Stockport and Ashton, one-tenth. Furthermore, children tended to be included with women in these calculations, rendering the proportion of women even lower. Rather than one-third, then, the proportion of women overall could not have exceeded one-eighth.[30] In all likelihood, a higher proportion of women to men were injured, partly because of their position on the ground – that is, with many close to the hustings, especially on the raised ground that bordered Windmill Street where a quick escape was impeded by the density of the crowd and the uninterrupted line of housing – and partly because of the indiscriminate manner in which the crowd was attacked, with no consideration shown for the fairer sex.

Position in the crowd was, in all probability, also important in determining the residential patterns evident among the injured. It is well known that the people from outside Manchester came to the meeting in processional parties, each drawn from a different area. Those coming to the field via Shudehill and Deansgate – such as the processions from Oldham and Bury – massed west of the hustings in the direction of Deansgate; and those coming in via Piccadilly and Mosley Street – such as the processions from Middleton, Stockport and Ashton – occupied the area to the east and north, in the direction of the continuation of Mount Street and Peter Street.[31] The first three processions to arrive – from Ashton, Stockport and Oldham – formed a tight protective cordon round the hustings.[32] This must account for the high casualty rates each suffered – 1 in 67 for Ashton,

1 in 30 for Stockport and and 1 in 71 for Oldham – as calculated by dividing the numbers estimated to be in each party by the number of injured each party sustained. Later processions to arrive – from Middleton and Rochdale, for example – came to be positioned at the perimeter of the crowd that surrounded

the hustings, over towards the Friends Meeting House in the north and the line of housing along the continuation of Mount Street in the east where the crowd remained thinly scattered even after all had assembled.[33] Able to find space in which to flee, they suffered a much lower casualty rate of 1 in 143 for Middleton and 1 in 750 for Rochdale (see Table 2). The same may well have been true for the Bury party, positioned away from the hustings towards Deansgate, which suffered a casualty rate of 1 in 308.[34]

Yet the question remains of why so many casualties were from Manchester and its immediate neighbourhood? Manchester people came to the field in two ways: many came individually and in small, neighbourhood groups. Arriving early, they used their local knowledge to take up an advantageous position on the raised ground behind the hustings and over towards Windmill Street. From there they could get a good view of the processions of outsiders as they poured on to the field as well as an oversight of, and proximity to, the hustings, which happened to be placed over to that side. It was in this densely packed area that many injuries occurred as the cavalry pursued the crowd, forcing the people to press against the railings of the houses in Windmill Street and tumble in heaps down the cellar steps as the railings gave way under their weight. In addition Mancunians formed part of the protective guard which accompanied Hunt to the field and who therefore arrived after the crowd had formed.[35] Another component of this guard had been the Middleton/Rochdale party which had been assigned the vanguard of Hunt's procession into Manchester. Heading the Hunt procession, they had marched along Blakely Street (now Dantzig Street), past St Michael's Church to turn left into Miller Street; but then became disconnected from Hunt through

Printed on cotton and based on the Wroe print, this image depicts the scene at a slightly later stage, with people knocked to the ground as they flee in the direction of Peter Street and the Quaker Meeting House.
MANCHESTER LIBRARY AND INFORMATION SERVICE: MANCHESTER ARCHIVES AND LOCAL STUDIES

failing to turn right down Shudehill. Instead, they continued along Swan Street to New Cross, turning right along Oldham Street to Piccadilly. As a result, whereas Hunt reached St Peter's Field via Shudehill and Deansgate, the Middleton/Rochdale party reached it via Mosley Street, arriving at least a quarter of an hour earlier.[36] In contrast, the Mancunian guard, prominently displaying a contingent of women in white, stuck by Hunt. With the crowd opening to admit Hunt's carriage, they were able, by following in its tracks, to take up, in spite of their late arrival, a position close to the hustings on the Peter Street side.

In addition, the predominance of Mancunians in the casualty lists must also have reflected the size of Manchester's population as well as the ease with which its people could get to the ground. It also stemmed from the radicalisation of its inhabitants, a process which had transformed the mentality of the town in the previous twenty years. Not so long before a dedicated subscriber to Jacobitism and violent practitioner of 'church and king' anti-Jacobinism, the town's working population had now become a major power-base of Radical Reform: the northern equivalent of what Birmingham was in the Midlands and London was in the South. Finally, the disproportion evident between the injuries sustained by Manchester residents and elsewhere may reflect the manner, already described, in which the lists were drawn up and have managed to survive: the result of the role of the Manchester Relief Committee and of James Wroe in furnishing names and the possibility that relief records for other large townships have failed to survive. For this latter reason, it would be unsafe to assume that the information the lists offer on residence reflects with any precision the proportions of supporters provided by the various townships of the North West.

Also questioning the existence of a simple correlation between injury and the character of the crowd is the large number of entries in the casualty lists which fail to give age and occupation. For age, this amounted to 48 per cent; for occupation to 58 per cent of all entries. Partly responsible for the latter's high omission rate was the frequent failure to supply the occupations of women: in fact, only 7 per cent of female casualties listed are assigned a trade. However, even if the male casualties are studied separately, the lists still leave 48 per cent with occupations undeclared. A trawl through trade directories for the period fails to remedy the matter. Adding this directory evidence to the data base provided by the casualty lists causes the casualties with unspecified occupations to fall only from 58 to 50 per cent – not enough to make a dependable sample. In sharp contrast, for gender only 4 casualties out of 654 are unspecified. For residence the information is also very good: the Bees found that only 10 per cent of the listed victims lacked a specified place of habitation. In fact, because 40 names in this category are known to have come from the Oldham area, this proportion falls to 3 per cent.

Residence of casualties

For a variety of reasons, then, the casualty lists could hardly be said to provide a true mirror of the Peterloo crowd. Yet the lists undoubtedly shed vital and vivid light on its background, especially in relation to residence, about which they make two challenging points. The surviving eye-witness accounts – the other major source for the study of the people at Peterloo – are inclined to emphasise the spectacular processions bringing reformers in from Ashton, Stockport, the Oldham area, Bury, Middleton and Rochdale. (See Map 1) By doing so, they give the impression that support for the Peterloo meeting mostly came from outside Manchester.[37] The predominance of outsiders was commented upon by several Mancunians, but they were bent on reclaiming Manchester for loyalism as well as on freeing its inhabitants from blame. It was therefore very much in their interest to depict the meeting as an invasion of Manchester by strangers.

Roger Entwisle, an attorney-at-law stated that he saw 'very few Manchester people on the ground'. Robert Mutrie, a merchant from Union Street and a

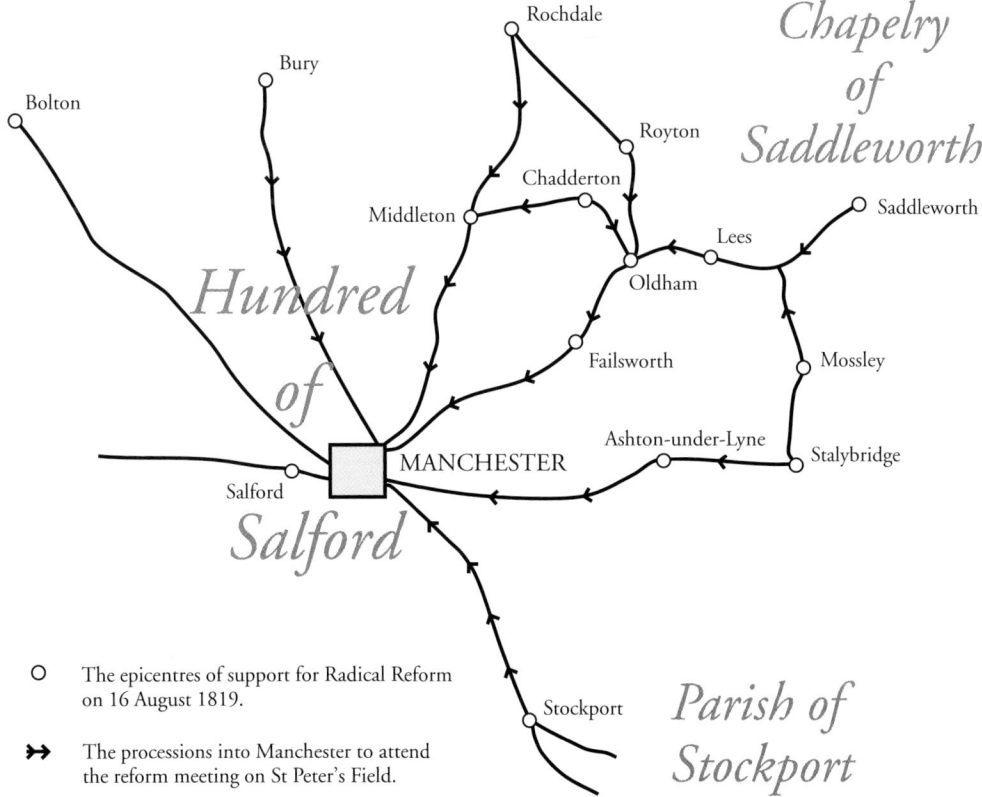

○   The epicentres of support for Radical Reform on 16 August 1819.

➤   The processions into Manchester to attend the reform meeting on St Peter's Field.

Map 1. The epicentres of support.

Special Constable, claimed that the people coming to the meeting 'appeared to me to be all strangers'. Edward Owen, another attorney, described the crowd on the field as consisting mostly of strangers, with 'the townspeople [standing] on the outside of the meeting as much as they could'. Robert Hall, a salesman in cotton, claimed that the crowd was formed by large bodies of people coming in 'from the country'. The Reverend Hay, a chief magistrate who had surveyed the meeting from a house overlooking the field, calculated that two-thirds of the crowd 'were strangers to Manchester'.[38] A contrary view was presented by the reformer John Shuttleworth, a local cotton manufacturer, who estimated that two-thirds of the crowd were Manchester residents; by William Thelwall, a builder from Lloyd Street, who claimed to have seen on the field 'a great number of Manchester people there, my townsmen and neighbours'; and by John Smith, a journalist for *The Liverpool Mercury*, who declared that many attending the meeting appeared to be 'inhabitants of Manchester from their dress and conversation'.[39] Exposing the reckonings of Mutrie, Owen, Hall and Hay as loyalist myth, and suggesting that even Shuttleworth had underestimated the number of Mancunians present at the meeting, is the fact that Manchester residents comprised 47 per cent of the injured (i.e. 282 out of the 596 casualties with places of residence specified) while constituting no more than 21.7 per cent of the population of the region from which the Peterloo crowd had been drawn.

If the casualty lists fail to define the precise residential composition of the crowd, they establish beyond all doubt the predominance of Manchester residents at the meeting. In addition, they reveal that the other participants were drawn from a much more extensive range of areas than the incoming processions would suggest.[40] They also indicate, much more specifically than the eye-witness accounts, the residential connections which existed between participants from a particular area. In the Manchester area – thanks to the fact that the actual addresses of the casualties are given – the lists reveal how they came from densely populated, working-class areas within the town itself; whereas in the surrounding mill-towns, they appeared to be heavily drawn from the neighbouring countryside.

In Manchester itself, the localities with the greatest number of casualties were as follows: New Cross – 80; Ancoats – 80; Deansgate – 38; Piccadilly – 37; Shudehill – 35; Bank Top – 32; around Miles Platting – 19; around St Michael's – 17; Newtown – 8 (see Map 2).

The same evidence shows that very heavy casualties were sustained by the inhabitants of certain streets: with 113 from the close vicinity of Great Ancoats Street; 10 from Cropper Street crossed by Pump Street, close to Miles Platting; and 8 apiece from the adjacent Loom and George Leigh Streets, both in Ancoats. The large number of casualties drawn from certain areas and streets of Manchester suggests not only that these streets and areas provided many participants of the meeting but also that, within Manchester itself, people came to St Peter's Field in communal parties which tended to stick together when there.

In addition to the 282 casualties from Manchester, a further 82 came from close by: mainly from Salford (36), Chorlton-upon-Medlock (10), Failsworth (9) and Ardwick (7). Another nine communities close to Manchester suffered between 1 and 3 casualties each: that is, Barton-upon-Irwell, Cheetham, Crumpsall, Flixton, Gorton, Hulme, Levenshulme, Rusholme and Stretford. This means that, of the casualties whose residence is known, 61 per cent came from within a three-mile radius of the centre of Manchester. What is clear is that the inhabitants of the parish of Manchester were especially affected by injuries received at Peterloo. (See Table 3) The same can be said for the residents of the manorial borough of Manchester. Among townships a higher rate of casualty was only evident in Failsworth, another constituent part of Manchester parish.

The casualty lists reveal that the Lancashire people attending the meeting were drawn from a very extensive area, with casualties recorded as far afield as Lancaster and Burnley. According to eye-witness accounts, their recruitment was transmitted through a series of epicentres situated to the north and north-east of Manchester: notably Bury, Rochdale, Middleton, Failsworth, Chadderton, Royton, Oldham, the Saddleworth–Lees–Mossley area and Ashton-under-Lyne, each of which had its own reform society and banner and organised on the day its own march into Manchester. They also make the point that large numbers were expected from Darwin and Blackburn but failed to arrive.[41] All this is confirmed by the casualty lists. But these lists also reveal a substantial attendance from the region north-west of Manchester as well: from Bolton, which suffered 19 casualties, and from Salford and its extensive neighbourhood of Whitefield, Prestwich, Irlams o' th' Height, Eccles, Pendleton with Charlestown, Pendlebury, Tyldesley and Worsley, with a total of 61 casualties.

Lancashire south-east of Manchester also furnished participants, notably from Reddish and Heaton Norris, evident in a total of 8 casualties, all but one, however, from Heaton Norris. Some of these participants were recruited by the incoming processions. For example, the Stockport procession on its way to Manchester must have attracted support in Heaton Norris, Reddish and Levenshulme; while the Bury procession must have enlisted people from Unsworth, Whitefield, Prestwich, Crumpsall and Cheetham. Incoming processions had the same effect to the north-east and east of Manchester, with the Middleton/Rochdale party recruiting support in Blackley and Newtown; the combined Royton/Oldham/Saddleworth parties drawing followers from Failsworth and Miles Platting; and the Ashton party enlisting support from Dukinfield, Droylsden and Ardwick. A large number of Lancashire communities, however, became involved in the Bolton or Salford manner: that is, unaided by an organised procession and simply because, either out of commitment, curiosity or business, some of their residents decided to visit Manchester on that

Map 2.
Manchester 1819, marked with the residences of Peterloo casualties

Table 3. Casualty rates per head of population, in descending order

By parish	Population[a]	Casualties[b]	Casualty rate
Manchester[c]	186942	364	1:514
Middleton	12793	21	1:609
Oldham	52510	82	1:640
Stockport	44957	49	1:917
Ashton	25967	28	1:927
Saddleworth/Quick[d]	13904	10	1:1390
Eccles	23331	16	1:1458
Bolton	50197	19	1:2642
Bury	34581	13	1:2660
Rochdale	47109	4	1:11777
By township or chapelry			
Failsworth	3358	9	1:373
Manchester[e]	108016	282	1:383
Crumpsall	910	2	1:455
Rusholme	913	2	1:456
Ardwick chapelry	3545	7	1:506
Stockport	21726	39	1:557
Cheetham	2027	3	1:676
Royton chapelry	4933	7	1:705
Salford	25776	36	1:716
Chorlton Row[f]	8209	10	1:821
Heaton Norris chapelry	6958	7	1:994
Middleton	5809	5	1:1162
Pendleton	5948	5	1:1190
Hulme	4234	3	1:1411
Blackley chapelry	2911	2	1:1455
Bolton town and chapelry	31311	18	1:1740
Oldham	21662	5	1:4332
Ashton	9222	2	1:4611
Bury	10583	2	1:5292

Notes

[a] These figures are taken from the 1821 census. Since the population of the region was growing rapidly over the previous decade, it would have been considerably less in 1819 and, for this reason, the casualty rate would have been generally higher at the time of Peterloo.

[b] Confined to casualties whose residence is identifiable.

c   These statistics include the township of Salford.
d   Technically it was a chapelry belonging to the parish of Rochdale, but here treated as a separate unit.
e   This is the old township defined manorially and kept separate from Ardwick, Chorlton Row, Hulme etc.
f   Alias Chorlton-upon-Medlock.

momentous day. On the other hand, important centres of parliamentary reform in Lancashire – notably Blackburn, Leigh, Wigan and Liverpool – failed to feature in the casualty lists. From their omission one can reasonably assume that their residents either failed to attend or did so in such small numbers as to make little difference to the character of the Peterloo crowd.

Besides identifying the range of participation in Lancashire, the casualty lists reveal attendance of people from Cheshire, Yorkshire and Staffordshire. Judged by the number of casualties, the participants from Cheshire were predominantly from Stockport, with 39 recorded, and its parochial suburbs of Edgeley, Gee-cross, Little Moor, Bullock's Smithy, Hyde, Dukinfield and Chadkirk supplying another 10; but some support also came from Macclesfield (1 casualty), Warrington (2), and Northwich (1). Support from Yorkshire was mainly raised by the Reform Union of Saddleworth, Lees and Mossley and mostly drawn from the relatively populous parish of Saddleworth with Quick which straddled the Lancashire/Yorkshire border (10 casualties). Leeds, Huddersfield and Ripponden suffered casualties, but only one apiece, suggesting a very limited participation. The same could be said of Staffordshire, reflected in two casualties from Burslem and one from Newcastle.

The processions into Manchester were organised by the reform societies of the larger mill towns. This gave the impression that they were manned principally by the inhabitants of these towns. The casualty lists, however, suggest that this was not so. For example, of the 30 casualties associated with Ashton-under-Lyne, only 2 came from the town itself. The remainder lived in villages and townships around Ashton: Charlestown (13 casualties), Hurst (4), Smallshaw Green (1), Taunton (2), Boston (1), Littlemoss (2), Haughton Green (1), Droylsden (2) and Dukinfield (2). The same was true of the other towns which organised processions into Manchester. Of the 24 casualties explicitly associated with Oldham, only 5 lived in that town; of the 21 casualties associated with Middleton, only 5 resided there; of the 13 casualties associated with Bury, only 2 were resident. In each case, the majority of casualties came from nearby villages, a reflection of the durability of the textile industry in the countryside, sustained by the survival of weaving as a domestic operation.[42]

Occupation of casualties

In seeking to identify the occupational background of the Peterloo crowd, the Bees claimed that 'the large "unspecified" category' in the casualty lists 'does not seriously weaken the conclusions drawn', even though they had to admit that 62 per cent (i.e. 384 of the 619 casualties they had traced) were of unknown occupation.[43] In point of fact, the number of casualties with occupations unknown is not as large as that, thanks to the evidence of trade directories; but, a problem remains. Of the 482 male casualties, 229 (48 per cent) are given no specified occupation in the casualty lists; and a trawl through contemporary trade directories

This print was commissioned by the London republican Richard Carlile who was on the speakers' platform at the time and represents his impression of the event. On the left it shows the house from which the local magistrates directed proceedings. Between this house and the platform it depicts the women in Hunt's carriage who are under attack. The print is dedicated to the Female Reformers of the region.
MANCHESTER LIBRARY AND INFORMATION SERVICE: MANCHESTER ARCHIVES AND LOCAL STUDIES

only brings this figure down to 193 (40 per cent). Of the 168 female casualties recorded, as many as 157 (93 per cent) are without specified occupation; and the evidence of trade directories reduces this figure only to 129 (77 per cent). In other words: supplementary research only reduces the proportion with occupations unknown from 58 to 50 per cent.

Can the casualty lists be taken as a useful guide to the principal occupations of those present at Peterloo? The Bees are surely right in assuming a predominance of weavers: in the lists 151 casualties are noted as following that trade, while the trade directories identify a further 16: comprising 50 per cent of all casualties whose occupations are known. No other occupation comes anywhere near this figure, the most frequently noted providing but a handful of casualties: with no more than 16 spinners, 13 labourers, 10 hatters, 10 shoemakers, 9 dyers and 8 tailors. Yet, since half the casualties are of unknown occupation, is the Bees' finding that 'a clear majority of male demonstrators were weavers' justified? Just as dubious, and for the same reason, is their second finding: that the support of factory workers 'was very limited', especially in view of the enormous number of casualties resident in areas where factory workers were known to live: e.g. New Cross and Ancoats.

Nonetheless, the crowd undoubtedly contained many handloom weavers, their livelihood once sustained by the factory system and the cheap yarn it was capable of producing, and the putting-out warehouse system and the plentiful weaving work it created, and now in 1819 threatened by excessive numbers in the industry and a recession in the cotton trade. In the circumstance weavers held responsible the government, and the upper classes who controlled it, for their misery: partly through upholding the price of bread by means of the Corn Laws, partly through imposing sales taxes on food and drink, partly through outlawing trades unions, partly through failing to set a minimum wage for weavers, and partly through fiscal policies which failed both to restrain spinners from selling their yarn abroad and to restrict the use of the powerloom at home. Intensifying the problem, as the weavers saw it, were sure signs that long-held fears were about to be realised and that, in the Manchester region, weaving would be taken over by the power-loom, making their misery chronic and their extinction inevitable. In search of salvation, they placed their faith in Hunt's campaign for parliamentary reform, in the naive belief that a political system made answerable to the people through its conversion into a proper democracy could not possibly ignore their plight.[44]

The conclusion to be drawn from the casualty lists – that handloom weavers were prominent in the reform movement of the North West – offers no more than the confirmation of a long-held view; yet one that deserves restatement in the light of a tendency, essentially a backlash against the views of E. P. Thompson, to regard handloom weavers at this time as intrinsically loyalist rather than radical and as supporting parliamentary reform essentially in response to the social distress created by a recession in the cotton trade. The predominance of weavers

The back of the black banner of the Saddleworth, Lees and Mossley Union. It was carried by John Ashton who was sabred to death. It is featured in the prints of Peterloo, positioned behind the speakers' platform. Unlike most of the banners, it was not suspended from a flag-pole but hung from a Roman staff. This meant that the Union's cap of liberty required its own pole, in defence of which both Edmund and William Dawson died from sabre wounds.
SADDLEWORTH MUSEUM AND ART GALLERY

in the casualty lists suggests, however, that they were very much to the fore in supporting Hunt's programme of reform, which was decidedly radical in view of its advocacy of universal suffrage – with its emphasis on the rights of man rather than of property – and its declared opposition to a political system controlled by gentlemen and clerics. The same predominance, moreover, would suggest that weavers were not deterred from supporting Hunt by loyalist attempts to present him as an ultra-radical bent on destroying king, church and aristocracy, by force if necessary, and of unleashing on polite society the vindictiveness of the propertyless. It would also suggest that Peterloo confirmed the radicalism of the weavers of the North West, their evident martyrdom on St Peter's Field leaving them committed in the blood and as a trade to the destruction the old regime.

One hundred years later a journalist, James Haslam, recalled conversations with Joss Wrigley, a handloom weaver and veteran of Peterloo, who, in the early 1870s, had worked a loom in the cellar of his parents' house, on the wall of which was a newspaper cut-out portrait of Henry Hunt. The subject of Peterloo came up regularly, leaving the weaver trembling with rage in spite of the passage of half a century. With uncompromising radicalism, Wrigley presented the meeting on St Peter's Field as 'for reets o' mon, for liberty to vote, an' speak an' write, an' be eawrsels [ourselves] – honest, hard-workin' folk. We wanted to live eawr [our] own lives an' th' upper classes wouldn't let us. That's abeawt it, lad'. Central to Wrigley's story was a clash of interest between 'the upper classes' and 'poor folk' that could only be resolved by parliamentary reform. Peterloo, moreover, according to the weaver, taught 'sommat as workin' folk should never forget': that is, to 'ston [stand] up an' feight for t'reets o' mon – t'reets o' poor folk'. In retrospect, Peterloo for him marked the beginning of a struggle for the transformation of the political system. All this stemmed from the weavers' attendance at Peterloo and the penalty of injury they suffered because so many weavers turned up, the result of their conviction that a radical reform of parliament was the best way to solve the problems besetting those who worked in cotton.[45]

The front of the banner shown opposite. The mention of 'Death' and its colour of black imparted a sinister message, implying a willingness to fight to the death for the cause of universal suffrage.
SADDLEWORTH MUSEUM AND ART GALLERY

The casualties of Irish extraction

As remarkable a feature of the casualty lists as the predominance of Mancunians and of weavers was the inclusion of large numbers of Irish. At least 97 of the recorded casualties were of Irish extraction – either immigrants from Ireland or born in England of Irish parents – against 19 Welsh and one or two Scots. Of the Irish casualties 63 came from Manchester, living north of Piccadilly, notably in Newtown; in the New Cross area; in the area around St Michael's Church; and in the lanes leading to right and left off Great Ancoats Street: the parts of Manchester, in fact, from which the Peterloo casualties were principally drawn. (See Map 2) Another 14 of the Irish casualties came from the close vicinity of Manchester, notably Stockport, Salford and Chorlton Row.[46]

E. P. Thompson felt that, 'while sympathising with the agitation of 1816–20', Manchester's Irish population 'did not become integrated with the movement' for parliamentary reform.[47] Yet the Peterloo casualty lists imply that large numbers of Irish did attend the meeting and, in doing so, demonstrated a deep commitment to its cause. Such evidence of support helps to explain the conduct of Hunt when on 9 August he was banned from holding a meeting on St Peter's Field and instead gave a public speech close to St Michael's Church where large numbers of Irish lived. Although the speech was unadvertised, one thousand people turned up to hear it, drawn from the population living thereabouts. Furthermore, a week later, on the day of Peterloo, Hunt, in travelling in from Smedley cottage, where he had been staying with the brush manufacturer Joseph Johnson, had the choice of proceeding along Red Bank to the north of the River Irk, so as to cross the river by Scotland Bridge, close to where it flowed into the Irwell; or of making the river crossing just below Collyhurst, by Vauxhall Gardens, and of coming to town down the Irk's southern bank. The latter route was less suited to the passage of a large body of people. As Bamford revealed, there was the 'long, hollow road' through Newtown and then the tight squeeze through 'the gully of a road below St Michael's Church'. But this route, which brought his party through two areas of concentrated Irish settlement – Newtown and St Michael's – was the one that Hunt chose to take.[48] The outcome was not sectarian strife or a confrontation of two alien forces but a warm affinity resting upon a shared faith in political reform, as Bamford's account of Peterloo makes clear.

Bamford's procession from Middleton and Rochdale came face to face with the Irish after Hunt had ordered it to veer west, away from the Rochdale Road, and to meet up with his party at Newtown. Travelling ahead of Hunt, the Middleton/Rochdale party reached Newtown first and received an ecstatic welcome from 'poor Irish weavers'. According to Bamford, the Irish 'came out in their best drapery', suggesting that they had already made the decision to attend the meeting on St Peter's Field and were simply waiting to latch on to the Hunt procession as it passed through. The Irish of Newtown were undoubtedly appreciative of the cause, and very excited by the event. According to Bamford, they 'uttered blessings and words of endearment'. Though he could not understand exactly what they were saying, the sentiments they expressed were unmistakable. In their excitement, some of the Irish took to dancing in the street, while, clasping their hands in adoration, others silently wept. Especially moving for the Irish, Bamford felt, was the Middleton party's green banner. In gratitude for the warmth of this reception, Bamford ordered the band to play 'Saint Patrick's Day in the Morning', a rendition that left the Irish 'electrified'. Bamford narrates how his party 'passed on, leaving those warmhearted suburbans capering and whooping like mad'.[49] But many from Newtown must have followed into Manchester. The casualty lists reveal 8 injured from Newtown – John Bell, Robert Carbett, Dennis Coil, Charles Harper, James Macconnel, Patrick Reynolds, Samuel Settle – all drawn from Flag Row, Dixon Street, Dimity Street and Portland Street, the main roads in this small but densely populated community that was also called Irish town.

In view of the evidence of the casualty lists, there can be no doubt that the Manchester Irish reached St Peter's Field in considerable numbers: numbers, moreover, disproportionate to their share of the town's population, for, if identified as immigrants and those born in England of Irish parents, the Irish comprised, in spite of a massive influx in the previous thirty years, only 15 per cent of the population of Manchester in 1851, whereas in 1819 at least 22 per cent of Manchester casualties had Irish names. This suggests that, in the manner of poor weavers – to which trade 36 out of the 45 Irish casualties with specified occupations belonged – they enthusiastically backed a political movement which appeared to offer them badly needed economic reforms, and, suffering heavily at Peterloo, had their commitment to the cause of democracy cemented by a consequent conceit of martyrdom.[50]

The judgment on Peterloo

Besides serving as a sample of the Peterloo crowd, the casualty lists have at least three further uses. In the first place, they provide detailed information on the rank and file of a radical popular movement: in the form of a large number of mini-biographies. Normally with such movements, detailed biographical information is confined to the leadership. For this reason, the lists are tremendously useful both to scholars of nineteenth-century radicalism and to family historians seeking to trace their ancestors in a period when the personal evidence of censuses has failed to survive.[51] In the second place, the lists throw some light on gender: thanks to the fact that the sex of all but 4 of the casualties is known, and because of what they reveal on the treatment of female reformers by military and police. Finally, the lists enable a judgment to be made on Peterloo.

A major problem in the study of Peterloo is the clash of discourse evident between reformist and loyalist narratives, and the irrepressible need to use the event either to justify or condemn parliamentary reform. Only by means of a close analysis of those wounded and injured – and the casualty lists make this possible – can the advocacy inherent in eye-witness accounts be exposed and a glimmer of the truth revealed. Helpfully for this purpose, 92 per cent of the casualties listed have their injuries described.

Treatment of the women

An iconic image of Peterloo – one prominent on the surviving prints, illustrated handkerchiefs, medals and commemorative pottery, as well as in contemporary descriptions of the event – is of mounted men, sabres raised and dressed in extravagant uniforms, riding down defenceless women and girls; just as the encapsulating sound of Peterloo – stressed in numerous contemporary accounts – is the female shriek. Thanks to the casualty lists, these characteristic impressions can be properly tested against what actually happened.

Print produced by J. Evans of London. It depicts the arrest of Hunt by the constables and therefore a later stage than the prints already shown.

MANCHESTER LIBRARY AND INFORMATION SERVICE: MANCHESTER ARCHIVES AND LOCAL STUDIES

Of the 654 persons recorded as injured in the casualty lists, at least 168 were women, 4 of whom died of their wounds. True, the lists show that only 1 in 3 of the casualties were women; yet this has to be measured against the proportion of women present at the meeting, which was less than 1 in 8.[52] The chances of injury, on this evidence (Table 4), were 2.8 times greater for women as for men: that is, 1.8 times greater for weapon wounds, 3.1 times greater for being trampled by horses, and 4.2 times greater for being crushed by the crowd.

Table 4. Male and female casualties	
8 times as many men as women were present at the Peter's Field meeting	
3 times as many men as women were injured	[482 : 168 = 2.9].
4 times as many men as women were wounded by weapons	[266 : 60 = 4.4].
3 times as many men as women were trampled by horses	[136 : 52 = 2.6].
2 times as many men as women were crushed by the crowd	[122 : 65 = 1.9].

The relatively heavy casualties suffered by women was noted at the time and given three possible explanations. Richard Carlile, radical journalist, republican and, as a long-term prisoner, martyr for the cause of free thought and a free press, was present at the meeting and able to observe the crowd from the vantage point of the speaker's platform at the time of the first cavalry charge. In his opinion, the women were especially targeted.[53] A second contemporary view claimed that the attack on the crowd was indiscriminate – that is, 'without distinction of age or sex' – and, as a result, children, the elderly and women were treated with the same ferocity as the men.[54] A third view sought to exonerate the magistrates, the military and the police with the claim that the injuries to women mostly resulted from the crush of the crowd, implying that the additional sufferings of the women, as with the elderly, was due to their physical frailty.[55]

The latter view, with its emphasis upon accident, has been particularly favoured by historians. Yet it is not supported by the injury evidence. (See Tables 1 and 5) The casualty lists reveal a large number of women with weapon wounds: 59 out of the 150 female casualties whose injuries are known, with 31 sabred, another 21 truncheoned, 1 bayoneted, 1 shot and a further 8 either shot or sabred. In addition, Ann Scott was badly kicked by a constable. Another 44 women were injured by the cavalry's horses – knocked down or trampled underfoot – as were 8 of the women already cited as having been sabred or truncheoned. In this respect, 104 women are known to have been physically assaulted by the military and the police. In contrast, only 44 were simply the victims of crowd pressure.[56]

Bearing in mind that at least eight times as many men as women were present on the field and only three times as many men as women were injured, the women can be said to have experienced the greater pain. They suffered disproportionately from being crushed in the crowd, with 1 woman to at least 2 men injured in this manner. They also suffered disproportionately from wounding, with 1 woman to 4 men the victim of a weapon attack. The death toll, moreover, reveals 1 woman to 4 men dying of their injuries. Pulling in one direction was the greater likelihood of men being shot (9 men to 1 woman) or bayoneted (15 men to 1 woman); yet pulling in the other was, as the Bees discovered, the high incidence of women truncheoned (22 women against 47 men).[57] Much greater numbers of men sustained sabre wounds (187 men against 31 women) but the overall ratio of 6 sabred men to 1 sabred woman was still below the ratio of men to women on the field.

Nonetheless, does this prove that women were deliberately singled out for attack? The sabring of women was undeniably brutal. Frequently a purposeful act, rather than the accidental result of military incompetence, it sprang from the conviction that women behaving like men should be treated accordingly. One woman (Margaret Downes) bled to death from a sabre-slash to the breast; another (Elizabeth Farren) sustained two sabre-cuts to the head that left a three inch gash from crown to brow; another (Alice Heywood) suffered an almost severed wrist. At least 26 women received sabre cuts; and 5 more suffered a beating with the flat of the blade.

Some women suffered serious arm injuries in seeking to protect their breasts and faces from the slash of the sabre (e.g. Ann Bardsley, Mary Jones, Bridget Monks); and several suffered cuts to the lower part of the body, suggesting that when sabred they had already fallen to the ground (e.g. Sarah Morton, Ellen Harvey). Another indication of the brutality deliberately inflicted lies in the fact that several women were sabred more than once: thus, the body of Sarah Howarth was wounded in twenty places while Elizabeth Farren suffered two cuts to the head. The cavalry not only attacked women with their swords; they also ran them down. 52 women were knocked over or trampled upon by horses ridden at a gallop into the crowd.

To the fore in the cavalry's attack on women were the Yeomanry Cavalry, a group of Manchester and Salford shopkeepers, publicans, manufacturers and professional men who had volunteered for military service on horseback in the cause of maintaining order and resisting revolution. Some women [e.g. Farren and

Captain Hindley's sword: the type of sabre wielded by the cavalry as they charged the crowd.
SALFORD MUSEUM AND ART GALLERY

Goodwin] claimed that they knew their attackers and were known by them – a moment of recognition which seemed to incite rather than restrain acts of violence. Assisting the Yeomanry Cavalry in the task of dispersing the crowd was another body of volunteers, the Special Constables. Temporarily appointed to assist the regular town officers and magistrates at times of crisis, they were recruited from the same social stratum as the volunteer cavalry.[58] At least 22 women were beaten up by truncheon-bearing Special Constables (see Table 1) – again often by men they knew – one (Sarah Jones) so badly that she later died. In attacking the fleeing crowd, constables appeared to operate in packs, even when truncheoning women. Several women (e.g. Hannah Barlow, Elizabeth Bond, Elizabeth Chambers, Mary Fildes, Elizabeth Gaunt, Ann Hall, Mary Horton, Ann Peel) alleged a simultaneous assault by several constables, beating them, usually on the head, shoulders and back, with truncheons or staves. Other women (Mary Jervis, Ann Scholes, Sarah Keenan) were attacked by constables after having been knocked over by the charging cavalry or the fleeing crowd and when they were lying on the ground. The constables appeared to assault any woman within range, whether on or off her feet, and irrespective of age. However, like the cavalry, they paid particular attention to the women on prominent display: those, for example, standing on the platform (e.g. Mary Fildes), or sitting in Hunt's carriage alongside the hustings (Elizabeth Gaunt and Mary Horton), or holding flags.

Accounting for the violence committed against the women was not simply the fact that they were inescapably in the way but that the considerations of protection, respite and mercy that men were normally expected to show to women – in accordance with deeply imbedded notions of gallantry, chivalry and paternalism – failed to come into operation. This was undoubtedly in reaction to the obtrusive behaviour of female reformers at recent political meetings in the North West – an unprecedented and successful invasion by women of a world traditionally accepted as a male prerogative. Deeply disturbed by this startling innovation in the practice of politics, loyalists came to link the cause of reform with a novel fear of sexual revolution, as well as with the old fears of social disruption and collapse. In self-protective disgust, they recast the image of female reformers, depicting them not as caring mothers, dutiful wives and obedient daughters but as harlots and drunks who deserved to be severely punished for neglecting their homes and families.[59] In this respect, the physical assault on women was justified and driven by a sense of moral crusade as well as the need for a counter-revolutionary defence of the old order.

Treatment of the men

Yet the view that women were especially targeted at Peterloo is questioned by the savagery which the cavalry and constables also showed towards the male reformers

Table 5. Male and female injuries with specified cause*

By weapon:	287 of 546 male injuries:	53 per cent
	61 of 178 female injuries:	34 per cent
By horse:	136 of 546 male injuries:	25 per cent
	52 of 178 female injuries:	29 per cent
By crowd:	123 of 546 male injuries:	23 per cent
	65 of 178 female injuries:	37 per cent

* Based on evidence of injuries set out in Table 1.

present. For men the ratio of casualties caused by weapon wounds was much higher than it was for women.

Taking all the known injuries received by men (see Tables 1 and 5), one finds that the proportion inflicted by sabre, truncheon or musket was 53 per cent; whereas taking all the known injuries received by women 34 per cent of them were weapon-inflicted. Creating the difference was the extensive sabring of men. Of the 266 men wounded by weapons, at least 187 were injured by the sabre. Another 28 were either shot or sabred, the evidence failing to distinguish between the two but inclined to suggest that they were victims of the sword. Of the sabred 7 died of their wounds.[60] 57 per cent of sabred men received head wounds. A further 26 per cent of sabred men sustained injuries to limbs, usually arms slashed as the victims sought to protect their heads from the flashing blade, but also legs and feet through being struck by swords when already knocked down by charging horses or the fleeing crowd. Several men were sabred repeatedly: e.g. James Berry, Thomas Billington, James Chiswall, Frederick Graves, Samuel Kay, James Lees, Matthew Macglade, Peter Warburton. Three of the sabred men (John Ashton, William Entwistle, Thomas Redford) stood out in the crowd as flag-bearers, and another two (Edmund and William Dawson) distinguished themselves by defending a pole surmounted by a cap of liberty, but the great majority were mere rank-and-file. In addition, the number of men definitely shot, or bayoneted, or clubbed with musket-butts by the infantry was relatively high, amounting to 24 (against 2 women wounded in this manner). Finally 47 men (against 21 women) were truncheoned by constables, many of them, like the women, attacked by several constables simultaneously (e.g. Thomas Barron, John Black, John Boulter, John Coates, John Edwards, John Foster, James Higgins, Joseph Jones, Bernard McMaghan, John Scholfield, Thomas Webster).

Whereas weapon wounds accounted for a larger proportion of injuries received by men than those received by women – 53 per cent for men against 34 per cent for women – it was the other way round for injuries inflicted by horses (25 per cent for men against 29 per cent for women); and for injuries inflicted by crowd pressure (23 per cent for men against 37 per cent for women). (See Table 5) In the light of this evidence, men, it would seem, were better able to escape the trampling and the crush; but were – just as much as the women – the target of

TREATMENT OF THE MEN

Medal struck to commemorate Peterloo. The massacre was also commemorated with plates, jugs and handkerchiefs, all depicting cavalrymen with drawn swords slashing at defenceless women.
MANCHESTER LIBRARY AND INFORMATION SERVICE: MANCHESTER ARCHIVES AND LOCAL STUDIES

the military and police: in their case, because of the contempt they had shown for the society of orders by asserting the sovereignty of the people, and because it was suspected that their advocacy of democracy was really a ruse to seize the property of the rich and to substitute for the British liberty of order the French liberty of civil strife.

Treatment of youth and age

Underlining the brutality with which the crowd was attacked was the treatment of the elderly (i.e. those aged fifty and above) and the young (i.e. those yet to attain the maturity of twenty-one). To neither groups were any favours shown by the magistrates, the military and the police. The over-50s comprised only 10 per cent of the region's population.[61] What is more, they were less likely than, say, the 21–40 age group to be present at the meeting, simply because of the infirmities and conservatism to which age had made them prone. Nonetheless, they comprised 27 per cent (92 out of 342) of all casualties with ages given. Moreover, 36 per cent of their injuries were weapon wounds; as large a proportion as the injuries sustained from being crushed in the crowd. Their injuries therefore cannot be simply attributed to frailty and slowness. In all 65 per cent of their injuries were caused by horse or weapon, the larger proportion by weapon. (See Table 6) This rather suggests that, in attacking the elderly, the military and police were prepared to break a social taboo by making no allowance for age, presumably on the grounds that the victims should have known better and therefore were doubly to blame.

Table 6. Injuries to the old (50 years of age and over)

By weapon:	44 of 123 injuries:	36 per cent.
By horse:	36 of 123 injuries:	29 per cent.
By crowd:	43 of 123 injuries:	35 per cent.

Youth was treated with the same unconcessionary rigour, essentially to teach it a lesson it would not forget. Yet on the face of it, this group appeared to be let off lightly: in spite of forming 54 per cent of the region's population, they comprised only 10 per cent of casualties with specified injuries (i.e. 34 out of 342) – although this may well have reflected their low attendance at the meeting. A harsher picture, however, emerges from studying their injuries and how they happened. For the elderly, as for women, a relatively large proportion of injuries – 35–36 per cent in contrast to 23 per cent for men and 26 per cent for all casualties – resulted from crowd pressure. This was not the case with the young. (See Table 7)

Table 7. Injuries to the young (21 years of age or under)

By weapon:	30 of 50 injuries:	60 per cent.
By horse:	15 of 50 injuries:	30 per cent.
By crowd:	5 of 50 injuries:	10 per cent.

Only 10 per cent of their injuries had this cause. Instead, the great majority – 60 per cent – were weapon wounds – much the highest proportion for any group – with 71 per cent sabre-inflicted. Their remaining injuries, amounting to 30 per cent of all the known injuries they received, were due to horse-trampling. Six casualties in this youth group (17 per cent) were under sixteen, the youngest aged eleven, four of them being sabred (John Elliott, Isabella Harvey, Edward Lancaster, Richard Wilde); four trampled upon by the cavalry (Elliott, Harvey, Lancaster, Rose Maccobe); and one crushed by the crowd (Mary Mackennagh).

The casualty lists reveal, then, two major features in the attack upon the crowd. In the first place, the behaviour of the soldiers and police was unconventional and a shocking affront to paternalist custom, in offering no concessions to vulnerable groups, whether it be women, the elderly or the young. In the second place, it expressed a great deal of deliberation: so much so that the damage inflicted at Peterloo on the reformers of the North West cannot be attributed simply to panic, incompetence or the immensity of the task, but also sprang from premeditation, design and determination.

Motives for attack

The ostensible aim of the cavalry charge was to terminate the meeting and enable the police to arrest Hunt. But, in the circumstances, its practical purpose was to instil terror and to humiliate. Inciting the cavalry and the magistrates to take rigorous action was the reformers' initial triumphalism: evident both in the processions of men marching to St Peter's Field in military formation and step – men who were known to have drilled on the hills and moors prior to the meeting – and in the boisterous behaviour of a monstrous crowd on the field itself with intimidating displays of flags, caps of liberty, sticks, music and noisy unisons of sudden clapping, hissing and huzzaing. Especially provocative was the deeply disturbing sight of forward women inappropriately dressed in modest white and of belligerent working men spuriously wearing top hats falsely decorated with sprigs of laurel, the token of peace. That women who were thought to have forsaken the plinth of female virtue by advocating political reform should publicly present themselves as vestal virgins, and that labouring men should derogate the dress code, as well as lie about their intentions, by adopting the guise of peaceful gentlemen reverential of tradition when clearly bent on taking measures – violent if necessary – to abolish gentility and private property: all this was seen as outrageous expressions of popular impudence which, in view of its revolutionary implications, could not go unpunished. But then the triumphalism of the crowd suddenly collapsed, giving way to abject submission, the result of Hunt's emphasis upon 'peaceableness' and his control of the crowd which rendered resistance to the cavalry and constables impossible to organise. With the crowd on the run and incapable of mounting an effective counter-attack, there was nothing to stop the military and police from assaulting with impunity those whom they caught.

Peterloo, of course, did not happen in isolation. The hostility which raged between loyalists and reformers on that day derived from earlier conflicts and confrontations in and around Manchester, prominent among which was the Blanketeers meeting on St Peter's Field on 10 March 1817 when a large crowd of 12,000 assembled to send off a party of 300 men to London to present a petition to the Prince Regent; on that occasion the military and police disbanded the meeting and stopped the march with a show of force.[62] The Peterloo meeting, moreover, had two forerunners in 1819: a monster meeting on 18 January, also held on St Peter's Field under the chairmanship of Hunt, which unanimously voted against petitioning and opted instead for a remonstrance. A further meeting occurred on 21 June, on the same field but not attended by Hunt. On this occasion an assembly of weavers were dissuaded from petitioning for assisted emigration as the solution to their problems, and were won over instead to the cause of demanding parliamentary reform.[63] The Peterloo meeting itself, moreover, was the realisation of a St Peter's Field meeting originally scheduled for 9 August. This the municipal authorities had successfully banned on the grounds that, following Birmingham's example, its aim was to alter the constitution by illegally electing an MP for Manchester. Hunt arrived for the first meeting and stayed on for the second which, in return for a promise that it would merely discuss parliamentary reform, was officially sanctioned.[64]

Magnifying the fears of Manchester loyalists was a series of reform meetings held in various parts of Lancashire over the previous two months, notably at Oldham, Ashton and Stockport in June; at Blackburn, Rochdale, Macclesfield in July; and at Leigh in early August: meetings which attested to the massive popular support which Radical Reform enjoyed in the region and revealed how well the movement had become organised, with Reform Unions flourishing in the major townships and clearly capable of recruiting a large and enthusiastic membership from the local industrial workforce and of inciting it to make public protest.[65]

Such meetings generated a great deal of loyalist propaganda which found expression in the local press and in circulated handbills, propaganda that created beliefs to which social elites – from manufacturers, shopkeepers and lawyers to clerics and gentlemen professing to have neither trade nor profession – readily subscribed.[66] Thus, under the influence of this propaganda, loyalists came to see reformers as bent not simply on admitting the propertyless to the parliamentary electorate by giving all mature males the vote, but also on abolishing private property, on upsetting the balanced constitution by removing monarchy and aristocracy, on demolishing the moral basis of society by disposing of the Christian religion and on wrecking the family, the bedrock of a well-run state, by encouraging women to engage directly in public affairs. The outcome, as predicted by this propaganda, was the rule of a mindless, rampaging mob, a state of chronic anarchy and the termination of England's prized liberty: achieved and upheld over the centuries by its capacity to reject the tyranny of the fickle multitude as well as that of wicked monarchs.

Proof of what could happen if the state became answerable to the propertyless, it was pointed out, was glaringly evident in the example of Jacobin France. To counteract these charges, Hunt stressed his patriotism, his monarchism, his Christianity, his allegiance to the ancient constitution and his attachment to peaceableness and private property; but, for loyalists, this was to no avail: in spite of what he professed they saw him as the associate of Spenceans – that is, the opponents of private property – the friend of republicans like William Sherwin, the ally of atheists like Richard Carlile; and as such the enemy of king, church and aristocracy and the advocate of physical force. As a Manchester handbill put it: Hunt's reform programme would 'fill the land with violence', turn women against their family duties and convert 'the open, honourable Englishman into the dark and degraded assassin'.[67]

Giving credibility to these loyalist fantasies were accounts of military preparations made by people in the North West and also news of a series of street incidents in Manchester, all occurring shortly before the Peterloo meeting. The former was incited by an order from the magistrates of Manchester on 21 July 1819 authorising, for the defence of the constitution and to prevent 'the miseries of a revolution', the formation of an armed association in which the loyal inhabitants of Manchester and Salford were invited to enrol 'for the preservation of Public Peace'. This followed an order of 9 July in which the municipal authorities had identified the reform societies as a revolutionary threat, authorising in counteraction the appointment of additional constables and a committee to preserve the peace.[68] Enraged by these loyalist preparations, reformers resorted to military measures of their own, justifying them as defensive safeguards against the loyalist threat of direct action. They took to drilling on the hills and moors, not in the use of weapons but in the discipline of marching in military formation and responding to military commands. These exercises also had the purpose of refuting the loyalist presentation of popular politics as intrinsically unruly and prone to violence and theft. They were meant, then, to demonstrate the people's capacity for order and self-control. Their specific aim was to prepare reformers for the meeting at St Peter's Field on 16 August, when the order and discipline of the people would be on public display and a glorious opportunity would present itself to expose loyalist rhetoric as a pack of lies. Not surprisingly, these military preparations had just the opposite effect, confirming the loyalist belief that the reformers were planning a violent overthrow of the old regime, and fully justifying military counteraction.

Certain offensive incidents, all occurring in Manchester in the weeks leading up to Peterloo, further fuelled loyalist fears and fantasies, especially by appearing to indicate that the municipal authorities had lost the capacity to maintain order. At the real root of the problem was the anachronistic system of local government, based upon the manor which was naturally fit to run a small face-to-face society but not the dense mass of humanity suddenly dumped upon Manchester by industrialisation and the migrants it attracted from Ireland and the surrounding countryside. But, unwilling to countenance reform, loyalists blamed the problem on Hunt and his reform movement, especially the way in which it persuaded men and women to act above their station and to forget their duty of obedience.

These incidents occurred in a small part of Manchester called New Cross. Centred on an elaborate cross positioned at the junction of Oldham Road and Great Ancoats Street the area comprised the narrow lanes branching off Oldham Road, Oldham Street, Swan Street and Great Ancoats Street. (See Map 2) New Cross was described in an article that appeared in the *Manchester Observer* for 30 August 1819. By then it had acquired a national importance for daring to resist the military occupation imposed upon Manchester after Peterloo, with stone-throwing crowds attacking not only troops but also shopkeepers and publicans who had served as Special Constables. The *Manchester Observer* described it as 'the

St Giles of Manchester' – in other words, as resembling one of the poorest parts of London – and the home of 'labourers of some of the largest factories of the town'. It found the inhabitants to be mostly spinners and weavers, with not a few Irish. Many lived in cellars and most were wretchedly poor. It noticed that every third house was a pawnbroker's shop which held in pledge much of the furniture, bedding and clothing of those resident in the neighbourhood. So great was their distress in late 1819 that, having nothing to lose, the *Manchester Observer* thought the inhabitants of New Cross were 'fit for everything' and therefore 'the most turbulent' in Manchester. It went on to say: 'their wretchedness seems to madden them against the rich who they dangerously imagine engross the fruits of their labour', adding in illustration: 'A well-dressed person ... is so obnoxious to them that they sometimes throw stones at them when passing'.

The New Cross residents' reputation for impudence and violence was not born at Peterloo. For the local authorities it had become a no-go area some time before. This was made evident on 2 August when a bill-poster sought to stick up a royal proclamation at New Cross. Anticipating trouble, he arrived under the guard of two beadles. When they found themselves attacked by a substantial crowd, reckoned at 500 strong, the boroughreeve, the chief manorial officer, and his constables were obliged to rush to their assistance. However, in doing so, they met with a hail of stones and were driven out of the quarter.[69]

The casualty lists reveal that New Cross provided a large number of those present at Peterloo. The anarchic, communally aggressive and individually insolent behaviour of its inhabitants would seem to bear out the loyalist propaganda that presented popular parliamentary reform as turning men into thugs and women into harlots, whereas in reality the disorder of the area sprang from the extreme distress caused by high levels of unemployment and the absence of adequate local relief.

Driven on by fantasies far removed from reality but real enough in their own minds, and grimly determined to settle old scores arising from earlier conflicts, the loyalists of the town, dressed up as troops and constables, sought to disperse the Peterloo crowd with measures soft and hard. For example, they proceeded against the insignia of reform: flags and caps of liberty were confiscated or destroyed, and top hats were tipped off or slashed.[70] But because the cavalry had moved into the crowd with drawn sabres, these 'soft' measures easily led to serious injury. The ensigns, for example, had to be physically assaulted to make them release their flags: as was the case with John Ashton and the black flag of Saddleworth; Thomas Redford and the green flag of Middleton; William Entwisle and the black flag of Bury, its pole surmounted with a distinctive tin fleur de lis provocatively painted red; and Mary Fildes and the white flag of the Manchester Female Reform Society. Consequently, they all sustained serious wounds from sabre or truncheon. Edmund and William Dawson died from injuries received when defending the Saddleworth cap of liberty. Moreover, sabre attacks upon top hats led to injury (as with Thomas Brown, Thomas Clark, Thomas Jones, Stephen Pollitt, John Shields, James Slater, Richard Southern and Peter Wood). John Shields, for example, had his hat knocked off by a constable. Infuriated by his cheek in trying to retrieve it, a cavalryman cut him with a back-handed blow. John Slater's hat was cut to tatters by four cavalrymen who chased him round the yard of the Friends' Meeting House after he had sought sanctuary in a small outhouse, only to find it crammed with other refugees. In the process, they cut his chin. The exception was John Brierley who had come in that morning from Saddleworth, his mid-day meal of bread and cheese safely stored under his hat. When struck by a sabre blow which cleft the hat, his head remained unharmed, protected by his yet to be eaten lunch, and the injuries he suffered came only of being thrown down by the crowd and ridden over by a horse.

Another 'soft' measure that the attackers employed was to use their sabres for beating rather than cutting: that is, by applying the back or flat of the blade instead of the edge or point.[71] The casualty lists show that, rather than an idle claim concocted by the cavalry to repudiate the charge of brutality, this measure was actually put into practice. On the other hand, it could cause considerable injury, especially to women. Sarah Graves, for example, suffered a broken collar bone from one blow of the back of a sabre and was left disabled for 10 weeks. The thirteen-year-old Isabella Harvey was so badly beaten on the left arm with the back of a sabre that the following January it remained, according to one casualty list, 'still bandaged and partially useless'. Daniel Hall, a clog-maker of Deansgate, was put out of work for three weeks, the result of a member of the Manchester Yeomanry Cavalry beating him severely with a sabre on his back and shoulders. Moreover, the lists reveal only eight instances of the sabre used in this manner: i.e. on James Barrett, Thomas Brown, Daniel Hall, William Jerron, Ann Bardsley, Sarah Graves, Isabella Harvey and John Nuttal. Much more common was cutting with the edge or stabbing with the point. In taking action against the crowd, the military and police were directed by a clear idea of what they needed to do: essentially to deter popular support for parliamentary reform by branding their mark, in blood and bruises, on the fleeing crowd, and to make reformers pay dearly for their rude behaviour in the work and income their injuries caused them to forfeit.

A massacre?

Peterloo was soon presented as a massacre. 'Peterloo Massacre' was the title James Wroe gave to a weekly journal devoted to the event which he started in September. In December he publicly justified its choice: 'This title was given to the Work from a wish to fall in with the common feeling which the proceedings of the 16th of August elicited, and not on account of its classical elegance'.[72] In doing so he revealed its popular provenance, and then sought to dissociate

View of St Peter's Plain, drawn by T. Whaite, engraved by J. Sudlow and advertised for sale in the *Manchester Observer* for 22 October 1819. The platform has been cleared of reformers, the caps of liberty and the banners have been seized, and the crowd is vacating the field, but with acts of violence still being committed against isolated individuals in the foreground.

MANCHESTER LIBRARY AND INFORMATION SERVICE: MANCHESTER ARCHIVES AND LOCAL STUDIES

himself himself from its usage by dismissively declaring: 'Its quaintness is its only recommendation'. None the less it caught on. Shortly afterwards, John Wade published without apology his *Manchester Massacre!! An Authentic Narrative of the Magisterial and Yeomanry Massacre at Manchester* (London, [?1820]).

The perception of the event as a massacre, however, has been questioned in view of the small number of injuries resulting in death. Donald Read in the preface

to his *Peterloo* stated: 'The successful designation of Peterloo as a "massacre" represents another piece of successful propaganda. Perhaps only in a peace-loving England could a death-role of only eleven persons have been so described'. Influential in dismissing the event as a massacre was the eye-witness account of Sir William Jolliffe, a lieutenant in the 15th Hussars who had taken part in the attack on the Peterloo crowd. He recollected: 'Beyond all doubt... the far greater amount of injuries were from the pressure of the routed multitude', implying that most of the injuries were inflicted by the crowd upon itself. This has become ensconced in the historiography of Peterloo, with Read making the point that, as 60,000 were dispersed in ten minutes, it was 'little wonder that hundreds were hurt, and many more by crushing than by sabring'. To clinch his case, he added that, of the 400 people injured, all – with the exception of 140 cut by sabres – 'were crushed or thrown down as a result of the pressure of the crowd'. This conclusion was echoed by Alan Kidd in his *History of Manchester*. According to him, 'most of the injuries' resulted from 'being trampled on or crushed in the panic of dispersal'. Robert Walmsley, apologist for William Hulton, the magistrate who authorised the military action taken against the crowd, made the same point.[73] Yet the surviving casualty lists reveal something else. In showing that most injuries were inflicted by the military and police (see Table 8), and how deaths and severe injuries resulted from the sabring, bayonetting and truncheoning of unarmed people, they render the term 'massacre' – though technically an overstatement in that Peterloo did not witness a large number of killings – an appropriate expression which encapsulates the enormity of what actually happened.

Table 8. Injuries with specified cause*

By weapon:	350 of 726 injuries:	48 per cent
By horse:	188 of 726 injuries:	26 per cent
By crowd:	189 of 726 injuries:	26 per cent

* Based on evidence of injuries set out in Table 1.

On the subject of death, the point needs to be made that the standard figure of 11 dead is a gross underestimation. In all likelihood, 18 deaths resulted from Peterloo. (See Table 9) Not all, however, were due to the attack made upon the crowd in St Peter's Field. In addition there was the killing of Robert Campbell, a Special Constable, by a mob on 18 August in Newton Lane, in reprisal for the violence committed by constables at Peterloo; and Joshua Whitworth was shot by the military on the evening of 16 August, several hours after the event and in New Cross, well away from St Peter's Field. Also to be viewed apart is the death of Martha Partington which was not a killing. Pressed by the crowd, she fell into a cellar and, buried under other bodies, probably died from suffocation. On the other hand, her death occurred at the top of Bridge Street, some distance from the field, suggesting that the crowd panic which caused it resulted from the presence of pursuing cavalrymen. If so, it makes the cavalry indirectly responsible.

This leaves at least 15 deaths, which were the direct result of acts of violence committed on or near the field by armed cavalry and police. Of these fatalities, two were Special Constables – John Ashworth and William Evans – the former sabred, the latter trampled by horse. The injuries they sustained, it can be assumed, were unintended. Then there was William Fildes, a baby accidentally knocked out of his mother's arms by a cavalryman galloping along Cooper Street in response to the magistrates' original order to sort out the crowd on the field. Of the remaining 12 deaths, all were caused by injuries inflicted on the field and resulted from the force with which the troops and police attacked the crowd.

A MASSACRE?

Eight were sabred by the cavalry – John Ashton, Thomas Buckley, William Bradshaw, Edmund Dawson, William Dawson, Margaret Downes, John Lees and John Rhodes – and Buckley was bayoneted as well, while Lees was also bludgeoned by constables with truncheons and the staff of an abandoned banner. Constables were responsible for two other deaths: that of Sarah Jones of Silk Street, severely beaten on the head by Thomas Woodworth, who lived just round

Table 9. Peterloo death list

Name	Residence	Cause	Location of fatal injury	Date of Death*
John Ashton	Nr Oldham	Sabred	On field	16 Aug.
John Ashworth	Manchester	Sabred	On field	?
Wm. Bradshaw	Whitefield	Sabred	On field	29 Apr. 1922
Buckley, Thos.	Chadderton	Sabred/bayoneted	On field?	16 Aug.?
Robert Campbell	Manchester	mob violence	Newton Lane	18 Aug.
James Crompton	Barton	Trampled by cav.	On field	By 1 Sept.
Edm. Dawson	Saddleworth	Sabred	On field	31 Aug.
Wm Dawson	Saddleworth	Sabred	On field	1 Sept.
Margaret Downes	Manchester	Sabred	On field	?
Wm. Evans	Hulme	Trampled by cav.	On field	?
Wm. Fildes	Manchester	Trampled by cav.	Cooper Street	16 Aug.
Mary Heys	Chorlton Row	Trampled by cav.	On field	17 Dec.
Sarah Jones	Manchester	Truncheoned	On field	?
John Lees	Oldham	Sabred and Truncheoned	On field	30 Aug.
Arthur Neil	Manchester	Truncheoned and crushed	On field	?
Martha Partington	Barton	Crushed in cellar	Bridge Street	16 Aug.
John Rhodes	Nr. Oldham	Sabred	On field	19 Nov.
Joshua Whitworth	Hyde	Shot	New Cross	20 Aug.

* Not all these deaths were subjected to a coroner's inquest. Three remain disputable: Margaret Downes was presented as 'supposed dead'; William Evans was declared to be 'in a dying state'; while only the casualty list produced by Hunt in 1831 declared that Sarah Jones was killed. Margaret Downes' injuries were sufficient to cause death but concealed by her friends, presumably to avoid prosecution. That Evans probably did die of his wounds: see n. 26. The deaths subjected to a coroner's inquest were found to be accidental or natural and therefore not indictable for manslaughter or murder: that is with the exception of the death of John Lees. In his case, the coroner's court was adjourned after much deliberation without reaching a verdict. An additional death was possibly that of John Hulme, a member of the Manchester Yeomanry Cavalry who fell from his horse on the Field and died of a fractured skull. See ch. II, under Hulme.

the corner from her in Newton Lane, and Arthur Neil, who was badly bruised by the constables and then incarcerated without trial in the New Bailey prison. The remaining deaths – of James Crompton and Mary Heys – were the work of the cavalry. Crompton was trampled to death; Heys, a mother of six with another on the way and an almost blind husband, was knocked down and trodden on by a cavalry horse, leaving her badly bruised and prone to fits. Her condition led to a premature birth from which she died. This made the cavalry responsible for at least 13 deaths. In contrast, the crowd caused but one death (that of Martha Partington) and contributed to another (that of Arthur Neil). The constables likewise caused but one death (that of Sarah Jones) and contributed to two others (those of John Lees and Arthur Neil). Manchester people suffered the highest number of fatalities, 6 in all, but this was equalled by the Oldham party. The number of deaths associated with Peterloo should not be dismissed as a small matter, especially as so many of them were killings caused by deliberate attempts to inflict severe injury.

Seen in the context of armed men deliberately attacking a defenceless and unresistant crowd, the issue of whether or not Peterloo was a massacre hinges on what proportion of the injured were deliberately wounded, as well as on what proportion were severely wounded. The evidence of the lists shows that, of all injuries specified, 48 per cent were inflicted with weapons deployed by the military and police. In addition, 26 per cent of all specified injuries resulted from people being knocked down or trampled upon by horses. Some of these injuries might have been accidental, the result of people getting in the cavalry's way; but, nonetheless, most were due to a decision which originated with the local magistrates and the way they instructed the cavalry to charge the crowd, knowing full well that serious injury would inevitably follow. As for the proportion of injuries principally caused by the crowd itself, this amounted to no more than 26 per cent of specified injuries.

The casualty lists include eight constables injured by the cavalry, proving that on the field the troops on horseback were somewhat accident-prone and not completely in control of themselves; but two facts point to a deliberately perpetrated atrocity.[74] In the first place, a large number of casualties were wounded in a very short period of time: the result of the crowd being broken up and driven off the field in the space of ten to fifteen minutes by charging and pursuing cavalry. In the second place, the lists cite woundings inflicted by constables and soldiers off the field and after the crowd's dispersal. By doing so, the lists reveal that the action taken by military and police was not simply the application of a short, sharp shock to truncate the meeting, but a campaign of attrition waged over the following twenty-four hours. Some of it comprised justifiable reprisals against attempts at counteraction: notably against the riots in New Cross which broke out on the evening of 16 August. But several injuries resulted from cavalry and constables pursuing and harassing reformers who had passively accepted defeat and were quietly making their way home. Some were attacked on the edges of the field, notably in Windmill Street and around the Friends' Meeting House; others further afield. James Richardson, for example, was sabred in Jackson's Row; John Foster was attacked and severely beaten by ten drunken constables in Deansgate. John Hargreaves was ridden down by cavalry near the infirmary in Piccadilly; the sixty-seven-year-old Mary Jones was sabred one mile from Peter's Field; Patrick Reynolds was driven into a lime-hole by the cavalry and badly scalded; Richard Wilde, aged fourteen, was cut in Oldham Street. All this suggests that, as well as attacking the crowd in order to stop the meeting, the military and police had vindictively hunted down fugitives from the field, not because the latter posed a threat to authority but because their vulnerability rendered them an easy target for an act of gratuitous violence.

To measure the severity of injuries inflicted at Peterloo, the Bees produced a table entitled 'Duration of Incapacitation'.[75] Its evidence was taken from the casualty lists concerned with the dispensation of relief and the information they provide, essentially to decide the level of payment, on the period of disability suffered by the injured. In this context disability meant incapacity to work. Of the casualties with specified periods of disability, the Bees' table reveals that 67 per cent suffered severe injury, leading either to death or at least three weeks out of work. The problem with the Bees' findings, however, is that they include 'all injuries'; whereas, in order to assess whether or not a massacre had occurred, one needs to separate those wounded by weapons from those injured by the crowd.

For the purpose of assessing the severity of injury, each case has to be taken on its own merits, and considered in the light of how the lists describe the wounds inflicted and whether or not the degree of disability stated in the description was caused by weapons or accidental factors, such as the force of the crowd or collision with a passing horse. The lists reveal 53 per cent of those with weapon wounds to have been severely injured. Broken down, this accounted for 48 per cent of those sabred, 45 per cent of those truncheoned, 64 per cent of those bayoneted, 100 per cent of those shot, and 72 per cent of those unresolvably placed in a category of 'shot or sabred'. Since no one was shot at Peterloo itself but only in the riots which followed the same evening and on the next day, and also in connection with a related incident in October, these figures require revision.[76] The outcome is that on the field, or in fleeing from it, 49 per cent of those injured by weapons were severely wounded. This included the eight persons who died from sabre wounds (John Ashton, John Ashworth, William Bradshaw, Edmund Dawson, William Dawson, Margaret Downes, John Lees, John Rhodes), plus a woman who died from a beating with truncheons (Sarah Jones) and a man who died from having been bayoneted and then struck with a sabre (Thomas Buckley). The tally of those dying from wounds inflicted by weapons on or near St Peter's Field stands at ten, against three who died from being ridden down by the cavalry (William Fildes, James Crompton, Mary Heys), and two who were crushed to death by the crowd (Martha Partington, Arthur Neil). Some were so badly wounded as to leave them, in the doctors' opinion, disabled for life, as with Samuel Jackson and Edward Jones; while the wounds of others put them out of work for two to three months.[77]

Another means of evaluating the atrocity committed at Peterloo is to relate the number of casualties to the size and behaviour of the crowd. The Bees believed that the numbers attending the meeting is calculable from the casualty lists.[78] As suggested earlier, this is highly questionable. Nonetheless, their point that the size of the crowd was much exaggerated at the time is surely valid. In commenting on Peterloo, both sides had a strong incentive to maximise: with reformers keen to demonstrate that their cause commanded an enormous following in the region; and with loyalists needing to stress a massive attendance in order to justify and excuse the military action taken. For this reason, the figures supplied at the time for the size of the crowd have to be treated with a great deal of scepticism. That they were exaggerated is evident in the surviving eye-witness accounts of Peterloo and the way they attest to the relatively small number of women and children in attendance.[79] If 16 August 1819 had been a gala day with people present as families and dressed in their best as though participating in a local annual festival such as a wakes or rush-cart procession – the impression given by several eye-witness accounts sympatic to reform – it would have been a different matter; and the accuracy of the estimates made for the size of the crowd could have been tested by relating them to the total population of the region from which the crowd was drawn: that is the parish of Stockport, the Hundred of Salford and the chapelry of Saddleworth with Quick.[80] But the crowd was not a composition of families; and the fact that relatively few children and women were present calls for a considerable scaling down of the region's population base. The extent to which this has to be done can be roughly gauged from the 1821 census. By separating men from women, and children from adults, this census reveals that about half the population were female and that as many as 39 per cent of the population were children under fifteen. For this reason, a grand total population of 534,000 provided a cohort of no more than 198,000 males aged fifteen or above: that is, the group which furnished the great majority of those in attendance. As the Bees proposed with slightly different figures, this renders a crowd of 150,000 at Peterloo utterly improbable; even more so as the census was taken two years after the event. In view of the fact that the population of the region was experiencing rapid growth at the time – for example, the parish of Manchester grew from 136,000 persons in 1811 to 187,000 persons in 1821 – its size must have been a good deal less in 1819.[81] A crowd of about 50,000 would appear to be a more realistic estimate, especially if related to the limited space available within the field's perimeter – that is, the triangle formed by Peter Street, Mount Street and Windmill Street, the area now occupied by Peter Street which in 1819 had yet to be extended to cross the field, and the area beyond leading to the high wall surrounding the Friends' Meeting House. Estimates of the extent of the ground vary from 29,000 to 12,000 square yards. The reformer John Wade produced the former figure in order to justify a crowd of 150,000; but in calculating the area he wrongly multiplied its length and breadth and misleadingly assumed that the field was a rectangle whereas it was principally a triangle – that is, the area formed by Peter Street, Mount Street and Windmill Street – supplemented by a quadrangle of land bounded by the Peter Street extension, Bootle Street, Mount Street and South Street. Correctly multiplied and adapted to account for the shape of the field, Wade's measurements produce a figure close to the magistrates' calculation of 14,000 square yards and not too far removed from the Bees' reckoning of 12,000 square yards.[82] Also to be considered is a point made at the time by many eye-witness accounts that, prior to the attack, the crowd was dense only round the hustings and that several areas of the field were thinly populated, especially over towards Mount Street where the cavalry first positioned itself and consequently had sufficient room to build up a gallop before crashing into the crowd; and over towards Bootle Street, an area, strewn with loose timbers, which was not packed with people until after the cavalry charge when many fled in that direction, only to find their escape thwarted by the high wall of the Friends' Meeting House and a cordon of infantry guarding the exits on either side of the wall with drawn bayonets. It would seem that the crowd was densely packed only within, at most, a fifty-yard radius of the hustings, the result of the decision of the first contingents to arrive – that is from Ashton, Stockport and Oldham – to form a protective barrier of men around the hustings and the wish of others to get near enough to hear what was said from the platform.[83]

Yet the smaller the crowd only serves to magnify the atrocity. Put together the lists reveal, as we have seen, a much larger number of casualties than was previously calculated: with 654 persons injured rather than the normally accepted number of 400, and with 18, rather than 11, deaths. Moreover, as we have seen, this casualty figure is likely to be an underestimation. The reasonable assumption that there were 700 casualties and that the Peterloo crowd numbered 50,000 produces a high casualty rate of 1 in 71. Assuming casualties of no more than 654, the casualty rate is still remarkable: 1 in 76. Viewed in this light, the casualty lists suggest that the physical assault on the peaceful crowd assembled in Peter's Field on 16 August 1819 represented a terrible act of suppression.

Compounding the offence was the fact that, at the point of attack, the crowd was without weapons, other than walking sticks, and prepared to abide by a policy of peaceful assembly and passive resistance. Accordingly, the arrest of Hunt and the other occupants of the platform passed unopposed. In view of this, and the high proportion of people wounded by weapons or trampled by cavalry, it could be aptly termed a 'massacre'.

The perpetrators

In describing the injuries sustained, the casualty lists frequently identify those responsible for inflicting them. It is generally accepted that to the fore in the attack on the crowd were 60 volunteers from the Manchester and Salford Yeomanry Cavalry, backed up by 400 or so Special Constables, another voluntary group.[84] The casualty lists bear this out, presenting in some detail the armed onslaught of these volunteers – all recruited from the shopkeepers, publicans, manufacturers and professional men of Manchester – upon the unarmed working class of the town and its vicinity. But what gave this relatively small number of men the courage to proceed so vigorously against such a large and confident crowd?

The answer lies in the proximity of other troops, regular as well as volunteer: notably 340 cavalry of the 15th Hussars, 420 members of the Cheshire Yeomanry Cavalry and another 60 volunteers from the Manchester and Salford Yeomanry. With sabres drawn – the blades flashing in the sunlight through the clouds of dust stirred up by the horses' hooves – these additional troops galloped on to the field from the Windmill Street side immediately after the initial charge of the Manchester and Salford Yeomanry, allegedly because the latter had become stranded in the crowd and needed to be rescued. Moreover, guarding the routes to and from the field were, to the south, another 150 Hussars, half of them positioned in Lower Mosley Street in the company of a troop of Royal Horse Artillery equipped with two six-pounders, and the other half stationed to guard the road to Hulme which led to the barracks. To the north and positioned along Dickinson Street were 160 troops of the 88th Foot with bayonets at the ready, for the sinister purpose of blocking off what was the most direct route home not only for fleeing Mancunians, most of whom lived in the Ancoats area, but also for the participants from Bury, Middleton, Rochdale, Oldham, Stockport and Ashton. Also to the north, and for the same interceptory purpose, were 250 troops of the 31st Foot, at first positioned in Brazenose Street and at the time of the attack used to block off Bootle Street. (See Map 3) This made a total of about 1,500 troops deployed on the day, 1,000 of whom were regulars.[85] Knowledge of the near presence of these extra troops must have instilled the local Yeomanry and constables with the confidence and courage to attack the crowd. In addition, as the casualty lists reveal, many of these extra troops became actively engaged in the onslaught.

Twenty-six years later, one of the Hussars present, Sir William Jolliffe, recollected that nine-tenths of the cuts inflicted by cavalrymen at Peterloo were the work of his regiment.[86] Although the casualty lists do no bear this out, attributing 55 of the cited sabre wounds to the Yeomanry Cavalry and only six to the Hussars, they do not deny that the Hussars were heavily involved in attacking the crowd. Many of the sabrings noticed in the casualty lists fail to mention either

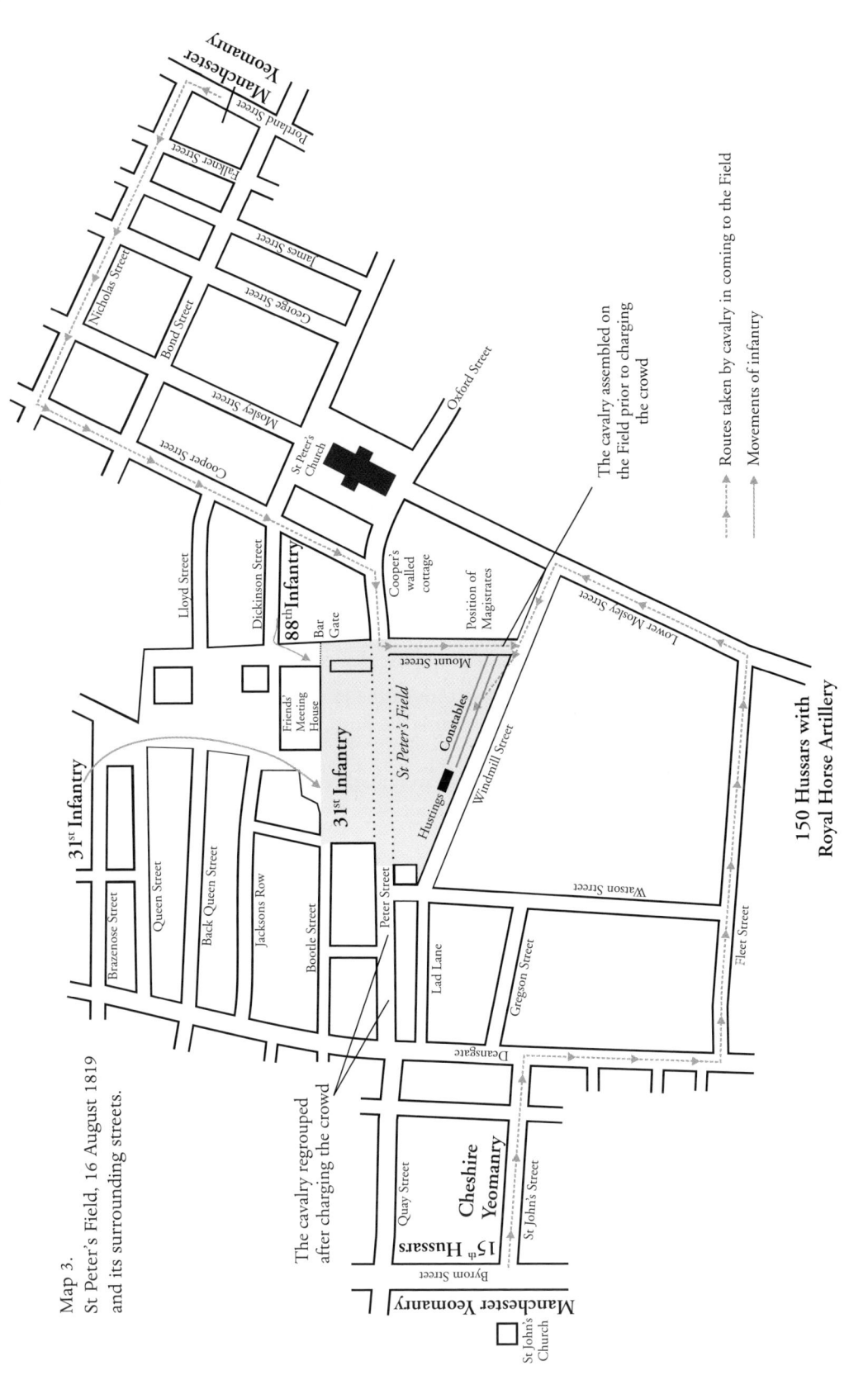

Map 3.
St Peter's Field, 16 August 1819 and its surrounding streets.

the Yeomanry or the Hussars but simply refer to the cavalry and its part in beating, stabbing and cutting people with the sword. In fact, only 27 per cent of the sabre casualties are specifically attributed to the Yeomanry Cavalry. 70 per cent of them could be equally attributed to the Hussars. Another eye-witness, John Railton, blamed the Hussars for injuries inflicted, this time on the Special Constables, at least eight of whom fell victim to cavalrymen. Railton's account went as follows: 'Some of the constables, being between the Manchester cavalry [i.e. the Yeomanry Cavalry] and the Barracks cavalry [i.e. the Hussars], on the latter entering the ground, with the constables being indistinguished, were trampled upon or otherwise wounded and two or three of them were killed'.[87] The casualty lists throw light on this account. Nowhere in the lists are injuries inflicted upon constables attributed to Hussars. Moreover, of the eight constables mentioned as cavalry victims, the injuries of two of them (William Evans and John Routledge) are attributed to the Yeomanry Cavalry and those of another (James Chesworth) to 'possibly the Cheshire Corps', that is the Yeomanry Cavalry of Cheshire. Of the rest, one, Samuel McFadden, appeared to be a victim of the Manchester Yeomanry in view of his claim that all was quiet when the cavalry that trampled him charged, which rather suggests that he fell at the very first attack. Nonetheless, of the remaining four – three of whom were sabred (John Ashworth, Robert Darbyshire and Henry Froggatt) and one trampled (Petty) – they could well have been victims of the Hussars as, following the initial charge by the Manchester Cavalry towards the hustings from Mount Street, they galloped across the field from Windmill Street. This would have brought them crashing through what remained of the avenue of Special Constables leading up to the hustings from the house on Mount Street where the magistrates were placed.

Yet, at the time, the Hussars were seen as more restrained than the Yeomanry, largely because of their military experience, self-discipline and expertise as professional soldiers. They were presented as using the flat of the sword to drive people off the field, not the cutting edge to inflict a wound. They were also seen as acting with a forbearance which limited the number of woundings, and even of intervening to protect people against the savagery of the Yeomanry and the Special Constables. In the map which he produced and appended to his Peterloo Massacre journal, James Wroe noted at the far end of Windmill Street: 'Manchester Yeomanry cutting at men and women heaped on each other before the houses', adding: 'Some lives were saved here by the officers of the 15th Hussars'. Hunt himself stated that the massacre 'would have been worse' but for the regulars 'who were heard to threaten these cowardly fellows with summary justice if they did not desist from cutting down the fleeing people'.[88] Three entries in the casualty lists offer support for these claims. Thus, Thomas Brown was bruised 'by the flat of the swords' of 'some of the 15th'; Samuel Allcard, 'an interesting lad' of 18, was saved by a Hussar who threatened to sabre a Yeoman to prevent him from striking the boy a second time; while William Barnes, having been sabred and then placed in prison, was released on the admission made by Captain Whitfield of the Hussars that he had been 'very ill-used'.

Other entries in the casualty lists, however, show the Hussars acting with brutality and in keeping with the remark of John Fell, a Manchester shopkeeper, that 'the Hussars dispersed themselves in all directions, not in line, and cutting the same as the others had done'. The same witness also revealed that the Hussars were the second band of cavalry to attack the crowd, followed by the Cheshire Yeomanry. Whereas the latter 'went straight across the field', presumably because it was now, but for prone bodies, virtually empty of people, the Hussars appeared to target the individuals and groups whom the initial charge of the Manchester Yeomanry had failed to disperse.[89] Moreover, not all Hussars used the flat of the sword: thus James Greaves was stabbed by a Hussar's sabre, while both Sarah Taylor and James Lees were described as cut by a Hussar, suggesting the use of the sabre's edge. Lees was cut twice. The entries for Peter Warburton and Charles Washington reveal the predatory aggression of the Hussars, especially around the Quaker Meeting House in Mount Street where the high wall of the chapel yard and a barrier across the street had blocked the way for the fleeing crowd as the cavalry pursued it from the field. Warburton's entry showed how, pinned against the chapel wall, he sustained seven cuts to his head and body, some from the bayonets of the 88th Foot, some from the sabres of the 15th Hussars. Washington's entry described how six of the Hussars entered the chapel yard, cutting at the people who had sought refuge within its walls.[90]

Since 300 or so Hussars had charged the crowd shortly after the 60 Yeomanry had done so, they must bear some responsibility – along with the 420 Cheshire Yeomanry Cavalry and a further 60 Manchester and Salford Yeomanry Cavalry, both of whom had accompanied the Hussars to the ground – for the large number of people ridden down, even though the lists cite only one instance (i.e. Charles Washington) of an injury specifically caused by a Hussar's horse. Jolliffe's account of the Hussars' initial charge and its impact implies the damage done. According to him, the charge 'swept this mangled mass of human beings before it ... so that by the time we had arrived at the end of the field the fugitives were literally piled up to a considerable elevation above the level of the ground'.[91] Of all the injuries inflicted by the cavalry, no more than 21 per cent were attributed to the Yeomanry. As for the rest, which are presented in the lists as caused by 'cavalry' or 'horse' – presumably due to the difficulty on the day of distinguishing between regulars and volunteers, whose uniforms were very much alike and whose identity was obscured by the dust that the horses kicked up – a considerable number must have been the work of Hussars.

The casualty lists also reveal something of the damage done by the 88th Foot who were involved not only in opposing the New Cross riots which occurred the same evening, but also in the military operation against the crowd on St Peter's

Field itself. Hunt arrived at the field just as the clock of St John's Church struck one. A few moments later, people in the crowd sighted, with some consternation, troops from the 88th Foot formed along Dickinson Street, the far side of the Quaker Meeting House.[92] The role of the infantry was to intensify the terror of the crowd by preventing people from making their escape from the field along the most direct routes home. With fixed bayonets, they formed a bristling barrier across the street exits on the north side, inflicting wounds on the press of people by stabbing with the bayonet blade and clubbing with the musket-butt. Encountering the line of bayonets, people turned back only to find themselves under attack from the sabres of the cavalry. This was described by an anonymous eyewitness:

> The 88th troop were marched to a station at the south end of the Quaker Meeting House to intercept the people who might fly in that direction and here there was indeed most dreadful slaughter [as] crowds passed to this quarter and were forced back by the bayonets of the infantry, the cavalry cutting them in the rear.

Another eye-witness, John Railton, saw the same thing:

> The cavalry were pursuing the mob and they were met and goaded by the infantry who were advancing upon and pricking them with fixed bayonets.[93]

Fifteen entries in the casualty lists reveal the work of the 88th Foot: William Batsan, John Boulter, John Brookes, Joseph Brookes, Thomas Buckley, Mary Evans, John Goodwin, John Hardman, Mark Howard, William Hurdies, William Moores, Joseph Ogden, John Pimblet, John Smithies, Peter Warburton. They show how the 88th stabbed people in the head, belly, back and arms with their bayonets or clubbed them to the ground with the butts of their muskets. Their deliberate fencing in of the fleeing crowd to prevent its escape from the pursuing cavalry must have increased the number of wounded on or near the field.

The brutality of the infantry's conduct is illustrated by the entries in the casualty lists for Mary Evans, Joseph Ogden and William Batsan. Accompanied by her niece, Mary Evans was seeking to return to her home in Style Street near St Michael's Church when stopped by a soldier of the 88th and stabbed in the thigh. The same man also attacked the niece, piercing her clothing with his bayonet. Only the intervention of another soldier saved her from injury. Joseph Ogden was also making his way home, to George Leigh Street in Ancoats, when he encountered the 88th. He had already been cut, either by sabre or horse's hoof. One of the 88th then stabbed him in the head with a bayonet whose blade either snapped off or became ineffectually loose in its holder. Undeterred, the soldier reversed his musket and felled him with the butt, leaving him disabled for six weeks. William Batsan's entry was of more general import since he himself miraculously escaped wounding by the military only to be injured by the crowd.

He showed how he and others were trapped, in the vicinity of the Quaker Meeting House, between the cavalry and the 88th Foot. According to him, the latter were 'charging bayonets at the people as they endeavoured to pass ... sometimes as if to frighten them, at other times wounding them in the thighs'.

None of this detracts from the importance of the Yeomanry Cavalry in initiating the attack, but it does suggest that many of the wounds inflicted were the work of the regular cavalry – charging across the field and then attacking people trapped under the wall of of the yard round the Friends' Meeting House and in the yard itself where they had sought refuge – and of the regular infantry standing fast across the streets by the Quaker chapel with bayonets fixed and at the ready.

The payment of compensation

Finally, the casualty lists usefully reveal the amounts of money awarded in relief to the injured. What is remarkable about this evidence is first the favour shown by relief committees to women casualties: 67 per cent of them were granted relief, against 63 per cent of male casualties; while 26 per cent of all females relieved – against 19 per cent of all males relieved – received above £2. (See Table 10)

Table 10. Relief dispensed to male and female casualties

Relief dispensed	£2 or less	over £2	Total
Men	237	55	292
Women	81	29	110
Total	318	84	402

The second remarkable feature of this evidence for relief is the paltriness of the amounts dispensed to the injured. As the Bees revealed in their table 7, over 80 per cent of the payments were £2 or less, with 50 per cent £1 or less. Payments above £5 were made to no more than 3 per cent of the injured.[94] Bearing in mind that many of the casualties required medical care and were obliged to take weeks off from work, these payments were, with a few exceptions, parsimonious in the extreme.

The third remarkable feature about the relief dispensed to the injured is that it consumed only 31 per cent of the money raised for Peterloo victims. By February 1820 some £3,408 had been collected, thanks to subscriptions from London, Birmingham, Liverpool, Leeds, Norwich and Manchester; but by this time as much as 42 per cent of this money had been spent upon legal proceedings and administrative costs, leaving a surplus of £768 which was swallowed up in further legal fees, notably related to the trial of Hunt and others in March 1820 at York.⁹⁵ All this reflects the social prejudices of the fund's bourgeois and aristocratic organisers, especially their low opinion of working people. They clearly preferred to use the money for promoting the cause of parliamentary reform and the interests of its leaders, rather than to compensate adequately the injured rank and file. For this reason, the victims who were reasonably well relieved tended to be the ones prepared to bring legal actions against the perpetrators of the massacre (e.g. William Butterworth of Middleton, Margaret Goodwin, Elizabeth Farren, Alice Kenyon, John Leigh and William Leigh) or who suffered imprisonment for serving as leaders on the day (e.g. Elizabeth Gaunt, Ann Scott, William Billinge, James Green, Thomas Kelly, Arthur Neil). In contrast, the claims of other victims – predominantly workers, their wives and offspring – were viewed with suspicion and scepticism, no matter how serious the injury, and they consequently received payments inappropriate to the gravity and consequence of their disability. This even applied to some of those receiving relatively large sums of money: such as Mary Jervis who was granted £8 but had to pay doctors' bills of £4 and was left lame for life; or Samuel Jackson who received £15 but was in the Infirmary for over a month and suffered an amputation of the leg; or Owen McCabe who received £9 but was now condemned to walking on crutches; or John Millard who received £3 after having his arm almost cut off; or Benjamin Seed who received £8 but was obliged to spend two months in Manchester Infirmary. The payments made to relatives in compensation for death were similarly inadequate: notably the £5 paid to the husband of Martha Partington who was killed in the crush; the £6 6s. 0d. paid to the father of John Rhodes who died of a sabre wound; or the £4 paid to the father of Joshua Whitworth who was shot dead.

The outcome was that, having publicly demonstrated their commitment to democracy by attending a meeting in St Peter's Field on 16 August 1819, the purpose of which was to promote parliamentary reform, the workers of Manchester and its vicinity suffered maltreatment not only from those loyal to the old regime but also from the reformers themselves whose cause of universal suffrage, annual parliaments and voting by ballot they had enthusiastically embraced, and for which they underwent, unwillingly but without much resistance, a thankless martyrdom in the form of a ruthless slaughter.

Notes to Chapter I

1. See M. I. Thomis and J. Grimmett, *Women in Protest, 1800–1850* (London, 1982), ch. 5; Ruth and Edmund Frow, *Political Women, 1800–1850* (London, 1989), ch. 2; James Epstein, *Radical Expression* (London, 1994), pp. 88–92; Anna Clark, *The Struggle for the Breeches: Gender in the Making of the British Working Class* (London, 1995), ch. 9. Also see M. L. Bush, 'The Women at Peterloo: the Impact of Female Reform on the Manchester Meeting of 16 August 1819', *History*, 89 (2004), pp. 209–32.
2. The *Manchester Observer* report appeared on 23 Aug., the *Star* report, on 17 August.
3. G. M. Trevelyan, 'The Number of Casualties at Peterloo', *History*, VII (1922), pp. 200–5.
4. E.g. Donald Read, *Peterloo: the 'Massacre' and its Background* (London 1958); Robert Walmsley, *Peterloo: the Case Reopened* (Manchester, 1969); Joyce Marlow, *The Peterloo Massacre* (London, 1970); Robert Reid, *The Peterloo Massacre* (London, 1989); J. Riding, *Peterloo* (London, 2018) and Graham Phythian, *Peterloo* (Stroud, 2018).
5. See Malcolm and Walter Bee, 'The Casualties of Peterloo', *Manchester Region History Review*, III (1989), pp. 45–6. Five years earlier Robert Glen had provided an analysis of casualties confined to the Stockport area. See his *Urban Workers in the Early Industrial Revolution* (London, 1984), ch. 10. For the standard view of numbers of injured and cause of injury, see Read, *Peterloo*, p. 140.
6. Rylands English MS. 1197 (28).
7. Reid, *Peterloo Massacre*, pp. 190–1. For the Infirmary Register, see *State Trials* new series, I (London,1888), p. 1262, note a.
8. Rylands English MS. 1197 (41), (44), (45); Reid, *Peterloo Massacre*, p. 190.
9. Rylands English MS. 1197 (41).
10. Ibid., (41) and (45).
11. *Peterloo Massacre*, issues 12 and 13 (Manchester, 1819), pp. 177–92 and 193–216.
12. Wroe supplied the total at the end of the list in the 29 January issue.
13. Wroe promised a list of the dead, to be published in the 5 February issue, but it never appeared.
14. See below, p. 9.
15. For the published list, see pp. 90–6. For Hunt's comments on it, see pp. 89–90.
16. Samuel Bamford, *Passages*, I, pp. 224–5. The omitted names are William Kershaw of Rochdale, Thomas Barlow of Blackley and, from the Middleton area, John Barlow, James Barrett, Samuel Hilton, William Kay, Robert Lancashire, Ellen Lees and John Smithies.
17. See *Bee*, pp. 43–4.
18. For first list, see Rylands English MS. 172. The second list appears as Appendix IV in the publication entitled *Report of the Metropolitan and Central Committee Appointed for the Relief of the Manchester Sufferers* (London, 1820).
19. A. Prentice, *Historical Sketches and Personal Reminiscences of Manchester* (Manchester, 1851), p. 167; *MCC Report*, p. 11; John Edward Taylor, *Notes and Observations by a Member of the Manchester Committee for Relieving the Sufferers of 16th August* (London, 1820), p. 170.
20. *MCC Report*, pp. 11, 15–16; Taylor, *Notes and Observations*, p. 170.
21. *MCC Report*, pp. 2, 5–6, 13–15.

22. Ibid., pp. 17–18. The casualty lists reveal 8 of the injured with more than one address: Samuel Allcard, Charles Harper, William McGairathy, Catherine O'Neal, Stephen Pollitt, John Prince, Ann Roberts, Bernard Seed.
23. For the manuscript list, see Rylands English MS. 172. For processing of applications, see *MCC Report,* pp. 17–18, 22.
24. The *MCC Report* declares that it received 200 new applications (pp. 17–18) and was obliged to leave 140 of them to be sorted out by the Manchester Relief Committee (p. 22).
25. Ibid., p. 19.
26. See Read, *Peterloo*, p. 140; Marlow, *Peterloo Massacre*, p. 152; Prentice, *Historical Sketches*, p. 168. Making a death tally of 18 was the likely death from trampling by the Yeomanry Cavalry of the Special Constable, William Evans. John Railton in his recollected account of Peterloo (see *Manchester Guardian*, 18th Aug. 1919) claimed that 2 or 3 constables had been killed in this way, whereas the casualty lists cite only one case of a constable killed by the charging cavalry: John Ashworth. As for Evans, one list claimed that he 'appears to be in a dying state' and another stated that he was 'still dangerously ill'. In all likelihood he died shortly afterwards of the injuries incurred at Peterloo and his death was noted by Railton.
27. *MCC Report*, pp. 17–18; Taylor, *Notes and Observations*, p. 171.
28. Rylands English MS. 1197 (25).
29. *Bee*, pp. 46–7.
30. For Mutrie, see *Report*, Lees Inquest, pp. 438–9. For Hunt, see *Peterloo Massacre*, p. 95. For Bury, see *Report*, Trial of Hunt, p. 248. For Oldham, Royton and the High Moors, see *Report*, Redford v. Birley, pp. 27–8. For Stockport and Ashton, see *Report*, Lees Inquest, p. 443 and *Report*, Trial of Hunt, p. 130.
31. See Read, *Peterloo*, pp. 128–30.
32. See John Walker's account, *Report*, Trial of Hunt, p. 112; and J. Mills' account, ibid., p. 77.
33. See James Dyson's account, *Report*, Trial of Hunt, p. 179. There are suggestions, however, that the party did not stick tightly together. In spite of Bamford's exhortation at Barrowfield that the Middleton party should on arrival remain as one unit – 'keep yourselves as select as possible, with your banners in your centre' (see Dyson's account, *Report*, Trial of Hunt, p. 178) – Dyson declared that soon after reaching the field 'our line broke' and 'every man went where he liked' (*Report*, Trial of Hunt, p. 180), although this might refer to the breaking up of the column of men that, arranged in military formation, had brought the Middleton party to Manchester. There is also evidence that some of the Middleton women became separated from the Middleton party by taking up position behind the hustings on the raised ground verging upon Windmill Street. Standing at a distance of twenty yards from the platform, they found themselves surrounded by strangers. See Elizabeth Sheppard's and Mary Yates' accounts, *Report*, Trial of Hunt, p. 185; and Jemima Bamford's account in Bamford, *Passages*, I, p. 221.
34. See John Hamer's account, *Report*, Redford v. Birley, p. 81.
35. See *The Champion*, 22 Aug. 1819.
36. See Bamford, *Passages*, I, pp. 201–2.

37. The eye-witness accounts are mostly connected with evidence given at the three trials associated with Peterloo: i.e. the coroner's inquest on John Lees; the trial of Hunt and others; and the private action brought by one of the victims, Thomas Redford, against Hugh Birley and other members of the Manchester Yeomanry Cavalry (see Abbreviations for full titles and details of publication). In addition, there are the newspaper reports of Peterloo: notably by Charles Tyas in *The Times*, 19 Aug. 1819; in *Wheeler's Chronicle*, 21 Aug. 1819; the report written for the *Manchester Courier* which was suppressed by this paper but then published by Wroe in his journal devoted to Peterloo (see *Peterloo Massacre*, no. 4); in *Exchange Herald*, 17 Aug. 1819; and the letter from Manchester printed in *Morning Chronicle*, 3 Sept. 1819. For reports of Richard Carlile, see Bush, *The Friends and Following of Richard Carlile*, ch. 7. Further eye-witness accounts eventually surfaced: notably by Bamford; the three narratives printed by Bruton (by Jolliffe, Stanley and Smith); Swift's Narrative (copy in Manchester Central Library); John Railton's account, printed in *Manchester Guardian*, 18 Aug. 1919; Francis Philips' account in *An Exposure of the Calumnies* ... (London, 1819); Archibald Prentice's account in his *Historical Sketches and Personal Reminiscences of Manchester* (Manchester, 1851); Absalom Watkin's account in *Extracts from Absalom Watkin's Journal, 1814–1856*, ed. A. E. Watkin (London, 1920), ch.11; James Weatherley's recollection, to be published by Michael Powell and Terry Wyke; and Joseph Barrett's account in R. Poole (ed.) *Return to Peterloo* (Manchester, 2014), pp. 134–6.
38. *Report*, Lees Inquest, pp. 376 (Entwisle), 423 (Mutrie), 446 (Owen), 317 (Hall); Rylands English MS. 1197 (67) (Hay).
39. *Report*, Redford v. Birley, pp. 155, 161–2 (Shuttleworth); *Report*, Trial of Hunt, p. 239; ibid., p. 193 (Smith) The Bees note the preponderance of Mancunians in table 6, p. 46.
40. See below, p. 19.
41. *Wheeler's Chronicle* on 21 August claimed that 'many were from Blackburn'. But that they had failed to arrive was evident in Bamford's remark that when the cavalry first approached the field their noise made people say: 'it was the Blackburn people coming' (*Passages*, I, p. 206).
42. See Geoffrey Timmins, *The Last Shift: the Decline of Handloom Weaving in Nineteenth-century Lancashire* (Manchester, 1993), p. 22 and ch. 1 *passim*.
43. *Bee*, p. 46.
44. For the impact of spinning developments, see R. Lloyd-Jones and M. J. Lewis, *Manchester and the Age of the Factory* (Beckenham, 1988), chs 4 and 5. For the factor of an oversupply of labour, see Duncan Bythell, *The Handloom Weavers* (Cambridge, 1969), pp. 106–7. For powerloom developments in the Manchester region at the time of Peterloo, see ibid., p. 91. For weaver fears about powerlooms, see ibid., pp. 198–9.
45. For weaver radicalism and Peterloo, see Read, *Peterloo*, p. 24; Glen, *Urban Workers in the Early Industrial Revolution*, pp. 246–7. For the attempt at revision – in reaction to E. P. Thompson's *The Making of the English Working Class* – see Bythell, *Handloom Weavers*, ch. 9. For Haslam's article, see *Manchester Guardian*, 13 Aug. 1919.
46. The Irish have been identified from their names, using Edward Maclysaght's *Guide to Irish Surnames* (London, 1965). For identifying the Irish areas in Manchester, see Mervyn Busteed and Rob Hodgson, 'Coping with urbanisation: the Irish in early nineteenth-century Manchester', in S. J. Neary, M. S. Symer and F. E. Brown (eds), *The*

Urban Experience (London, 1994), fig. 41.1, p. 472.
47. For Thompson's view, see his *The Making of the English Working Class* (London, 1970 ed.), pp. 707–8.
48. For a historiographical consideration of this point, see Roger Swift, 'The historiography of the Irish in nineteenth-century Britain' in Patrick O'Sullivan (ed.), *The Irish in the New Communities* (Leicester, 1992), pp. 62–8. For Hunt's conduct on 9 Aug., see *Report*, Hunt's Trial, p. 38. For Hunt's conduct on 16 Aug., see Bamford, *Passages*, I, pp. 201–3.
49. Bamford, *Passages*, I, pp. 202–3. For a critique of this account and the first published attempt to relate the Irish to Peterloo, see Michael Herbert, *The Wearing of the Green: a Political History of the Irish in Manchester* (London, 2001), pp. 29–30.
50. See Mervyn Busteed, '"I shall never return to Hibernia's Bowers": Irish migrant identities in early Victorian Manchester', *The North West Geographer*, II (2000), pp. 16–17.
51. Prior to the 1841 census, details relating to individual persons were systematically destroyed, leaving no more than the statistical conclusions.
52. See above, n. 30 for the calculations made at the time of the relative numbers of women to men.
53. See *Sherwin's Political Register*, V (1819), p. 242.
54. See *MCC Report*, pp. 19–20; *Champion*, 22 Aug. 1819, p. 528.
55. *Bruton*, p. 53; a report on the Yeomanry in Rylands English MS. 1197 (26).
56. Another 21 women were crushed in the crowd as well as injured by weapons or horses.
57. *Bee*, p. 45.
58. See Read, *Peterloo*, pp. 81–2, 237.
59. For the illustration of this attitude in contemporary prints, see Diana Donald, *The Age of Caricature* (London, 1996), pp. 192–5. For its expression in the press, see *Cowdroy's Manchester Gazetteer*, 7 August 1819; *Wheeler's Manchester Chronicle*, 10 and 17 July 1819; *Manchester Comet*, 30 October 1822.
60. See below, p.45.
61. See 1821 census returns. The region referred to is the area of the North West from which the majority of the Peterloo participants were drawn: principally the Hundred of Salford, the parish of Stockport and the chapelry of Saddleworth with Quick. Unfortunately the 1821 returns from the townships of Manchester and Salford did not provide information on age. It has to be assumed that the age profile provided for the rest of the region is applicable to Manchester and Salford.
62. Read, *Peterloo*, p. 100.
63. For the January meeting, see Read, *Peterloo*, p. 106. That he understates the size and significance of this meeting is evident in a contemporary account by J. Knight entitled *A Full and Particular Report of the Proceedings of the Public Meeting held in Manchester on Monday, 18th January, 1819* (Manchester, n.d. but 1819). For June meeting, see Read, p. 109 and *Manchester Observer*, 26 June 1819, p. 620.
64. Read, *Peterloo*, p. 113.
65. Read, *Peterloo*, pp. 109–10; Rylands English MS. 1197 (89), pp. 2, 4.
66. See the rich collections of material in Rylands English MS. 1197 and in the Hay Scrap Box, Chetham's Library, Manchester.

67. Rylands English MS. 1197 (38).
68. Ibid., (9) and (3).
69. Ibid., (89, pp. 6–7).
70. For Flags, see *Bruton*, p. 18; *Report*, Lees Inquest, pp. 137, 172; *Report*, Redford v. Birley, pp. 450–2. For caps and hats, see *Report*, Lees Inquest, p. 179; *Report*, Redford v. Birley, pp. 39–41.
71. See, for example, *Report*, Lees Inquest, pp. 312–15.
72. See *Peterloo Massacre . . . edited by an Observer* (Manchester, 1819), p. ii.
73. *Bruton*, p. 53 (for Jolliffe's observation); Read, *Peterloo*, pp. 139–40; Alan Kidd, *Manchester* (Manchester, 1993), p. 94; Walmsley, *Peterloo: the Case Re-opened*, ch. 15. Undaunted, the two full-length studies of Peterloo that followed – by Marlow and Reid – were both entitled *The Peterloo Massacre*. In commenting on the fact that 15 deaths resulted from Peterloo, Marlow commented: 'hardly much of a massacre! Yes and no. The definition of a massacre is general slaughter, a carnage, which was what occurred on Saint Peter's Field' (p. 151).
74. Names of constables injured by cavalry: John Ashworth (killed by sabre), James Chesworth (sabred), Robert Derbyshire (sabred), William Evans (trampled and dying), Henry Froggatt (sabred), Samuel McFadden (trampled), Mr Petty (trampled), John Routledge (trampled and nearly killed).
75. *Bee*, p. 45.
76. The October incident resulted from a leading member of the Yeomanry Cavalry, Edward Meagher, firing a gun from the window of his house at the crowd outside who were taunting him with the nickname 'Peterloo butcher'. He injured two men (Joseph Jones and John Robinson). See Read, *Peterloo*, p. 149 and the eye-witness account by Weatherley.
77. E.g., of those wounded by soldiers or police, John Bridges was disabled for ten weeks, John Coates, for eleven weeks, Jeremiah Holden, for eight weeks, Samuel Kay, for twelve weeks, Edward Lancaster, for twelve weeks, William Leigh, for eight weeks, John Thompson, for ten weeks, Peter Warburton for eight weeks.
78. *Bee*, p. 47.
79. See above, n. 30.
80. For this 'family' image, see Samuel Bamford, *Passages*, I, p. 200; *Bruton*, pp. 65–6 (Smith); *Peterloo Massacre*, p. 95.
81. See *Bee*, p. 47. For statistics on population growth, see *Baines' Lancashire Directory*, II, p. 128.
82. For Wade's estimate, see his *Manchester Massacre*, p. 8. For the magistrates' calculation, see English MS. 1197 (67). For the Bees' reckoning, see their n. 36. On the question of the maximum size of crowd that could be accommodated, much depends on the extent to which, prior to the attack, the crowd occupied the area north of Peter Street: that is, the considerable space that extended to the high south wall of the Friends Meeting House.
83. See above, p. 13.
84. Read, *Peterloo*, pp. 133ff; Reid, *Peterloo Massacre*, pp. 28–9. Figures vary for the number of constables present from 200–500. *The Times* reckoned that 300–400 marched on to the field, while *Manchester Mercury* put the figure at 400–500. See Walmsley, *Peterloo: the*

Case Reopened, pp. 152–3.
85. For various contemporary calculations of the troops present, see *Bruton*, pp. 49–50 (by Jolliffe) and *Report*, Redford v. Birley, p. 473 (by L'Estrange).
86. *Bruton*, p. 53 (Jolliffe's account).
87. See Railton's account in *Manchester Guardian*, 18 Aug. 1919.
88. For the Hussars' alleged steadying influence, see *Champion*, Aug. 22 1819 (p. 528); *Bruton*, p. 53; *Peterloo Massacre*, the frontispiece map; a letter from Hunt in *Manchester Observer*, 6 Sept. 1819.
89. *Report*, Lees Inquest, p. 173; *Report*, Hunt's Trial, p. 231.
90. *Report*, Lees Inquest, p. 173.
91. *Bruton*, pp. 52–3.
92. *Report*, Hunt's Trial, p. 213 (John Brattargh); ibid., p. 200 (John Shuttleworth); ibid., p. 234 (Robert Wright).
93. Railton's account in *Manchester Guardian*, 18 Aug. 1919; Bamford, *Passages*, I, p. 209; John Swift's narrative [manuscript in Manchester Central Library], p. 16; Stanley's account in *Bruton*, p. 18; *MCC Report*, p. 20; *Morning Chronicle*, 3 Sept. 1819 (letter from Manchester).
94. *Bee*, p. 47.
95. *MCC Report*, p. 6. The total sum distributed to sufferers was £1,206 13s. 8d. However £200 of it went to compensate several who were victims of imprisonment, not casualties.

II The Peterloo casualty lists

In the following lists the superscript numbers at the left refer to the following sources:

[1] Hunt's List: *Henry Hunt's Addresses to Radical Reformers*, nos 11 and 12 (1831). The dead are named in no. 11; the injured in no. 12. This is largely a copy, with a few extra names, of the list that appears in the journal *Peterloo Massacre* (Manchester,1819), pp. 199–214.

[2] Peterloo Relief List: Rylands English MS. 172.

[3] List of Persons taken to the Manchester Infirmary on 16/17th August 1819: Rylands English MS. 1197(28) and printed with a few extra details in *Wheeler's Manchester Chronicle*, 21 Aug. 1819.

[4] Pearson's List of the Killed and Wounded: Rylands English MS. 1197(41) and printed in *The Times*, 3 Sept. 1819.

[5] Samuel Bamford's List of 'wounded and badly bruised who went with the Middleton party': *Passages in the Life of a Radical* (1844), I, pp. 224–5.

[6] *Appendix to MCC Report*: *Report of the Metropolitan and Central Committee Appointed for the Relief of Manchester Sufferers* (London, 1820).

[7] *Manchester Observer* List: the *Manchester Observer*, 22 and 29 January 1820.

NB Newton-lane refers to Oldham-road. Chorlton Row is Chorlton-on-Medlock. The residences designated 'Manchester' refer to what Manchester township was in 1819: that is, the manor of Manchester clearly bounded on three sides by the Rivers Irwell, Irk and Medlock. It did not as yet include Ardwick, Chorlton-on-Medlock, Hulme, Cheetham or Beswick which were added when Manchester became converted into a corporate borough in the 1830s. See Map 2.

[1] **Ackerley, Samuel**, 29 Lever-street [Manchester]: badly cut and wounded in both legs.
[2] ditto but of 3 Gregson-street, Deansgate: a sabre cut on his left leg, knocked down and trampled on. A tailor, 61 years of age. 20/– final.
[6] ditto: aged 61 and a tailor. Disabled 1 month. Sabre-cut on his left leg, right leg bruised. Knocked down and trampled on by the cavalry. £1 received in relief.
[7] ditto but of 29 Lever-street.

[1] **Adshead, Elizabeth**, 6 Thomas-street [Manchester]: bruised very badly.
[2] ditto but 6 St Thomas-street: much crushed and trampled on, legs and body much bruised. A young woman. Manchester Committee 20/–. 20/– final.

⁴ ditto as Adshead, E. (female): wounded by sabre or shot.
⁶ ditto, 6 St Thomas-street: aged 43 with 1 child. Ribs and body bruised, her legs also hurt. Disabled 1 month. Thrown down and trampled on by the crowd. Received £1 of relief, with relief also from local committee.
⁷ ditto, 6 Thomas-street.

---

² **Ainsworth, John**, 2 Duncan-street, Bolton: a severe sabre cut on his right cheek and two other cuts. Was five weeks disabled. 30/– final.
⁶ ditto: aged 24 and a weaver with 2 children. Disabled three weeks. Received £1.10.0. in relief.
⁷ ditto but of 2 Duncan-street, Bolton Moor.

---

¹ **Allcard [Alleard], Samuel**, 240 Newton-lane [Manchester]: sabred and trampled on.
² ditto but of 11 Portugal-street: cut on the hand and elbow severely, the man saved by the 15th Hussars. An interesting lad, a plasterer. 20/– final. Manchester Committee 20/– and 20/–. The above is the youth saved by one of the 15th who threatened to cut the Yeoman down if he struck him again.
⁴ ditto but Alleard, S. (male): wounded by sabre or shot.
⁶ ditto as Allcard, 11 Portugal-street: aged 18 and a plasterer. Right elbow and head cut severely, his finger nearly cut off by the sabre of a Yeoman, thrown down and trampled on. Still disabled. Received £1 of relief, with relief also from local committee.
⁷ ditto as Allcard, Samuel, 240 Newton-lane.

---

² **Allecock [Allcock], William**, Heaton Norris, Stockport: right arm much hurt by a blow from one of the 15th Hussars and otherwise bruised. 30/– final.
⁶ ditto but Allcock: aged 33 and an ironfounder with 4 children. Disabled 1 month.
⁷ ditto, Stockport.

---

¹ **Allen, John**, 59 Loom-street [Manchester]: trampled on very badly.
⁴ ditto as Allen, J. (male): badly wounded by sabre or shot.
⁷ ditto.

---

⁴ **Allward, S. (male)**: badly wounded by sabre or shot.

---

⁷ **Amer, John**, Tottington, near Bury.

---

² **Armstrong, Vincent**, 20 German-street [Manchester]: thrown down by the crowd and much trampled, his knee hurt and body bruised. A young man. 20/– final.
⁶ ditto: aged 22 and a weaver with 1 child. Hurt in the knee and body. Disabled 2 weeks. Thrown down by the crowd. £1 received in relief.
⁷ ditto.

---

¹ **Ashcroft, Mary**, 10 Griffith's Court, Salford: trampled upon and bruised very badly.
² ditto, 10 Griffon Court, Chapel-street, Salford: trampled on and the skin off her knees and legs. Her hips hurt. 20/– final.

⁴ ditto as Ashcroft, M. (female): badly wounded by truncheons of the Special Constables or crushed by the multitude.
⁶ ditto of Griffin's Court, Chapel-street, Salford: aged 41 with 2 children. Knees cut and bruised in the body. Disabled 2 weeks. Received £1 of relief.
⁷ ditto of 10 Griffith's Court, Salford.

¹ **Ashton, John**, Cowhill, near Oldham: sabred – dead.
² ditto: carried the black flag. He was killed on the field but the jury returned a verdict of accidental death. 20/– received in relief by Samuel, his son.
³ ditto but of Manchester: dead. [copy of this list in *Wheeler's Manchester Chronicle*, 21 August 1819 describes him as from Oldham].
⁶ ditto of Cowhill, Oldham: sabred. Killed.

⁷ **Ashton, Thomas**, 15 Loom-street, Bank Top [Manchester].

¹ **Ashworth, Abel**, Church-stile, Rochdale: ankle-bone and leg severely crushed.
⁵ ditto: [but injury unspecified].
⁶ ditto: aged 37 and a labourer. Left ankle and leg hurt severely. Disabled 3 weeks. Thrown down by pressure of the crowd. £1 received in relief.
⁷ ditto.

¹ **Ashworth, John**, Bull's-head Inn [Manchester]: Special Constable. Killed by the cavalry.
⁶ ditto: sabred and trampled on – dead in consequence.
[Green's deposition at Hunt's trial, see *Report*, pp. 99–100, presented him as killed in the crush, not by sabre. Rylands MS. 1197(26) states that he died as a result of being thrown down and trampled upon.]

⁷ **Ashworth, Samuel**, of Mr Bell's Butcher Yard, Wood-street [Deansgate, Manchester]. *Pigot's Manchester and Salford Directory, 1819*: smallware weaver, Bell's Court, Spinningfield.

² **Back, Robert**, 2 William-street, Higher Ardwick: knocked down by the crowd, rib broken and right hip much bruised. A weaver. 20/– final.
⁶ ditto: aged 41 and a weaver with 4 children. Rib broken and right hip much hurt. Disabled 2 weeks. £1 received in relief.
⁷ ditto.

¹ **Baine [Baines], William**, 7 Ancoats-street [Manchester]: very much crushed in the breast.
² ditto: crushed in breast by the crowd and trampled, a very poor and wretched old man of 60. 20/–.
⁶ ditto but Baines: aged 60 and a weaver. 6 weeks disabled. Trampled on by the crowd. £1 received in relief.
⁷ ditto as Baines.

² **Baker, John**, 3 Pump-street [Manchester]: this poor man was beat by the constables but his principal injury was an overstrain by carrying William Taylor of Boardman-lane off the Field who was wounded and lost much blood. 40/– final.

² *repeated* with: much hurt by carrying William Taylor of Middleton who was dreadfully hurt and skull laid open. 40/– final [40/– more in pencil].

⁶ ditto: weaver with 6 children. Beat on the head and body by constables. Still disabled. £4 received in relief.

⁷ ditto.

⁷ **Ball, Thomas**, New Mount-street [Manchester].
Baines' Lancashire Directory, II, p. 163: rope and twine manufacturer, 15 Mount-street.

⁶ **Banks, William**, Chester Gate, Stockport: aged 49 and a machine maker with 1 child. Left hip and foot hurt, head hurt by constables' truncheons. 5 days disabled. Thrown down by the pressure. 10/– received in relief.

⁷ ditto.

⁴ **Banndylor, B. (male)**: badly wounded by sabre or shot.

⁷ **Bantler, John**, John-street, Stockport.

Barber, see Barton, Richard

² **Bardsley, Ann**, Bamford-street, Stockport: sabre cut on her right arm and beat about the head by swords. 20/– final.

⁶ ditto of Bamford-street, near Stockport: aged 20. Beat about the head and a sabre cut on the right arm. 2 weeks disabled. £1 received in relief.

⁷ ditto as Bamford-street, Stockport.

⁴ **Barker, J. (male)**: badly wounded by sabre or shot.

⁴ **Barlow, F. (male)**: badly wounded by trampling of cavalry.

¹ **Barlow, Hannah**, Coldhurst Hollow [Oldham]: breast-bone broke.

² ditto, but Ann of Coldhurst Lodge, Oldham: this poor woman who is a widow with seven children was beat by some of the constables, thrown down and trampled on, her breast-bone broke. She was in the infirmary 3 weeks and is still very ill. £4.

³ ditto but Ann of Oldham: fractured ribs and much bruised.

⁶ ditto but Ann of Coldhurst Lodge, near Oldham: 7 children. Crushed by the crowd and had her breast-bone broken. Bruised by the constables' staves. Now ill. Was 3 weeks in the Infirmary, a deplorable object. £4 received in relief.

⁷ ditto of Coldhurst Hollow, Oldham.

⁶ **Barlow, John**, Middleton: aged 32 with 2 children. Left foot hurt by a cavalry horse, head and shoulders bruised. 2 weeks disabled. Was knocked down by a cavalry horse. £1 received in relief.

⁷ ditto of Barrowfields, Middleton.
[Gave evidence at Hunt's Trial, see *Report*, pp. 181–3, where he declared himself a weaver.]

² **Barlow, Mary**, Lancashire Hill, Stockport: thrown down and trampled on, right leg and left foot a good deal hurt. A single woman. 20/–final.
⁶ ditto of Lancashire Hill, near Stockport: aged 30. Right hand and left foot hurt by being trampled on. 5 weeks disabled. £1 received in relief.
⁷ ditto.

⁶ **Barlow, Sarah**, Stockport near the Windmill: aged 50 with 4 children. The flesh of her right leg loosened from the bone, her back much bruised. Still disabled. Knocked down and trod on by a cavalry horse. A poor widow. Received £2 in relief.
⁷ ditto of Weavers' Row, Stockport.

¹ **Barlow, Thomas**, Boardman-lane, near Blackley.
⁴ ditto as Barlow, T. (male): wounded by sabre or shot.
⁷ ditto.

¹ **Barlow, Thomas**, Little Heaton, Middleton: sabred in the head and much crushed.
² ditto but near Middleton: a cut on the head. 3 weeks disabled. 20/–final. Manchester Committee 20/–.
⁵ ditto.
⁶ ditto of Little Heaton, near Middleton: aged 30 and a weaver with 3 children. Sabre-cut on the top of his head by a Yeoman. 3 weeks disabled. £1.5.0. received in relief. Relief also from local committee.

² **Barnes, William**, 33 Brown-street, Salford: sabre cut on the right side of his head, his eyes hurt and legs trampled. 40/– final.
⁶ ditto: a weaver with five children. Sabre-cut on left eyebrow and right side of his head, legs trampled on. Imprisoned for five days. Taken into custody but discharged on evidence of Captain Whitfield, 15th Hussars, and Mr Wadkins, his master, who said he had been very ill-used. Mr Ethelstone said, notwithstanding, that he thought him a very dangerous fellow. Received £2 in relief.
⁷ ditto.

⁶ **Barrett, James**, Chadderton Mills, near Middleton: aged 28 with 3 children. Internally injured and spit blood for some time, his head hurt. 10 days disabled. Beat on the head with the back of a sabre and thrown down by pressure. £1 received in relief.
⁷ ditto.

² **Barron, Thomas**, 6 Edge-street [Manchester]: trampled on and hurt. A respectable man, a plasterer. 20/– final.
⁶ ditto: aged 67 and a plasterer. Severely beat on the head with truncheons. Disabled 3

weeks. Since fallen from a scaffold, supposed in consequence of his head being bad. £1 received in relief.
7 ditto.

---

4 **Barry, B. (female)**: badly wounded by sabre or shot.

---

1 **Barton [Barber], Richard**, Gorton: right ankle crushed, sabre cut on right hand and trodden upon by the cavalry.
2 ditto but Barber, Richard, Gorton: right ankle crushed, a slight wound or cut on the right hand, trampled. A slight case. 20/– final. Manchester Committee 20/–.
6 ditto: aged 30 and a weaver with 3 children. Sabre-cut on right hand and ankle hurt by tread of a cavalry horse. Still partially disabled. £1 received in relief. Also relief from local committee.
7 ditto.

---

1 **Barton, Thomas**, Swan-court, Stockport: rode down and two ribs broken.
2 ditto: two of his ribs broke on the left side by being thrown down and trampled on. 30/– final.
6 ditto: aged 38 and a spinner. Two ribs broken in the left side and much crushed. 3 weeks disabled. Thrown down by the pressure of the crowd and trampled on. £1.10.0. received in relief.
7 ditto.

---

1 **Batsan [Bateson, Batson], William**, Rusholme Green: bruised on the side.
2 ditto but Bateson: crushed in the breast by the pressure of the crowd. In his attempts to get away was 10 minutes betwixt 2 bodies of troops. Was repeatedly struck at by a cavalryman but avoided it by stooping. The foot soldiers were charging bayonets at the people as they endeavoured to pass next the wall, sometimes as if to frighten them, at other times wounding them in the thighs. 20/– final. Manchester Committee 20/–.
6 ditto but Batson: a weaver with 6 children. Hurt in the breast by the pressure of the crowd. Disabled 1 week. Was struck at repeatedly by a cavalry man but avoided the blows by stooping. Saw the foot soldiers charging the people as they attempted to pass. £1 received in relief. Also money received from local committee.
7 ditto as Batson.

---

1 **Beard, James**, Levenshulme, much bruised by being thrown down among the timber.
2 ditto: had his clothes torn off but a person of very indifferent character.
7 ditto.

---

6 **Beard, William**, Heaton Norris: aged 44 and a weaver with 8 children. Stabbed in the left elbow by a sabre, his hands injured by being trampled on. 1 week disabled. £1 received in relief.
7 ditto of Lamb-fold, Heaton Norris, Stockport.

---

1 **Beatley [Betty, Beattie], Mary**, 4 Union-street, Darlington Square [Manchester]: trampled upon and bruised very badly.

⁴ ditto but Mary Betty: trampled on by cavalry – seriously wounded.
⁶ ditto but Beattie of 36 Union-street, Ancoats: aged 40 with 3 children. Left side, knee and thigh badly bruised. Disabled 1 month. Was knocked down by one of the horses and trod on by the crowd. £1 received in relief.
⁷ ditto but Beattie, Mary, 36 Union-street beyond the bridge.

¹ **Bell, James**, Town Star, Ancoats Hall [Manchester]: crushed in the body and arms very badly.
² ditto, Ancoats Lane, near the Hall: a weaver crushed and thrown down. Disabled a month, his loins still painful. A widower with 2 children. 20/–.
⁴ ditto: badly wounded by truncheons of Special Constables or crushed by multitude.
⁶ ditto of New-street, near Ancoats Hall: aged 64 and a weaver with 2 children. Legs and body hurt by trampling of the crowd. Disabled a month. A widower. £1 received in relief.
⁷ ditto of Town Star, Ancoats Hall.

¹ **Bell, John**, 12 Flag-row, Newtown [Manchester]: thrown down by the horses.
⁴ ditto as Bell, J. (male): badly wounded by trampling of cavalry.
⁶ ditto: aged 20 and a weaver. Breast hurt and spit blood for a month. Trampled on by the crowd. Disabled 2 weeks. Five weeks an out-patient of the Infirmary. £1 received in relief.
⁷ ditto.

⁶ **Berry, Bridget**, 49 Primrose-street [Manchester]: aged 35 with 5 children. Left breast and back hurt by being down under the crowd. Disabled 1 month. £1 received in relief.
⁷ ditto, 49 Primrose-street, Manchester.

¹ **Berry, James**, Stockport: three cuts on the head.
² ditto, Carrington Fields, Stockport: a sabre cut on the left side of his face and two cuts on his head, bruised inwardly. Three weeks totally disabled. 31/– final.
⁶ ditto of Carrington Fields, near Stockport: aged 60 and a weaver with 3 children. Two sabre-cuts on the head and one on the left side of his face and inwardly bruised. 3 weeks disabled. £1.11.0. received in relief.
⁷ ditto.

¹ **Beswick [Berwick], James**, 2 Lomax-street [Manchester]: sabred in the arm.
² ditto but 3 Lomax-street, Ancoats-street: cut on the arm, thrown down and trampled on. Was detained by falling. For some time 5 or 6 of the Manchester Cavalry were off their horses and cutting at the people as they passed. He held up his arm and received the above cut. 40/–.
² *repeated* with sightly different account: thrown down and trampled on. 7 weeks under Dr Taylor. Was cut on the arm as he was rising from among some timber. 5 or 6 of the Yeomanry were dismounted and cutting at the people as they passed. He held up his hand and received the above.
⁴ ditto but Berwick, J. (male): badly wounded by sabre or shot.

⁶ ditto of 3 Lomax-street: aged 22. Severe sabre-cut on his elbow, and trampled on by the crowd. 7 weeks disabled. Saw five or six of the Manchester Yeomanry Cavalry off their horses, cutting at the people as they passed. He held up his arm and received the cut as stated. £2 received in relief.

⁷ ditto, 3 Lomax-street.

Betty, see Beatley, Mary

---

² **Bickerstaff, Ann**, 63 Cropper-street [Manchester, near Miles Platting]: was thrown down and trampled on and so much exhausted as to be carried off the field for dead. 20/– final [20/– more pencilled in].

⁶ ditto of 63 Cropper-street: aged 22; thrown down and trampled on; was carried off the field for dead. 7 weeks disabled. £2 received in relief.

⁷ ditto, 63 Cropper-street.
Pigot's Manchester and Salford Directory, 1819: Henry Bickerstaff, weaver of same address.

---

¹ **Billinge, William**, Barton's Yard [i.e. Barlow's Yard, Manchester]: cut on the head and body – hat cut through by a Yeoman.

² ditto but 7 Barlow's Yard, Long Millgate: cut and bruised and prisoner still in the New Bailey. 20/–, 20/–.

⁶ ditto of 7 Barlow's Yard, Long Millgate: aged 26 and a weaver. Cut on the head and beat by constables severely. Still in the New Bailey. £2 received in relief. [Statement C reveals that he was indicted for rioting and confined to the New Bailey for 5 months for want of bail, for which he received £5.10.0. relief.

⁷ ditto of Barlow's Yard, Long Millgate.

---

¹ **Billington, Thomas**, Chapel-street, Ardwick: sabred very badly.

² ditto: a dreadful cut on the head which went to the skull. 4 other wounds. Was chased round the chapel yard repeatedly and just at the gate going out received the above. 32/– final. Manchester Committee 20/–.

² *repeated* as 7 Chapel-street, Ardwick: cut to the skull and 3 other cuts. Was disabled about 3 weeks. Certified by Dr Woods. 3 children.

⁴ ditto as Billington, T. (male): badly wounded by sabre or shot.

⁶ ditto: aged 38 and a weaver with 3 children. Severe sabre-cut on the top of his head which went to the skull and both arms bruised. 2 weeks disabled. Was repeatedly chased round the Chapel yard and going out at the gate received his cut on the head. £1.12.0. received in relief. Relief also received from local committee.

⁷ ditto.

---

¹ **Birley**, captain of the Yeomanry: his coachman very much bruised and trampled upon.

⁷ ditto – Birley's coachman.

---

¹ **Black, John**, Stockport: rode down and struck by the constables.

² ditto, 10 Union-street, Stockport: beat by constables on the head and trod on by the cavalry. An old man. 21/– final.

⁶ ditto: aged 67 and a weaver. Beat on the head by constables; knocked down and trampled on by a horse. 10 days disabled. £1.1.0. received in relief.
⁷ ditto.

---

¹ **Blair, Peter**, New-street, Eccles: sabred very badly.
² ditto: severe sabre cut on the right shoulder. Knocked down and a good deal bruised. 40/– final.
⁴ ditto but Blair, P. (male): wounded by sabre or shot.
⁶ ditto: a weaver with 2 children. Severe sabre-cut on his right shoulder, knocked down and bruised. Disabled 1 month. £2 received in relief.
⁷ ditto.

---

¹ **Blair [Blears], Thomas**, Eccles: leg badly wounded by pressure of the crowd.
² ditto, New-street, Eccles: thrown down and trampled on, his leg and ankle much injured. A respectable man. 40/– final [20/– more pencilled in].
⁶ ditto of New-street, Eccles: aged 50 and a weaver with 3 children. Right leg and ankle hurt very severely. 6 weeks disabled. Thrown down by the crowd and trampled on. £2 received in relief.
⁷ ditto but Blears.

Blindston [Blinston], see Bludstow, Thomas

---

¹ **Bloom, J.**, 34, Edge-street [Manchester]: sabred on the head by a cavalry man on 17 August.
⁷ ditto.

---

¹ **Bludstow [Blindstone, Blinston, Blunstone], Thomas**, 7 Back Turner-street [Manchester]: trampled upon and both arms broken.
² ditto but Blindstone: both arms broke and much injured. 7 weeks in the Infirmary. An old man but not a good character. Repeatedly had money from the Manchester Committee to go to his parish at Warrington. 40/– final. Manchester Committee 20/–, 10/–, 20/–, 10/–.
³ ditto but Blinston of Manchester: both arms fractured.
⁴ ditto but Blunstone, F. (male): badly wounded by truncheons of the Special Constables or crushed by the multitude. Aged 74.
⁶ ditto but Blinstone: aged 74 and a blacksmith. Both arms broken and much bruised in the body. Disabled for life. Received in relief £2, with relief also from local committee.
⁷ ditto but Blindstone.

---

¹ **Boles, James**, Whitworth [Manchester]: wounded in the temples.
⁴ ditto: badly wounded by sabre or shot.
⁶ ditto of 9 Whitworth Court, New Mount-street: aged 47 and a weaver with 3 children. Sabre-cut on left eyebrow, arm bruised by being trampled on when down. 2 weeks disabled. £1 received in relief.
⁷ ditto of Whitworth Court, Angel Meadow.

Bolton, see Boulter, John

² **Bond, Elizabeth**, 16 Prussia-street [Manchester]: struck by truncheons on the right shoulder, much bruised. 10/– final.

⁶ ditto: aged 25. Right shoulder hurt by constables' truncheons. Disabled 2 weeks. 10/– received in relief.

⁷ ditto, 11 Prussia-street.

¹ **Boon [Boond, Bound], Martha**, Heaton Lane, Stockport [? Heaton Norris]: seriously hurt by the crowd and military.

² ditto but Boond, Bridge [i.e. Ridge] Field, Stockport: foot crushed and bruised in the breast and fingers but was repeatedly thrown down. 30/– final.

⁶ ditto as Boond of Bridge Field, Stockport: aged 53. Right foot trod on by a cavalry horse, slight sabre-cut on finger and crushed inwardly. Still unwell. A widow. £1.10.0. received in relief.

⁷ ditto but Bound of Bridge Field, Heaton-lane, Stockport.

⁷ **Booth, George**

¹ **Booth, John**, Pitsworth [i.e. Pilsworth] Moor, near Bury: wounded in the back and under the right ear.

⁷ ditto, Pilsworth Moor.

¹ **Booth, Margaret**, 126 [i.e. Great] Ancoats-street [Manchester]: thrown down and trampled.

² ditto: much trampled on. 9 weeks confined. Back and sides still sore. A married woman attended by Dr Harriss. Paid 20/–. Manchester Committee 20/–, 10/–.

³ ditto of Manchester: contusion.

⁶ ditto, 126 Great Ancoats-street: aged 39 with two children. Dreadfully crushed in the body by the crowd. Disabled 9 weeks. She is still unwell. £3 received in relief. Relief also from local committee.

⁷ ditto, 126 Ancoats-lane.

¹ **Booth, Richard**, Royton.

⁷ ditto.

¹ **Booth, William**, 63 London-road [Manchester]: sabred in the head.

² ditto: sabre cut on the left side of his head to the skull, left knee hurt. Now a prisoner in the New Bailey for a bastard child. 40/– final.

⁴ ditto as Booth, W. (male): badly wounded by sabre or shot.

⁶ ditto: aged 45 and a carder with 3 children. Severe sabre-cut on the left side of his head to the skull, left knee hurt. 2 weeks disabled. Was knocked down and trampled on. Is now a prisoner for debt. £2 received in relief.

⁷ ditto.

¹ **Bostock, Peter**, Stockport: sabre-cut on the hand.
² ditto, Petty Car Green, Stockport: a sabre cut on the back part of his right hand by one of the Yeomen. 20/– final. Manchester Committee 20/–.
⁶ ditto of Pettycar Green, Stockport: aged 32 and a tailor. Sabre-cut on the back of the right hand. Disabled 2 weeks. £1 received in relief.
⁷ ditto.

¹ **Bottomley, Joseph**, New Breaks, Oldham: sabred on the shoulder.
² ditto but of Knowsley [i.e. High Knowl], near Oldham: sabre cut on the right shoulder and beat about the head with truncheons. 20/– final.
⁴ ditto as Bottomley, J. (male): badly wounded by sabre or shot.
⁶ ditto but of Knowlesley, near Oldham: aged 22 and a spinner with 1 child. Sabre-cut on the right shoulder and beat on the head. 2 weeks disabled. £1 received in relief.
⁷ ditto.

¹ **Boulter [Bolton, Boulton], John**, John-street, Stockport: wounded by the cavalry and constables on the arm, back and shoulder.
² ditto, 7 John-street: beat by the constables' staffs and by the butt of a musket. An old man of 60. A shoemaker. 26/– final.
⁶ Bolton, John, 7 John-street, Stockport: aged 60 and a shoemaker with 4 children. Beat on the head and shoulders by the butt of a musket. £1.6.0. received in relief.
⁷ ditto but Boulton.

¹ **Bower [Bowers, Bowey], Harriet**, Back Garden Court, Shudehill [Manchester]: bruised very badly in the leg and thigh.
³ ditto but Bowers of Manchester: contusion.
⁴ ditto but Bowey, H. (female): trampled on by cavalry – badly wounded.
⁷ ditto.

¹ **Bowker [Bouker], Thomas**, Bowker-bank, Crumpsall, stabbed in the belly with bayonet, wounded in the leg and left arm and knee bruised.
⁴ ditto but Bouker, T (male): badly wounded with sabre or shot.
⁶ ditto but Bowker, Thomas: aged 30 and a weaver. Stabbed in the belly by a bayonet near the Quakers' Chapel, leg and side hurt. 1 month disabled. Knocked down by a yeoman cavalry horse which trod on him. £1 received in relief. Relief also from local committee.
⁷ ditto of Bowker-bank, Crumpsall.

¹ **Bradshaw, James**, 6 Bank Top [Manchester]: trampled on, much bruised.
² ditto but 6 London-road: thrown down and trampled on, chest and legs hurt. A slight case. 5/–. Manchester Committee 10/–.
⁶ ditto, 6 London-road: aged 45 and a weaver with 1 child. Chest and legs bruised and trampled on. 3 days disabled. 5/– received in relief. Relief also from local committee.
⁷ ditto, 6 Bank Top.

[1] **Bradshaw, William**, Lilly Hill, Whitefield: wounded by a musket. [Hunt declared him killed, see his *Addresses to Radical Reformers*, 12 (1831), p. 87].
[4] ditto as Bradshaw, W. (male): wounded by sabre or shot.
[7] ditto.
[Confirming that he died of a sabre wound, see the *Manchester Observer*, 11 May 1822, p. 263. This source gave his age as 21 and his date of death as 29 April 1822.]

Brannagan, see Bunnogan, Bryan

Brayford, see Brosford, Andrew

[1] **Brearley, Benjamin**, Stockport: severe sabre-cut on the cheek, rode over and trampled on by the crowd.
[7] ditto.

[1] **Bridge, John**, Tottington: sabred very badly and crushed.
[3] ditto, near Bury: much bruised.
[6] ditto: Tottington, near Bury: aged 57 and a weaver with 2 children. Knocked down by Yeoman Cavalry horse, which trod on his right side and face, his right shoulder dislocated etc., the bone broken. His shoulder was set by Dr Taylor after he left the Infirmary and five weeks after the accident. Disabled 10 weeks. £2.10.0. received in relief.
[7] ditto.

[4] **Brient, T (male)**: badly wounded by sabre or shot.

[2] **Brierley, John**, Valiant Castle, Saddleworth: thrown down and trampled by the cavalry and crushed by the crowd, breast hurt. He had some bread and cheese in his hat which saved him from being cleft with the stroke of a sabre. 20/– final.
[6] ditto: aged 31 and a spinner with 4 children. Breast crushed by being down in the crowd and hurt by Cavalry horses going over him. Disabled 1 week. This man's hat was completely cut through, but happening to have some bread and cheese in the crown saved his head. £1 received in relief.
[7] ditto.

[2] **Brierley, Joseph**, Coldhurst-lane [Oldham]: thrown down into a cellar and inwardly crushed, cut on the palm of the hand and left arm. A hatter. 20/–.
[6] ditto of Coldhurst-lane, near Oldham: aged 36 and a hatter with 5 children. Slight sabre-cut on the palm of the hand and inwardly crushed. 2 weeks disabled. Was driven by the pressure of the crowd into a cellar. £1 received in relief.
[7] ditto of Coldhurst-lane, Oldham.
[He gave evidence at Redford v. Birley Trial, see *Report*, pp. 48–54. He described himself as a journeyman hatter of 25 years service, with his own shop and Mr Barker as his employer. He went to Manchester with the Oldham party. He had drilled at Bolton in a red coat like a soldier. At the meeting he was thrust into a cellar as the railing broke under pressure from the crowd.]

⁷ **Brierley, Joseph**, Charlestown, Ashton.

¹ **Brindle, Ellen**, Failsworth.
⁶ ditto of Dob-lane, Failsworth: aged 23. Left side much bruised and still painful, was taken to a neighbouring house insensible. 4 days disabled. Thrown into a cellar. £1 received in relief.
⁷ ditto.

⁷ **Britland, John**, Boston in Ashton.

¹ **Broadhurst, Nathan**, Manchester: sabred on the leg very badly.
⁶ ditto but of Preston: 2 children. Sabre-cut on his leg. A widower. £1 received in relief. Also received relief from local committee.
⁷ ditto, Manchester.
[He gave evidence at the Lees Inquest, see *Report*, pp. 179–81, revealing that he served as a soldier for 14 years, that at Peterloo he assisted in 'forming the hustings', and that he was cut for refusing to give up a cap of liberty. He was also a witness at the Lancaster Inquest, see *Peterloo Massacre*, p. 85. In 1832 he wrote to William Benbow from prison: see *Cosmopolite*, 29 (22 Sept.). He became a follower of Richard Carlile: see *Newgate Magazine*, I, p. 95 and *Gauntlet*, p. 335. In 1833 he lived in St George's-street. See *Gauntlet*, p. 335.]

⁴ **Broadhurst, W. (male)**: wounded by sabre or shot.

¹ **Bromely, W.**, 10 Union-street, Salford: sabred and crushed.
² ditto but William, 10 Union-street, Salford: cut on the nose and crushed. A weaver with 3 children. 20/– final. Manchester Committee 20/–.
⁶ ditto: aged 47 and a weaver with 3 children. Cut on the nose and crushed in the body. Disabled 2 weeks. £1 received in relief.
⁷ ditto.

¹ **Brookes, John**, 10, Loom-street [Manchester]: wounded in the head with a bayonet, and knocked down with the butt-end of a gun several times.
² ditto: two cuts on the head, bruised and buffeted by a musket. 20/–.
⁴ ditto but Brookes, J. (male): badly wounded by sabre or shot.
⁶ ditto: aged 20 and a weaver. Two sabre-cuts on his head and arm hurt by butt-end of a musket. Disabled for two weeks. A single man. Received £1 in relief. Also received relief from local committee.
⁷ ditto.

² **Brooks, Joseph**, Quick, Saddleworth: slight sabre-cut on the forehead. Had a tooth knocked out by the butt of a musket and his elbow dislocated: 20/– final.
⁶ ditto: aged 27 and a weaver. Slight sabre-cut on forehead, left elbow dislocated and a tooth knocked out. This man was severely knocked about by the butt of a musket. £1 received in relief. Relief also from local committee.
⁷ ditto

1. **Brosford [Brayford, Braford, Bruford, Brayfond, Brayford], Andrew**, Back Ash-street, Boardman Square [i.e. Manchester, Miles Platting]: wounded very badly and trampled upon.
2. ditto as Brayford: thrown down and left elbow hurt and hand hurt. 10/– final. Manchester Committee 10/–.
2. *repeated* as Braford: rather a slight case.
4. ditto as Bruford: badly wounded by trampling of cavalry.
6. ditto as Brayfond: aged 50 and a single man. Left arm and hand hurt by being trampled on. 8 days disabled. 10/– received in relief. Relief also from local committee.
7. ditto as Brayford.

1. **Brown, Thomas**, Copperas-street [Manchester]: severely cut on the head by a Yeomanry man.
2. ditto, 22 Copperas-street: head bruised by the flat of the sword, his hat cut. A poor infirm old man, a milk man. It seems to have been done by some of the 15th in the confusion. 20/–.
6. ditto, 22 Copperas-street: aged 60 and a milkman. Head bruised and beat with the flat sides of sabres. Still unwell. In a very bad state of health. £1 received in relief.
7. ditto, 22 Copperas-street.

1. **Brown, William**, North Moor, near Oldham: bayonetted on the head by a foot soldier.
7. ditto, North Moor, Bush [i.e. Busk], near Oldham.

1. **Bruce, Joseph**, 10 Boardman's Square, Miles Platting [Manchester]: stabbed in right shoulder by a Manchester Yeoman.
2. ditto but 10 Ash-street, Boardman's Square: stabbed with the point of a sabre by one of the Yeomanry, rather severe. A wife and 4 children. 20/– final. Manchester Committee 20/–.
4. ditto: badly wounded by sabre or shot.
6. ditto of 10 Ash-street, Boardman Square: aged 36 and a weaver with 4 children. Stabbed in the right shoulder by the sabre of a Yeoman. 5 weeks disabled. £1 received in relief. Also relief from local committee.
7. ditto, Miles Platting.

1. **Brunt, Thomas**, Brentriol [i.e. Brentnall] -street, Stockport: sabred very badly.
1. *repeated* but of Higher Hillgate, Stockport: ear cut by a Yeomanry man.
2. ditto, Brentnall-street, Stockport: sabre-cut on the right side of his head. An old man, a labourer. 20/– final. Manchester Committee 20/–.
6. ditto of Brentnall-street, Stockport: aged 65 and a labourer. Sabre-cut on the right side of the head. Disabled 3 weeks. £1 received in relief.
7. ditto, Brentnob-street, Stockport.
7. *repeated* but of Brentnall-street, Higher Hillgate, Stockport.

1. **Buckley, J.**, Woodbrook, Saddleworth: sabred on the shoulder by a man who rode a skewbald horse.

⁶ ditto but Joseph, Woodbrook, Saddleworth: aged 44 and a weaver with 4 children. Sabre-cut on the shoulder by the trumpeter. Knocked down and trampled on. Left leg hurt seriously. 2 weeks disabled. £1 received in relief.
⁷ ditto as Joseph.

⁶ **Buckley, Joseph**, Duckenfield Hall [Dukinfield]: aged 70 and a weaver. Sabre-cut on the top of his head, right leg much hurt. Disabled 3 weeks. Was thrown down by the pressure of the crowd near the Quakers' chapel. £1 received in relief.
⁷ ditto.

¹ **Buckley, Thomas**, Baretrees, Chadderton: sabred and stabbed with a bayonet. Dead.
⁴ ditto as Buckley, T. (**male**): badly wounded with sabre or shot.
⁶ ditto: sabred and stabbed. Killed.

¹ **Bullen [Bullin, Butler], Joseph**, Garden-street [Manchester]: bruised in the legs very badly and crushed inwardly.
² ditto, 16 Garden-street, Shudehill: legs and body crushed. Attended by Dr Lond of Shudehill. Legs still unwell. 20/– final. Manchester Committee 30/–.
⁶ ditto, 16 Garden-street: aged 25 and a weaver with 2 children. Legs badly hurt and body crushed. Disabled 6 weeks. His legs still unwell. £1 received in relief. Also relief from local committee.
⁷ ditto as Bullin of 16 Garden-street.
⁷ *repeated* but as Butler, Joseph, 16 Garden-street.

¹ **Bunnogan [Brannagan, Brannegan], Bryan**, Back Cock-street [Salford]: wounded in both legs.
² ditto as Brannagan of Back Cook-street, Salford: crushed by the railing giving way, the end of which was forced into his leg. A fustian cutter. 20/– final.
⁶ ditto as Brannagan of 6 Back Cook-street, Salford: aged 40 and a fustian-cutter with 3 children. Hurt by iron railing being forced into his leg. Disabled several days. £1 received in relief.
⁷ ditto as Brannegan, Brian, 6 Back Cook-street.

⁴ **Burnley, W.** (**male**): wounded by sabre or shot.

¹ **Burton, Thomas**, 52 Bridge-street [Manchester]: crushed and trampled upon.
² ditto as Under 52, Bridge-street: a carpenter. Down among the mob and much crushed. Bled by Dr Matthews. Lived in his present residence 8 years. 20/– final.
⁶ ditto: aged 58 and an umbrella-maker with one child. Crushed inwardly. Disabled for three weeks. Received £1 in relief.
⁷ ditto, 52 Bridge-street.

Butler, see Bullin, Joseph

⁴ **Butter, J.** (**male**): wounded by the truncheons of the Special Constables or the crush of the multitude.

1 **Butterworth, Jonah**, Carrington, near Flixton: head dreadfully cut by a sabre.
7 ditto.

1 **Butterworth, William**, Stake Hill, near Middleton: sabred in the arm very badly.
2 ditto, Stake Hill, near Middleton: a dreadful sabre-cut on the right arm just below the shoulder which was first false healed for want of proper medical aid but is still in a bad state. 45/– [40/– more in pencil]. Manchester Committee 20/–, 25/–, 20/–. Butterworth who attended the inquest (to identify the Yeomen) was taken up about 18 November for selling Hush beer on the charge of an infamous woman named Ann Taylor who subsequently went to the magistrates at Rochdale before whom the conviction took place with a determination to state the whole business. But they would not hear her. She has been with us and declared that she was prompted by the exciseman and supervisor who promised her £2 in case of conviction that she had not been in the village where he lived for some years.
4 ditto as Butterworth, W. (male): badly wounded with sabre or shot.
5 ditto of Stake Hill in Thornham: badly cut on the upper arm.
6 ditto: a weaver with 1 child. A desperate cut on the right arm just below the shoulder, which having been prematurely healed was very bad when we saw it – a frightful gash. Still lame. This man was one of the witnesses at Oldham. He was taken about 18 November, charged by an infamous woman of the name of Taylor with selling hush beer. She afterwards confessed she had not been in the village where he lived for two or three years. The magistrates refused to hear her a second time and sent Butterworth to Lancaster Castle where he still remains. £4.5.0. received in relief. Relief also from local committee.
7 ditto of Stake Hill, near Middleton.
[He is a witness at Lees Inquest, see *Report*, pp. 181–3, where he states that he was wounded 'amongst the timber' near the gates of Quaker meeting house, after running away from the hustings following the cavalry charge. He knew his attacker who said, in response to their plea of 'spare our lives', 'damn your bloody lives'.]

2 **Butterworth, William**, Bengal Square, Bolton: thrown down and trampled on. About a fortnight disabled. 35/– final.
6 ditto: aged 26 and a weaver with 1 child. Right shoulder and head much hurt. 3 weeks disabled. Thrown down by one of the horses which trod on him. £1.15.0.
7 ditto.

1 **Calbert, John**, Portugal-street [Manchester]: two sabre-cuts in the leg.
7 ditto.
Pigot's Manchester and Salford Directory, 1819: under John Calvert, shoemaker, 9B Portugal-street.

1 **Caldubank [Calderbank], John**, Coopers' Court, Back Mill-street [Manchester]: ruptured by being forced upon a post.
6 ditto but Calderbank, Cooper's Court, Back Mill-street. Forced by the crowd on a post and ruptured. No relief from Metropolitan and Central Committee. But relief from local committee.

⁷ ditto as Calderbank.
Baines' Lancashire Directory, II, p. 178: under Calderbank, earthware dealer, 106 Great Ancoats-street.

⁷ **Calloghan, John**, 2 Clay-street, Pothouses, Ancoats-lane [Manchester].

¹ **Campbell, Alexander**, 32 John-street, Salford: disjointed knee.
² ditto: knee fractured and dreadfully bruised. A respectable man, a warehouseman. 40/–.
⁴ ditto as Campbell, A. (male): wounded by truncheons of the Special Constables or crushed by the multitude.
⁶ ditto of 32 John-street, Salford: aged 50 and a warehouseman. Right knee fractured very badly by being trampled on by the crowd. Still disabled. £3 received in relief. More relief from local committee.
⁷ ditto.

¹ **Campbell, James**, 36 Jersey-street [Manchester]: sabred in the shoulder and bruised.
² ditto: sabre-wound on the shoulder. 5 small children. A poor man. 20/– [20/– more in pencil]. Manchester Committee 20/–.
⁴ ditto as Campbell, J. (male): badly wounded by sabre or shot.
⁶ ditto: aged 64 and a weaver with 5 children. Sabred on the shoulder and legs. Trampled on by horses. Disabled 5 weeks. £2 received in relief. Also relief from local committee.
⁷ ditto.

¹ **Campbell [Robert]:** Special Constable, killed by the populace in Newton-lane, on 18 August.
³ ditto as Mr Campbell of Manchester: dangerous. F.n. This person – a Special Constable – was dreadfully abused by the mob. [In printing this list *Wheeler's Manchester Chronicle*, 21 August 1819 gives his name as Robert.]
⁷ ditto.
Pigot's Manchester and Salford Directory, 1817: watchman of 18 Miller-street.

¹ **Canning, Sarah**, 19 Cornwall-street, Newton-lane [Manchester]: bruised by the constables.
⁷ ditto.

¹ **Carbett [Carbutt, Carbut, Corbett], Robert**, 7 Dixon-street, Newtown [Manchester]: severely cut in the left arm by a Yeoman in Mount-street.
¹ *repeated* as Carbutt, 7 Dickson-street: sabred in the arm.
² ditto but Corbett: stabbed in the arm. Was between two parties of Yeomanry. A rather severe wound. 20/– final. Manchester Committee 20/–.
⁶ ditto but Corbett, 7 Dixon-street, New Town: a weaver. Stabbed in the arm by a sabre. Disabled a month. £1 received in relief. Relief also from local committee.
⁷ ditto as Carbett.
⁷ *repeated* as Carbut.

6 **Carrol, James**, 15 Dean-street, Ancoats-lane [Manchester]: aged 35 and a calico printer. Sabre-cut on the back of his head, right shoulder hurt. 5 weeks disabled. Was knocked down and trampled on by crowd. £1 received in relief.
7 ditto.

1 **Carthy, John**, 2 Primrose-street [Manchester]: bruised by the trampling of the horses.
2 ditto: trod on by the cavalry and his ankle hurt. 10 days confined. A wife and 6 children. 20/– final.
4 ditto as Carthy, J. (male): wounded by trampling of cavalry.
6 ditto: weaver with 6 children. Ankle trod upon and hurt by a cavalry horse. 10 days disabled. £1 received in relief.
7 ditto.

1 **Cavenagh [Cavanagh], John**, 11 Loom-street [Manchester]: sabred in the shoulder.
2 ditto: sabre cut on the right shoulder and bruised. 20/– final.
6 ditto as Cavanagh: a weaver with 1 child. Sabre-cut on the right shoulder. 1 month disabled. £1 received in relief.
7 ditto [*repeated*].

Ceal, see Seal, John

Ceal, see Seal, Robert

1 **Chadwick, Thomas**, Stretford: trampled upon and much bruised.
7 ditto.

2 **Chambers, Elizabeth**, 17 John-street, Pothouses [Manchester]: beat by constable about the head and shoulders, a slight case. 10/– final.
6 ditto: one child. Beat about the head by the constables. Disabled 2 weeks. A slight case. 10/– received in relief.
7 ditto.

1 **Chantlen [Chantler], William**, Warrington: dreadfully crushed from the railing of a cellar giving way.
7 ditto as Chantler, William, at John Alderson's, Warrington.

1 **Chapman, James**, Barrow-street [Salford]: thrown down and trampled on, wrist crushed and finger broken.
2 ditto of Oldfield: thrown down and wrist broke, finger broke, disabled 10 weeks. Was repeatedly struck by Hughes one of the Yeomanry who lives near him. 40/– final.
6 ditto, 13 Barrow-street, Oldfield-road. A labourer with 1 child. Finger and wrist broken and much hurt by being trampled on. 10 weeks disabled. Says Hughes, a Yeoman, struck at him repeatedly. The parish officers of Pendleton refused him relief because he had been at the meeting. £2 received in relief.
7 ditto but of Oldfield-lane.

¹ **Cheetham, William**, Little Bolton: cut on the back of the neck very badly.
² ditto, Middle-street, Little Bolton: cut severely in the back of the neck by Meagher. He, and 4 or 5 others, was met by Meagher who damned them and told them to disperse. They requested him to let them pass and they would do so, Cheetham was the last. Meagher swore he would cut off his head and struck him as above. 40/– final. Manchester Committee 20/–.
⁴ ditto as Cheetham, W. (male): badly wounded by sabre or shot.
⁶ ditto of Middle-street, Little Bolton: aged 32 and a weaver. Severe sabre-cut on the back of the neck. Disabled 2 weeks. Was met by Meagher in Peter-street who said: Damn you disperse. Cheetham said: Give us room to pass. Meagher moved his horse a little and, as Cheetham went betwixt him and the wall, he cut him and said: I will cut off your damn'd head. £2 received in relief. Relief also from local committee.
⁷ ditto.
[He was a witness at the Lees Inquest, see *Report*, pp. 183–4, saying that he stood 30 yards from the hustings. He was severely wounded by a trumpeter when the Manchester Yeomanry 'charged upon the people'. Also a witness at the Redford v. Birley Trial, see *Report*, p. 57, where he admitted to having been dressed by a surgeon named Hanson and to have drilled on Cockey Moor.]

¹ **Cheetwood [Chesworth], S.,** Under 4 James-street [Manchester]: bruised very badly.
² ditto but Chesworth, Sarah, 4 Brierley-court, Angel-street: trampled on by cavalry and a good deal bruised. Certified by her employer. 20/– final.
⁴ ditto: badly wounded by truncheons of the Special Constables or crushed by the multitude.
⁶ ditto, 4 Brierley's-court: knocked down and trampled on. 3 weeks disabled. Certified by her employer Mr Foster. £1 received in relief.
⁷ ditto but Cheetwood, Sarah, 4 Brierley-court, Back Mill-street.

¹ **Chesworth, James,** Hanging Ditch [Manchester], a Special Constable: very much bruised and trampled upon.
² ditto as John Chesworth, 9 Hanging Ditch: cut by the cavalry and much bruised in the body. Has never recovered but in a declining state of health. Thinks it was the Cheshire Corps. A Special Constable. 40/– final.
⁶ ditto of 9 Hanging Ditch: a confectioner with 7 children. Sabre-cut on the head, crushed in the body by crowd. Still unwell, spits blood. A Special Constable. £2 received in relief.
⁷ ditto.

Chesworth, see Cheetwood, Sarah

Chisnall, see Chiswall, James

¹ **Chiswall [Chiswell, Chisnall], James,** Royton: wounded in the head very badly and had a double dislocation of the shoulders.
² ditto: a sabre-cut on the left arm and both shoulders dislocated. Was much trampled

⁴ ditto but Chiswell, J (male): badly wounded by sabre or shot.
⁶ ditto but Chisnall, James of Royton: aged 38 with 5 children. Both shoulders dislocated, sabre-cut on the left arm above the elbow, another on the right temple, right arm hurt by cavalry horse. Still disabled. £2 received in relief. Relief also from local committee.
⁷ ditto as Chisnall.

---

¹ **Clanrophy [Clanophy], Edward**, 59 Thomas-street [Manchester]: crushed and four ribs broken.
⁴ ditto as Clanophy, E. (male): badly wounded by trampling of cavalry.
⁷ Clannophy, Edward, 50 Thomas-street.

---

⁴ **Clark, F. (male)**: wounded by trampling of cavalry.

---

¹ **Clark, P.**, 15 Pump-street, Newton-lane [Manchester]: sabred in the arm.
² ditto but Philip: wounded in the hand. Confined in the New Bailey 4 days. Disabled 1 week. 20/– final.
⁴ ditto as Clark, P. (male): wounded by sabre or shot.
⁶ ditto: aged 17. Sabre-cut on the head and bruised by being trampled on. 4 days imprisoned and 1 week in bed. Says a Yeoman snapped a pistol at him. £2 received in relief. Statement B states that he was bailed out and then discharged by proclamation on 30 October].
⁷ ditto

---

¹ **Clark, Thomas**, Little Bridgwater-street [Manchester]: hurt on his foot.
² ditto, 9 Little Bridgewater-street: rode over by Burgess of the Hen and Chickens who also cut his son's hat. Bruised in the foot. Three weeks disabled. 20/– final.
⁶ ditto of 9 Little Bridgwater-street: aged 51 and a paviour [layer of pavements] by trade. Ankles and left foot hurt by being trampled on by a cavalry horse. 3 weeks disabled. Says it was Burgess that rode over him. £1 received in relief.
⁷ ditto.

---

² **Clarke, Jonathan**, Reddish, near Stockport: sabre-cut on the head and breast and body. Trampled on by the Cavalry 40/– final.
⁶ ditto of Redditch, Stockport: aged 36 and a hatter with 7 children. Sabre-cut on the head and breast, trampled on by a cavalry horse. 2 weeks disabled. His landlord sold his goods for £2.4.0. rent when his wife had lain in but a month, in consequence of his being a reformer. £2 received in relief.
⁷ ditto.

---

² **Clayton, John**, Charlestown [Ashton]: disabled about a week. Had his leg hurt and hand cut, body trampled on. 53 years of age and a weaver. 20/– final.
⁶ ditto, Charlestown, near Ashton: aged 63 and a weaver with 1 child. Hand cut and body trampled on by the crowd. Disabled 1 week. £1 received in relief.
⁷ ditto.

⁶ **Clegg, Francis**, Prestwich: thrown down and trampled on, seriously bruised by the pressure of the crowd. A person of some little property. [No relief awarded].
⁷ ditto.

---

¹ **Coates, John**, Royton: shockingly bruised by the constables in the head.
² ditto but Joseph: beat on the head by constables. Has had a delirium in consequence and been unable to work 11 weeks. 50/– final. Rochdale Committee 20/–.
⁶ ditto but Joseph: aged 23 of Royton: beat on the head by the constables' truncheons, which caused an inflammation of the brain. Disabled 11 weeks. Was confined to his bed the greater part of this time. £2.10.0. received in relief. Also relief from local committee.
⁷ ditto as Joseph.
Leigh's Lancashire General Directory, 1818–20: dyer and fustian finisher of Sandy-lane, Royton.

Cockshot, see Cookshot, Bridget

---

¹ **Coil, Dennis**, 9 Dimity-street, Newtown [Manchester]: crushed by the trampling of horses.
² ditto: thrown down and trampled on, leg hurt. Disabled in part 11 weeks. Relieved by the Manchester Committee. 20/– final. Manchester Committee 20/–.
⁴ ditto but Coyle: badly wounded by trampling of cavalry.
⁶ ditto but Coyle, 9 Dimity-street, Newtown: aged 40 and a weaver. Trampled on and leg much bruised. Leg still bad. £1 received in relief. Relief also from local committee.
⁷ ditto.

---

¹ **Coleman, Catherine**, 40 Primrose-street [Manchester]: bruised and three ribs broken.
² ditto: 3 ribs displaced in her right side and trampled on. 3 weeks totally disabled. A widow with 2 children. 20/– [£2 more in pencil].
⁴ ditto: badly wounded by truncheons of the Special Constables or crushed by the multitude.
⁶ ditto: two children. Three ribs on right side broken by being trampled on. Disabled 3 weeks. A poor widow. £3 received in relief.
⁷ ditto.

Collier, see John Collin and Sarah Collin

---

¹ **Collin [Collier], John**, Turner's Court [i.e. Garden-lane, St Mary's Church, off Deansgate, Manchester]: sabred upon the leg.
⁴ ditto as Collier, J. (male): wounded by sabre or shot.
⁶ ditto as Collier of Turner's Court: aged 36 and a hatter. Right arm bruised and knocked down by a Yeoman, left knee cut by the fall. 10 days disabled. £1 received in relief.
⁷ ditto as Collier.

¹ **Collin [Collins], Michael**, Kay-street, Bolton: cut in the hand.
⁴ ditto but Collins, M. (male): badly wounded by sword or shot.
⁷ ditto as Collin, Michael of Key-street, Bolton.

¹ **Collin, Sarah**, Back Prussia-street, Newton-lane [Manchester].
² ditto but Collier: [no entry].

⁵ **Collinge, Ann** of Bowlee, near Middleton: very much crushed and bruised.
⁷ ditto but Hannah.

¹ **Collins, Charles**: sabred in the cheek.
⁷ ditto.

¹ **Collins, Joseph**, Dukinfield: knocked down by the constables and trampled upon by the horses and dreadfully bruised.
⁶ ditto of Dukinfield, near Ashton: aged 21 and a weaver. Knocked down by a constable's staff when a cavalry horse trod off his shoe and hurt his foot severely. Right side hurt by being trampled on. Disabled 2 months. Was carried in an insensible state to the Infirmary where he was bled. £2 received in relief.
⁷ ditto.

¹ **Conway, Edward**, 4, Pot-street, Fairbotham [i.e. Fairbottom] Court [Manchester]: sabred very badly and his arm put out.
⁴ ditto as Conway, E. (male): badly wounded by sabre or shot.
⁶ ditto, 1 Fairbottom Court, Pott-street: aged 45 and a labourer. Collar-bone broken and right shoulder dislocated. 13 weeks disabled. Thrown down among the timber near the Quakers' Chapel by the crowd. £2 received in relief. Relief also from local committee.
⁷ ditto of Pot-street, Fairbotham Court.

¹ **Cook, James**, Greenacres, near Oldham: crushed and abused by the constables very badly.
² ditto but Greenacres Moor: thrown down into a cellar and his right leg severely bruised. 15/– final.
⁶ ditto of Greenacre's Moor, near Oldham: aged 31 and a weaver with one child. Thrown into a cellar by pressure of the crowd and right leg severely hurt. 9 days disabled. 15/– received in relief.
⁷ ditto.

¹ **Cook, John**, Royle-street, Stockport: trampled upon by the cavalry and leg hurt.
⁴ ditto as Cook, J (male): badly wounded by trampling of cavalry.
⁷ ditto.

¹ **Cook, Joseph**, Greenacres, near Oldham: bruised by the constables very badly.
² ditto but Greenacres Moor: thrown into a cellar and legs hurt. Beat with truncheons so as to be disabled a fortnight. 15/– final.

⁴ ditto: wounded by truncheons of Special Constables or crushed by multitude.
⁶ ditto of Greenacres Moor, near Oldham: aged 23 and a roller-maker. Right shoulder hurt by constable's truncheon and both legs bruised by falling into a cellar. 2 weeks disabled. 15/- received in relief.
⁷ ditto.

---

¹ **Cookshot [Cockshut, Cockshot], Bridget**, Swan [i.e. Span] Court, near St John's [Manchester]: severely crushed.
⁴ ditto but Cockshut: badly wounded by truncheons of the special constables or crushed by the multitude.
⁶ ditto of 16 Span Court: aged 63. Thrown down and trampled on by crowd, ankle dislocated and body a good deal bruised. 3 weeks disabled. £1 received in relief.
⁷ ditto as Cockshot, Bridget, Swan Court, near St John's.

---

¹ **Coop, John**, Hollinwood [near Oldham], trampled upon and wounded in the leg.
⁷ ditto but of Hollins, Hollinwood.

---

¹ **Cooper, James**, Leadyard, Stockport.
² ditto, Lad Yard, Millgate [i.e. Hillgate], Stockport: severe sabre-cut on his right shoulder-blade and a contusion on the back of his head. 20/- final.
⁶ ditto of Lad-yard, Hill Gate, Stockport: aged 22 and a weaver. Severe sabre cut on the right shoulder-blade, a contusion on the back of his head. 3 weeks disabled. £1 received in relief.
⁷ ditto of Lead Yard.

---

² **Cooper, Robert**, Cheetham Hill [Manchester]: was thrown down by the crowd and much crushed by the people, his breast hurt, one rib dislocated, spat blood for some time. A very decent old man of 63 years of age. 25/- final.
⁶ ditto of Cheetham Hill: aged 63 and a weaver with 2 children. A rib dislocated in his left side, breast hurt. 3 weeks disabled. Thrown down by the crowd; spit blood for some time. £1.5.0. received in relief.
⁷ ditto.

Corbett, see Carbett, Robert

---

⁶ **Cornwall, William**, Adlington Square, Stockport: aged 63 and a labourer. Sabre-cut on his left cheek, hip and groin hurt. Was knocked down by a cavalry horse which trod upon him. 15/- received in relief.
⁷ ditto.

---

¹ **Cordingly, William**, Failsworth.
⁶ ditto of Watch-Cot, Failsworth: aged 36 and a weaver with 5 children. Sabre-cut on the left shoulder, his left wrist bruised by a blow from a truncheon. Disabled 2 weeks. £1 received in relief.
⁷ ditto.

Coyle, see Coil, Dennis

- ² **Crabtree, Thomas**, Pitt [i.e. Pot] -street [Manchester]: thrown down by the crowd, trampled on. 2 days in the New Bailey. Disabled 10 days. 40/– final.
- ⁶ ditto of 5 Pott-street: aged 26 and a hatter with 3 children. Trampled on and crushed in the breast by the crowd. 10 days disabled. Was imprisoned 2 days in the new Bailey. £2 received in relief.
- ⁷ ditto of 5 Pot-street.

- ¹ **Croft, Ellen**, Cooper Court, Bradley-street, Back Mill-street [Manchester]: bruised with constables' staves.
- ² ditto, Back Mill-street, Bradley-street: crushed and bruised, very infirm. Thrown into a cellar and a good deal bruised. 20/– final. Manchester Committee 20/–.
- ⁴ ditto: wounded by truncheons of Special Constables or crushed by the multitude.
- ⁶ ditto of 3 Cooper's Court, Back Mill-street: aged 55 with 1 child. Internally injured by the crowd. Still unwell. Thrown into a cellar. £1 received in relief. Relief also from local committee.
- ⁷ ditto of Cooper Court.

- ¹ **Croft, George**, Cooper-street [i.e. Court], Broadly [i.e. Bradley] -street [Manchester]: bruised on the body by a constable's staff.
- ² ditto but of Back Mill-street, Bradley-street: sabre cut on the back and much hurt. Thinks it was Booth the Constable. 20/– final. Manchester Committee 20/–.
- ⁴ ditto as Croft, G. (male): badly wounded by truncheons of the Special Constables or crushed by the multitude.
- ⁶ ditto of 3 Cooper's Court, Back Mill-street: aged 42 and a weaver with 1 child. Sabre-cut on the back, bruised on the head and shoulders by constables' truncheons. 1 month disabled. Says he was cut by Booth, a Yeoman. £1 received in relief. Relief also from local committee.
- ⁷ ditto, Cooper's Court, Bradley-street.

- ¹ **Crompton, James**, Barton-upon-Irwell: trampled upon by the cavalry, dead. Buried 1 September.
- ⁶ ditto: trampled on by the cavalry. Killed.

- ¹ **Crompton, John**, Regent's-road [Salford]: trampled upon and severely bruised on the head.
- ⁷ ditto.

Pigot's Manchester and Salford Directory, 1817: weaver of 4 Glasking-street, Salford.

- ¹ **Cross, Mary**, 10 Cross-street [Salford]: bruised by constable's staff.
- ² ditto but adds Salford to address: trampled on by the cavalry and beat by the constables. Head and arms bruised. A cotton batter. 20/– final.
- ⁴ ditto: badly wounded by the truncheons of the Special Constables or crushed by the multitude.

⁶ ditto: head and arms much bruised and beat by constables. 1 week disabled. Was trampled on. £1 received in relief.
⁷ ditto.

---

⁷ **Crumblendene,** ———, Salford.

---

¹ **Cuman, John**, Ely-street [?Stretford]: bruised by the constables and trampled on by the cavalry.

---

¹ **Cunliff, Richard**, 10 Ross [i.e. Rowes] -street, Knott Mill [Manchester]: crushed by the trampling of the horses.
² ditto but Cunliffe, 10 Rowes-street: two horses went over him by which he was disabled for a fortnight. He has been in the 57th Regiment. 20/– final.
⁴ ditto: badly wounded by trampling of the cavalry.
⁶ ditto of 10 Rose-street: aged 26 and a carder. Legs and body severely bruised by horses trampling on him. 2 weeks disabled. £1 received in relief.
⁷ ditto of 10 Rose-street, Knott Mill.

---

⁷ **Curran, John**, 1 Clayton [i.e. Clay] -street, Pothouses, Ancoats-lane [Manchester]. *Pigot's Manchester and Salford Directory, 1817, 1819*: weaver.

---

² **Dale, Thomas**, 52 Jersey-street [Manchester]: beat on the head and injured by constables. Only a slight case. 10/– final.
⁶ ditto of 52 Jersey-street: aged 16. Beat by constables on the head. Disabled about 1 week. Slight case and not badly off. 10/– received in compensation.
⁷ ditto.

---

¹ **Dale, Susannah**, 52 Jersey-street [Manchester]: trampled upon.
² ditto: thrown down by cavalry and struck by a constable. 20/– final.
⁶ ditto: aged 45. Trampled on by the crowd and leg hurt. disabled about 1 week. Slight case and not badly off. 10/– received in relief.
⁷ ditto.

Daly, see Dayley, Mary

---

¹ **Daniels, Abigail**, 29 Boardman-street [off London-road, Manchester]: bruised very badly.
⁴ ditto: trampled on by cavalry – seriously wounded.
⁷ ditto.

---

¹ **Darbyshire [Derbyshire], Robert**, son of the Salford Deputy Constable: sabred in the head.
⁷ ditto but Derbyshire of Salford.
[A Special Constable – see *Report* on Lees Inquest, pp. 387, 392.]

¹ **Darlington, John**, Ancoats-street [Manchester]: wounded with a sabre.
⁷ ditto but of Factory-street, Ancoats-lane.
Pigot's Manchester and Salford Directory, 1817: spinner, 15 Back Mill-street; ibid., 1819: spinner, 9 Back Factory-street.

⁴ **Darlington, M. (female)**: badly wounded by sabre or shot.

¹ **Davenport, John**, Higher Hillgate, Stockport: sabre-cut on the forehead, bone extracted the size of half-a-crown.
² ditto, Barlow-street, Stockport: a clean cut off his forehead and part of the bone taken out. A single man, 20 years of age. 20/– final. Manchester Committee 20/–.
⁶ ditto, Barlow-street, Stockport: aged 20 and a weaver. Part of the skull on left side of forehead taken off by a sabre-cut. 3 weeks disabled. £1 received in relief.
⁷ ditto.
[Gave evidence in Redford v. Birley Trial, see *Report*, p. 68, claiming that he came to Manchester by himself, not in a party and that near the hustings he was struck by a mace as well as cut by a Yeoman. The bone was displayed by Hunt in the house of commons in 1831.]

² **Davenport, John**, Hargreaves, near Oldham: knocked down by a horse and the small of his back hurt by being trod on; left ankle cut by the horse's foot. Looks extremely ill. 40/– final.
⁶ ditto of Hargreaves, near Oldham: aged 22 and a weaver. His loins and left ankle hurt seriously by the Yeomanry Cavalry's horses trampling on him. Still unwell. £2 received in relief.
⁷ ditto.

⁴ **Davison, E. (male)**: badly wounded by sabre or shot.

¹ **Dawson, Ed. [Edmund]**, Saddleworth: sabred on the head. Dead.
³ ditto but Edmund: sabre wound on head. [*Wheeler's Manchester Chronicle*, 21 August 1819 adds 'of Saddleworth'].
[In a statement from Yeomanry (Rylands MS. 1197 (26, p. 8) about the dead: 'Edmund Dawson from Saddleworth died on 31st [August] from a sabre wound'. Coroner's Inquest on 4 September 1819 awarded 'verdict of wilful murder not allowed'. See Wade's *Manchester Massacre!!*, p. 29. He and William Dawson were, at the meeting, in possession of a pole surmounted by a cap of liberty. See Geoffrey Woodhead, *A Brief History of the Peterloo Massacre* (Saddleworth Museum publication), p. 5.]

⁷ **Dawson, Thomas**, 57 George Leigh Street [Manchester].

¹ **Dawson, William**, Saddleworth: killed by the cavalry. Died 1 September in the Infirmary.
⁶ ditto: sabred and crushed. Killed on the spot.
⁷ ditto.

- ¹ **Dayley [Daly, Doyley], Mary**, 11, Coop-street [Manchester]: sabred in the arm.
- ² ditto: a slight wound on the wrist. Disabled about a fortnight. Rather a slight case. 10/– final.
- ⁴ ditto as Doyley, M. (female): badly wounded with sabre or shot.
- ⁶ ditto as Daly, 11 Coop-street: sabre-cut on the wrist. 2 weeks disabled. Case rather slight. 10/–.
- ⁷ ditto.

- ⁷ **Dean [Deans], Edward**, Minshull-street [Manchester].
  Pigot's Manchester and Salford Directory, 1817: fustian-cutter ; *Baines' Lancashire Directory*, II, p. 189: cowkeeper.

- ¹ **Dean, James**, 4 Foundry-lane [Manchester]: sabred and bruised.
- ² ditto: hurt in the foot and laid up for a fortnight. A decent young man, a bricklayer. 20/– final.
- ⁴ ditto as Dean, J. (male): badly wounded by sabre or shot.
- ⁶ ditto but Deans, 4 Foundry-lane: aged 21 and a bricklayer. Thrown down and trampled on, head and leg bruised by the crowd. 3 weeks disabled. £1 received in relief.
- ⁷ ditto.
  Pigot's Manchester and Salford Directory, 1817: fustian-cutter.

- ¹ **Dennis, William**, Pendleton: legs much bruised and crushed inwardly.
- ⁷ ditto.

Derbyshire, see Darbyshire, Robert

- ⁷ **Dickie, James**

- ¹ **Ditchfield, Jane**, Ancoats-street [Manchester]: cut in the left leg on the wall of the [Quaker] Meeting House.
- ² ditto, Darlington's Buildings, Ancoats [i.e. Canal-street]: a severe sabre-cut on her left leg. 3 weeks disabled. A widow with 5 children. 25/–.
- ⁶ ditto of Darlington's Buildings: five children. Severe sabre-cut on the left leg. 3 weeks disabled. A widow. £1.5.0. received in relief.
- ⁷ ditto of Great Ancoats-street.

- ¹ **Dodd, Jane**, Williamson-street, Chancery-lane [Ardwick]: wounded in the leg and thigh.
- ² ditto: thrown down and trampled on by the crowd. 8 weeks disabled. 25/–.
- ⁴ ditto: badly wounded by sabre or shot.
- ⁶ ditto, Williamson-street, Chancery-lane. Two children. Thrown down and trampled on by the crowd, body bruised. 8 weeks unwell. £1.5.0. received in relief.
- ⁷ ditto.

- [1] **Dorley [Dooley, Dooly], Edward**, Stockport: wounded in both legs.
- [2] ditto but Dooley, Carrington-fields, Stockport: thrown down and trampled and his legs much hurt. A weaver, a single man. 26/– final.
- [6] ditto but Dooly, Carrington Fields, Stockport: a weaver. Legs much hurt by being trampled on by crowd and horses. 3 weeks disabled. £1.6.0. received in relief.
- [7] ditto as Dorley.

- [1] **Downes, Margaret**: dreadfully cut in the breast; secreted clandestinely, and not heard of, supposed dead.
- [7] ditto.

[Hunt claimed that her injury was 'concealed by her friends'. See *Henry Hunt's Addresses to Radical Reformers* (1831), p. 87.]

Doyley, see Dayley, Mary

- [4] **Droyer, E.** (male): badly wounded by sabre or shot.

- [6] **Duckworth, George**, Royton: aged 35 and a weaver with 5 children. Left leg seriously hurt and bruised by the trampling of the crowd. Disabled 1 month. £2 received in relief.
- [7] ditto.

- [1] **Duffy [Duffey], Henry**, 17 Clowes Buildings [in Jackson-street, Chorlton Row]: legs and body much bruised.
- [2] ditto: thrown down and trampled on. Left leg and groin hurt. A weaver. 20/– final.
- [6] ditto but Duffey, Clowes Buildings, Chorlton. Aged 34 and a weaver with 1 child. Left groin and leg hurt by being trampled on by the crowd. Disabled a month. £1 received in relief.

- [1] **Dyer [Dwyer], Edward**, 40 Jersey-street [Manchester]: crushed and cut in the back and hand.
- [2] ditto as Dwyer, 40 Jersey-street: sabred in the head and much bruised. Still unwell. A weaver, a poor man. 20/– [£2 more in pencil].
- [6] ditto as Dwyer: aged 67 and a weaver. Sabred on the head and bruised in the loins by being trampled on. 6 weeks disabled. A poor old man in a deplorable state. £3 received in relief.
- [7] ditto as Dwyer.

- [7] **Eccleson, Margaret**, 57 George Leigh-street [Manchester].
Pigot's Manchester and Salford Directory, 1819: John Eccleston, weaver of same address.

- [7] **Edwards, Edward**, Back-street, Macclesfield.

- [6] **Edwards, John**, 2 Back Henry-street [Manchester]: aged 24 and a carder with 1 child. Beat by the constables on the face and throat. Was unable to swallow solids for some

time. Disabled 1 week. Was four days imprisoned and then discharged. £1 received in relief.
7 ditto.

1 **Elliot [Elliott], John**, Tatton-street [Hulme]: sabred in the head.
2 ditto, 4 Tatton-street, Hulme: cut on the forehead and his legs trampled. A fine boy. 10/– final. Manchester Committee 10/–.
4 ditto: badly wounded by sabre or shot.
6 ditto but Elliott, 4 Tatton-street, Hulme: aged 14. Severe sabre-cut on the top of the head. 1 week disabled. 10/– received in relief. Relief also from local committee.
7 ditto, Tatton-street, near the Barracks.

1 **Ellis, David**, 72 London-road [Manchester]: sabre-wound in the left hand.
2 ditto: sabre-wound on the right arm and fingers of the left hand cut across. 20/– final.
6 ditto: aged 29 and a calico printer with 3 children. A severe sabre-cut on the right arm and one on his left hand. 2 weeks disabled. £1 received in relief.
7 ditto.

2 **English, William**, 20 Fawcett-street [Manchester]: bruised in the body and legs trampled on. 20/– final.
6 ditto of 20 Fawcet-street: aged 27 and a weaver. Bruised in the body and legs by being trampled on by the crowd. Disabled some time. £1 received in relief.
7 ditto.

1 **Entwisle [Entwhistle, Entwistle], James**, 23 Queen-street [Manchester]: sabred in the shoulder.
2 ditto as Entwhistle, 23 Queen-street, Deansgate: cut on the shoulder to the bone. A weaver, an old man. 3 weeks disabled. 20/– final.
4 ditto as Entwisle, J. (male): badly wounded by sabre or shot.
6 ditto as Entwistle of 23 Queen-street, Deansgate: aged 76 and a weaver with 1 child. Sabre-cut on the right shoulder. 3 weeks disabled. £1 received in relief.
7 ditto as Entwistle.

1 **Entwisle, William**, Bury: whilst holding the Bury Union Flag, received a sabre-cut in the head and in various parts of the body.
6 ditto of Back King-street Bury: aged 33 and a weaver with 1 child. Sabre-cut on the top of his head. Knocked down by a constable's truncheon and trampled on by the crowd and right knee much hurt. 10 days disabled. This man carried the Bury flag. £1 received in relief.
7 ditto.
[Serves as a witness in Redford v. Birley Trial. See *Report*, pp. 82–90. He carried the Bury flag, marching in the middle of the Bury party. On top of the flag pole was a metal fleur de lis painted red: see Burns' evidence at Hunt's Trial (*Report*, p. 259). He had taken part in drilling exercises. As a standard bearer he marched to the hustings and stood by them holding the flag.]

- ² **Epplestone, Joseph**, Edgely, near Stockport: crushed in the body, and toe of his right foot trod off by a cavalry horse. 40/– final. Manchester Committee 40/–.
- ⁶ ditto: aged 50 and a weaver with 2 children. Great toe on the right foot trod off by one of the cavalry horses. Crushed in the body by the crowd when down. 9 weeks disabled. £2 received in relief.
- ⁷ ditto.

- ¹ **Evans, Ellen**, Blackley: bruised very much.
- ¹ *repeated* under Walker, Ellen, Blackley: bruised in the breast and legs – finger cut.
- ² ditto as Evans or Walker: thrown down and trampled on. An outpatient in the Infirmary still. 40/– final. Manchester Committee 20/–.
- ⁴ ditto as Evans, E. (female): trampled on by cavalry – badly wounded.
- ⁵ ditto of Blackley. [Bamford thinks Evans and Walker are separate victims].
- ⁶ ditto but as Walker: aged 64. Legs and breast bruised severely by being trampled on. 5 weeks disabled. £2 received in relief.
- ⁷ ditto as Evans.

- ¹ **Evans, Mary**, 8, Style-street, near St Michael's [Manchester]: wounded in the thigh by a bayonet.
- ⁶ ditto: stabbed with a bayonet in the back part of the thigh by a soldier of the 88th Regiment. Disabled 1 week. Stopped by the 88th Regiment in getting away. Her niece had her clothes pierced by a bayonet, but another soldier interfered and saved her. £1 received in relief.
- ⁷ ditto.

Pigot's Manchester and Salford Directory, 1819: clear starcher.

- ² **Evans, William**, Queen-street, Hulme: a Special Constable in the employ of Pickfords. Appears in a dying state from the crushes and internal bruises called on him. 2 December he had not received anything but 20/– from Mr Shuttleworth and Mr Whitworth.
- ⁶ ditto of 1 Owen-street, Hulme: a carter. Much hurt internally by the Yeomanry Cavalry horses trampling on him. Still dangerously ill. A Special Constable. [No relief specified. But he receives relief from local committee].
- ⁷ ditto, 1 Owen-street, Hulme.

[In all probability, he died of his wounds. See above, ch. 1, n. 26.]

- ¹ **Fallrass [Fallows, Fallons], John**, Birch, near Middleton: knocked down by the cavalry and leg much bruised.
- ⁵ ditto as Fallows: cut in the head (later married Ann Heywood, another victim).
- ⁶ ditto as Fallows of Birch, near Middleton: aged 44 and with 7 children. Knocked down by a cavalry horse which trod on his right leg and foot. Disabled 5 weeks. £1 received in relief.
- ⁷ ditto as Fallons.

- ⁴ **Falmouth, J. (male)**: badly wounded by sabre or shot.

¹ **Farnworth James**, Jackson's Row [Manchester], sabred very badly.
⁷ ditto.

¹ **Farren, Elizabeth**, Lombard-street [Manchester]: cut in the head by a Yeoman.
² ditto at Thomas Kames Dudley, Worcestershire: severely cut on the head, the cut a very bad one by Tebbutt who has threatened her. £5 [40/– more pencilled in]. Manchester Committee 40/–.
⁶ ditto of Dudley, Staffordshire: two severe sabre-cuts on the head. She preferred an indictment against Tebbutt who cut her; but the bill was thrown out. £7 received in relief. Relief also from local committee.
⁷ ditto, Lombard-street.
[For the indictment against Tebbutt, see *Peterloo Massacre* (1819), pp. 84–5. This evidence declares her to be a neighbour of Tebbutt. Therefore the Staffordshire address given in ⁶ must be wrong. She received a 'deep sabre-wound, three inches long from the crown of her head to the top of the forehead'. She 'instantly fell from the shock of the blow' but Tebbutt 'repeated his attack, and struck at her with the sword as she was falling; the sword, however, got entangled in her clothes and did not do her further injury'. In giving evidence at the Lees Inquest, she presented herself as the wife of a velvet-dresser of Lombard-street and claims to have been attacked 30 yards from Buxton's house. See *Report*, pp. 177–8.]

Farren: a male child-in-arms of Elizabeth Farren. [See account of his injury in *Peterloo Massacre*, pp. 84–5: she was 'with her infant child at her breast ... Seeing Mr Tebbutt ... coming, she held her child down and prayed him to spare her infant'. As she was sabred on the head, 'her child fell from her arms, and received a severe contusion on the head, of which it is at this day suffering'.]

⁴ **Felsmere, W. (male)**: badly wounded by sabre or shot.

¹ **Fenton, Joseph**, 38 Spear-street, Ancoats-street [Manchester]: trampled upon and much bruised.
² ditto: Meagher made a blow at him. He cried out and fell when the horse sprung upon him and he was much hurt. A young man. 10/– final.
⁶ ditto: aged 20 and a shoemaker. Hurt by the trumpeter's horse which trod on his leg. Disabled for 3 days. 10/– received in relief.
⁷ ditto.

¹ **Ferguson, John**, 18 Bengal-street [Manchester]: shot in Newton-lane on 17 August.
² ditto: shot in the breast by the 88th Regiment on 17 August. Much hurt. A very respectable man. 40/– final [£2 more pencilled in]. Manchester Committee 20/–.
³ ditto of Manchester: shot. F.n. Struck by a spent ball as he was going to his work.
⁶ ditto: aged 69 and a weaver with 2 children. Shot in the breast by one of the 88th Regiment on the evening of 17th August. Received in relief £4. Also relief from local committee.
⁷ ditto.

² **Fielding, John**, Quick in Saddleworth: knocked down and trampled on, left knee much crushed. Attended by Dr Earnshaw, 7 weeks disabled. 30/– final.
⁶ ditto: aged 50 and a weaver with 1 child. Knocked down and trampled on by the crowd, his left knee seriously hurt. 7 weeks disabled. £1.10.0. received in relief.
⁷ ditto.

² **Mrs Fildes [Ann]**, 23 Kennedy-street [Manchester]: Mrs Fildes was knocked down by sergeant major who was riding after the others. The child thrown out of her arms lived till ten. [Her name is Ann, her child's name is William and her husband's name is Charles. For this and how she was accidentally knocked over, see Rylands MS. 1197 (82).]
Pigot's Manchester and Salford Directory, 1819, 1821: Charles Fildes, waiter of same address.

¹ **Mrs Fildes [Mary]**: who carried the flag in Mr Hunt's carriage and was wounded.
² ditto as Mary of Comet-street, Beswick Row [Manchester]: was much beat by constables and leaped off the hustings when Mr Hunt was taken. Was obliged to absent herself a fortnight to avoid imprisonment. Paid 40/– [40/– more in pencil].
⁶ ditto of 3 Comet-street: aged 27 with 5 children. Beat about the head and face by constables when escaping from the hustings. Her house was searched by the Police, and she was obliged to leave home for a fortnight. £4 received in relief.
⁷ ditto, 3 Comet-street, Beswick Square.
[See Mrs. G. Linnaeus Banks, *The Manchester Man* (first published in 1876; 1973), p. 120.]

¹ **Fildes [William, child of Ann Fildes]**: rode over and killed.
⁶ ditto: rode over by the cavalry. Killed.

² **Filmore, Sarah**, 6 Little Chapel-street, Bank Top [Manchester]: thrown down and trampled on, left knee and foot hurt. 20/– final.
⁶ ditto: aged 64: left knee and foot hurt by being trampled on by the crowd. Disabled 7 weeks. £1 received in relief.
⁷ ditto.

² **Finn, William**, 1 George Leigh-street [Manchester]: 13 cuts in different parts of the body. Disabled some time and imprisoned 3 weeks. 40/– final.
⁶ ditto, 81 George Leigh-street: aged 44 and a weaver with 2 children. 13 wounds in various parts of his body, principally by blows from the constables' truncheons. 18 days in prison. £2 received in relief.
⁷ ditto.

¹ **Firmstone, Joseph**: wounded on the thigh.
² ditto, Charlestown, near Pendleton: disabled 6 weeks by being trampled on the groin. A weaver with a wife and three children. Was 6 weeks disabled. 40/– final.
⁶ ditto: aged 34 and a weaver with 3 children. Trampled on and hurt in the groin by a Yeomanry Cavalry horse. 6 weeks disabled. £2 received in relief.
⁷ ditto.

² **Fletcher, James**, York-street, Bolton Moor: cut on the back of the hand by an artillery man. 10/– final.
⁶ ditto of York-street, Bolton: aged 24 and a weaver. Severe cut on the back of the left hand by an artillery man. 2 weeks disabled. £1 received in relief.
⁷ ditto.

¹ **Fletcher, John**, Eccles: wounded in the knee, being trampled upon by the cavalry.
² ditto: thrown down and trampled on. 1 week disabled, his knee hurt. 11/– final.
⁶ ditto: aged 31 and a weaver with 4 children. Thrown down and trampled on by Yeomanry horses; knee hurt and body crushed. 1 week disabled. 11/– received in relief.
⁷ ditto.

¹ **Fletcher, William**, Burnley: received a sabre wound on the head while, on the hustings, attempting to relieve the sick by giving them some water.
⁷ ditto.

¹ **Flint, George**, Cropper-street [Manchester, near Miles Platting]: bruised in his arm.
⁴ ditto: badly wounded by trampling of cavalry.
⁷ ditto but 3 Boardman's Square [Miles Platting].

¹ **Forpan [Forpar], Elizabeth**, 7 Dyer's-lane, Deansgate [Manchester]: wounded on the head.
⁴ ditto, but Forpar, E. (**female**): badly wounded by sabre or shot.

¹ **Foster [Forster], John**, 2 Blossom-street, Salford: wounded by a truncheon.
² ditto as Forster: head bruised in 4 places by constables about 10 of whom struck and knocked him down in Deansgate. They appeared drunk. He was much beat in the body. 20/– final.
⁴ ditto as Foster, J. (**male**): wounded by truncheons of the Special Constables or crushed by multitude.
⁶ ditto as Foster: a Calico printer with 1 child. His head much bruised by the truncheons of a party of constables in Deansgate. Disabled 1 week. £1 received in relief. A widower.
⁷ ditto.

¹ **Froggatt, Henry**, Church-street [Manchester]: Special Constable: injured by the cavalry.
⁴ ditto as Froggatt, H. (**male**): wounded by sabre or shot.
⁷ ditto.
Baines' Lancashire Directory, II, p. 198: victualler at the Unicorn, 45 Church-street.

⁴ **Fusner, M. (female)**: trampled by cavalry.

Gairathy, see McGairathy, William

⁴ **Ganalty, W. (male)**: badly wounded by sabre or shot.

² **Garside, Ellen**, Charlestown [Ashton]: thrown down and trampled on. Was under the horses feet some time. 20/– final.

⁶ ditto of Charlestown, near Ashton: trampled on by the Yeomanry horses and seriously bruised. 3 weeks disabled. £1 received in relief.

⁷ ditto.

² **Garside, Edmund**, Charlestown [Ashton]: shoulder hurt and his leg hurt. Trampled on. 20/– final.

⁶ ditto of Charlestown, near Ashton: weaver with 3 children. Shoulder cut, knocked down by a cavalry horse and bruised. 2 weeks disabled. £1 received in relief.

⁷ ditto.

² **Garside, John**, 119 Great Ancoats-street [Manchester]: thrown down and trampled on, his knee dislocated. An old man 62, with five children. 40/– final.

⁶ ditto of 119 Ancoats Lane. Aged 62 and a weaver with 5 children. Thrown down and trampled on by the crowd, his left knee dislocated. 1 month disabled. £2 received in relief.

⁷ ditto with addition of 'near the Hall'.

⁷ **Garside, Martha** [no address but follows Ellen Garside].

¹ **Gaunt, Elizabeth** [Manchester]: suffered much from bruises and solitary confinement in the New Bailey, whence she was discharged when Mr Hunt and his friends were examined.

² ditto: much beat by constables about the head and body and imprisoned 12 days. £10 final. Manchester Committee 20/–.

⁶ ditto: with two children. Severely beat on the head and back by constables. Imprisoned 12 days. One of those taken with Mr Hunt. £10 received in relief. Relief also from local committee.

⁷ ditto.

[She was described as 'a tall, pale woman about 45'. Her treatment was condemned by Hunt who claimed she was pregnant at the time. See *Peterloo Massacre* (1819), p. 99. For her taking refuge in Hunt's carriage, see ibid., pp. 41–2. For an indication that she was from Manchester, see *Republican*, V, p. 602. At her Final Examination in the New Bailey on 27 Aug, according to the *Manchester Observer*, 30 Aug. 1819: 'The prisoner came, or rather was carried from behind the dock where she had a seat ... She looked pale, emaciated and almost fainting for weakness in consequence of the wounds which she had received at the meeting and her subsequent solitary confinement'. A witness declared that 'he took her out of the carriage, she was then fainting ... Other constables came up and took her from me'. According to Gaunt's statement, 'in the confusion someone had put her into Hunt's carriage ... She had no right to be in the coach but was put in by two persons for safety. She fainted away and when she came to herself she found she had got a blow. She threw herself afterwards into a private house, and remained there for some time'. Awarded an immediate discharge.]

¹ **Gibbons [Gibbon], Anthony**, Chadkirk [near Marple]: sabre-wound on the head.
² ditto: sabre-cut on the head by one of the Yeomen. A young man. 20/– final.
⁶ ditto but Gibbon of Chadkirk. Aged 23 and a weaver with 1 child. Severe sabre-cut on the head by a Yeoman. £1 received in relief.
⁷ ditto as Gibbons.

¹ **Gill, Alice**, Hope-street, Oldfield-road [Salford]: bruised very badly.
² ditto of Oldfield-lane: 74 years of age. Thrown down and her ankle hurt. 20/– final.
⁴ ditto: trampled on by cavalry – badly wounded.
⁶ ditto of 30 Hope-street: aged 74. Ankle severely hurt and body bruised by being trampled on by the crowd. Disabled for 1 month. £1 received in relief.

¹ **Gillmore, William**, Deansgate [Manchester]: sabred in the head by Tebbutt.
⁷ ditto, but Quay-street.
[He brings an indictment against Tebbutt. See Rylands MS 1197 (58)].
Pigot's Manchester and Salford Directory, 1819: 53 Quay-street. [No occupation given.]

² **Gleve, Nappylinas**, Temple Bar, Stockport: two ribs displaced and her body trampled by the cavalry. 30/– final.
⁶ ditto but Nappylenas of Temple Bar, Stockport: aged 22. Body bruised and 2 ribs dislocated by being trampled on by Yeomanry Cavalry horses. Her clothes cut by the sabres of the Yeomanry. £1.10.0. received in relief.
⁷ ditto.

⁷ **Gobert, Thomas**, Charlestown, near Ashton.

⁷ **Goddard, William**, Ashton-on-Hurt [i.e. Hurst], Knowl.

¹ **Golding, Sarah**, 14 Cross-street [Salford]: bruised in the body and legs.
² ditto, 14 Cross-street, Salford: thrown down and trampled on, much crushed. An old woman. Made her escape without shoes. A decent person. 20/– [40/– more pencilled in].
⁴ ditto as Golding, S. (female): badly wounded by truncheons of the Special Constables or crushed by the multitude.
⁶ ditto: 67 years of age. Thrown down and trampled on by the crowd; severely crushed in the body. 6 weeks disabled. £3 received in relief.
⁷ ditto.

¹ **Goodwin, John**, Stockport: knocked down and cut in the leg.
⁶ ditto of Carrington Fields, Stockport: aged 28 with 1 child. Right leg hurt by being trampled on; received a violent blow from the butt-end of a musket by a foot soldier. Disabled 2 weeks. £1 received in relief.
⁷ ditto.

1. **Goodwin, Margaret**, 8 Bury-street, Salford: wounded by Shelmerdine in the head and back.
2. ditto, 18 Bury-street, Salford: trampled on by the horses, her eyesight much injured. Cut at by Shelmerdine. A widow with one child. One of the witnesses. Lost 3 families' washing and is much distressed. 20/– [40/– more pencilled in]. Manchester Committee 20/–, 20/–.
6. ditto, 8 Bury-street: 1 child. Sabre-cut on the head by Shelmerdine, a Yeoman; trampled on by the crowd; her back hurt. Still unwell. Went to Lancaster to prefer a bill of indictment against Shelmerdine whom she had known many years. Bill thrown out. £3 received in relief. Also relief from local committee.
7. ditto, 8 Bury-street.
[For her attempt to indict Shelmerdine, see Rylands MS. 1197 (58) where she is described as 'upward of 60 years old'. For her evidence at the Lees' Inquest, see *Report*, pp. 184–5 where she stated that she was well away from the hustings in the direction of St Peter's Church when attacked and 'knocked senseless' by Thomas Shelmerdine.]

1. **Goodwin, Thomas**, 11 Pump-street [Manchester]: trampled upon.
2. ditto: trampled on and bruised. 10 days disabled. A slight case. 10/– final.
6. ditto: aged 38. Bruised and trampled on by the crowd. 10 days disabled. 10/– received in relief.
7. ditto.

1. **Graham, Christopher**, Port-street [Manchester]: sabred on the head.
7. ditto.

1. **Graves [Groves], Frederick**, 4 Worsley-street [Manchester]: sabred and bruised very badly.
2. ditto, but Groves of 1 Worsley-street: sabre-cut in the back part of the head and on his arm. Legs also trampled. A hatter. 20/– final.
6. ditto as Groves of 1 Worsley-street: aged 40 and a hatter with 6 children. Sabre-cuts on the back of head and left arm; knocked down and trampled on by crowd; his legs hurt. 2 weeks disabled. £1 received in relief.
7. ditto as Groves.

1. **Graves [Greaves], Sarah**, Hollinwood: collar-bone broken by the blow of a sword from a Manchester Yeoman.
2. ditto but Greaves: left collar bone broke with the back of a sabre. Was 16 weeks disabled. 30/– final. Manchester Committee 30/–, 10/–.
4. ditto as Greaves, S. (female): badly wounded by sabre or shot.
6. ditto as Greaves of Hollingwood: aged 33. Left collar-bone broke by a blow from a Yeoman with the back of his sabre. 10 weeks disabled. £1.10.0. received in relief. Relief also from local committee.
7. ditto as Greaves.

2 **Greaves, Ann**, Oldham: thrown down and crushed in the body and her ankle dislocated. Certified by Mr Joseph Taylor. 15/– final.
6 ditto of Oldham: two children. Thrown down and trampled on by crowd; body bruised and ankle dislocated. 3 weeks disabled. 15/– received in relief.

1 **Greaves, James**, Hollinwood: stabbed with a sabre by a Hussar.
2 ditto: stab with a sabre behind his right hip, an awkward looking place. 30/– final. Manchester Committee 20/–.
4 ditto as Greaves, J. (male): badly wounded by sabre or shot.
6 ditto of Hollingwood, near Oldham: aged 58 and a weaver with 6 children. Sabre-stab by a Yeoman above the right hip. 1 month disabled. £1.10.0. received in relief. Relief also from local committee.
7 ditto.

1 **Green, E.**, Wild's Court, Shudehill [Manchester]: shot in the ankle.
2 ditto but Elizabeth, Wild's Court, Withy Grove: ankle shattered by a ball from the 88th at the New Cross about half-past seven. 2 pieces of bone taken out. A young woman. 40/– [40/– more pencilled in]. Manchester Committee 20/– at 5/– per week for a month.
6 ditto of 9 Wild's Court, Withy Grove: aged 24. Shot in the ankle by a soldier of the 88th Regiment at the New Cross on the evening of 16 August. Still disabled. Part of the ankle-bone taken out. £4 received in relief. Relief also from local committee.
7 ditto as Elizabeth of Wilde's Court, Shudehill.

1 **Green, J.**, Parliament-street [Manchester]: much bruised in the back and struck by the constables and Cheshire cavalry.
6 ditto, James of 1 Parliament Court, Deansgate: aged 28 and a tailor with 1 child. Severely beat on the back of the head by a Cheshire Yeoman. 10 weeks imprisoned. See imprisoned list. Says he was beat for hissing and for refusing to go on his knees to beg pardon. [No relief mentioned.] Statement B states that he was imprisoned for 10 weeks and 5 days – from 16 August to proclamation of 30 October. £3 in relief.
7 ditto as James, 1 Parliament Court, Parliament-street.

2 **Green, John**, 16 Long Milgate [Manchester]: thrown down and trampled on. Has lost the use of his limbs and is at present confined. 20/– [20/– more pencilled in]. Deserves further notice.
4 ditto as Green, J. (male): badly wounded by trampling of the cavalry.
6 ditto, 16 Long Millgate: aged 36 and a spinner with 3 children. Bruised and inwardly injured by being trampled on by a Yeomanry Cavalry horse. 3 weeks disabled. £2 received in relief.
7 ditto.

1 **Green, Joshua**, Poland-street, Newton-lane [Manchester]: bruised very badly.
7 ditto but Joseph.

[4] **Green, S. (female)**: badly wounded by sabre or shot.

[2] **Greenhalgh, Thomas**, 3 Back Rothwell-street [Bolton]: crushed in the body; horse fell on him when the rider was thrown off violently. 20/– final.
[6] ditto of 2 Back Rothwell-street, Bolton: aged 40 and a weaver with 2 children. Knocked down by a cavalry horse and much bruised. 3 weeks disabled. The horse fell on him and the rider was thrown violently on the ground. £1 received in relief.
[7] ditto.

[1] **Grice [but Grin], Mr**, Gravel-lane, Salford: bruised and trampled on.
[4] ditto as Grice, J. (male): wounded by trampling of cavalry.
[7] ditto as Grice, Mr of Gravel-street, Salford.

[1] **Griffiths, Mary**, 45 Fleet-street [Manchester]: violently struck by a constable and much trampled upon by the cavalry.
[2] ditto: hurt on the head. Does not live with her husband. A slight case not deserving notice.
[7] ditto.

[6] **Grimes [Grime], Jane**, 23 Aqueduct-street [Manchester]: aged 22. Thrown down by the crowd and left ankle hurt; body bruised. 3 weeks disabled. Her ankle still bad. £1 received in relief.
[7] ditto but Grime.

[4] **Grove, T. (male)**: badly wounded by sabre or shot.

Groves, see Graves, Frederick

[1] **Grub, John**, 9 Caygill-street, Salford: bruised in the body.
[2] ditto: his left wrist dislocated, thrown down and trampled on by the people, and much injured. 20/– final.
[4] ditto as Grub, J. (male): badly wounded by trampling of cavalry.
[6] ditto, 9 Caygill-street, Salford: aged 45 and a weaver with 4 children. Thrown down and trampled on by the crowd; left wrist dislocated and body bruised. 1 week disabled. £1 received in relief.
[7] ditto.

[1] **Hadfield, James**, Taflane [i.e. Turf-lane], near Royton: thrown down and his shoulder crushed.
[2] ditto but Turf-lane, near Royton: knocked down and trampled on, his right shoulder much hurt. 5 weeks disabled. 10/– final. Manchester Committee 30/–. Rochdale Committee 15/–.
[6] ditto of Turf-lane Royton: aged 32 and a weaver with 1 child. Knocked down and trampled on by the crowd; right shoulder hurt. 5 weeks disabled. 10/– received in relief.
[7] ditto, Turf-lane, Royton.

² **Hagan, Bridget**, 11 Lee [Lees-street or possibly Leigh-street, Manchester]]: still disabled. Was thrown down and trampled on, stomach hurt. Has had a miscarriage in consequence. Certified by Mr Houldsworth's putter-out. 40/– final. [Houldsworth was a cotton spinner].

⁶ ditto of 11 Lee-street: with 5 children. Thrown down and rode over by the cavalry; thighs and body much hurt. Still disabled. Had a miscarriage in consequence of the injury she received. £2 received in relief.

⁷ ditto.

⁷ **Hagerty, William**, Bolton.

¹ **Hall, Ann**, Miller's-lane [Salford]: bruised very badly.

² ditto but of Garden-street, Shudehill: knocked down and severely beat. A widow of 52 years of age. 20/– final. Manchester Committee 10/–, 10/–.

⁶ ditto of Garden-street, Shudehill: aged 52. severely beat about the head and shoulders by constables' truncheons. 6 weeks disabled. Received £1 in relief. Relief also from local committee.

⁷ ditto but of Miller's-lane.

¹ **Hall, Daniel**, Deansgate [Manchester]: struck and wounded by R. C. Sharp, a Yeoman.

⁶ ditto of Deansgate: patten-ring maker. Beat severely on the back and shoulders by the back of a sabre. 3 weeks disabled. Knocked down by a Yeoman Cavalry horse. £1.10.0. received in relief.

⁷ ditto.

Baines' Lancashire Directory, II, p. 205: a clog, patten and ring maker of 176 Deansgate.

¹ **Hamer, John**, Tottington: crushed in the body by the cavalry.

⁶ ditto of Tottington, near Bury. Aged 53 and a weaver with five children. Knocked down by a Yeomanry Cavalry horse and much trampled on. Was carried off the ground in an insensible state. 7 weeks disabled. Dr Fernely of Manchester stated that his countenance had assumed a deeper hue than he had ever known connected with a recovery. £2.10.0. received in relief.

⁷ ditto.

[Gave evidence at Redford v. Birley Trial, see *Report*, pp. 81–2. He claimed he went to Manchester with the Bury party but did not stay with it. On Peter's Field he stood at the Deansgate end.]

¹ **Hamilton, Hannah**, 54 Henry-street [Manchester]: sabred in the left elbow and knee and badly crushed.

² ditto Hannah (or Ann): thrown down and her knee much hurt. Is still under Dr Basonett's care. A cotton batter. 20/– [40/– more in pencil]. Per Manchester Committee 20/– 10/– 10/–.

⁴ ditto as Hamilton, H. (female): badly wounded by sabre or shot.

⁶ ditto: aged 18. Knocked down by the Yeomanry Cavalry horses and her knee much hurt. Still under care of Dr Basnett. £3 received in relief. Relief also from local committee.

⁷ ditto.
[Gave evidence at Lees' Inquest, see *Report*, pp. 186–7, declaring that she was wounded near the Quakers' Chapel. She had stood 1 yard from the hustings when Hunt was on stage. She lived with her mother.]

¹ **Hancock, Hannah**, Jones' [? Jackson's] Row, Deansgate [Manchester]: sabred by Birley.
⁷ ditto.

² **Hardman, John**, 24 Union-street, Stockport: thrown down by the crowd and stabbed in the right arm with a bayonet. 30/– final.
⁶ ditto: aged 38 and a weaver. Stabbed in the right arm with a bayonet by a soldier of the 88th Regiment, and trampled on by the crowd. 2 weeks disabled. £1.10.0. received in relief.
⁷ ditto.

¹ **Hardy, Mary**, New Windsor [Salford]: bruised.
⁴ ditto as Hardy, M. (female): badly wounded by sabre or shot.
⁷ ditto of New Windsor, Salford.

⁴ **Hargreave, J.** (male): badly wounded by truncheons of the Special Constables or crushed by the multitude.

¹ **Hargreaves, J.** [**John**], 2 Riders Row [Manchester]: trampled on and bruised.
² ditto but 12 Riders Row: rode over by the cavalry near the infirmary, left foot and right hip much hurt. Disabled a fortnight. 20/– final.
⁶ ditto as John of 2 Riders Row, Bank Top. Aged 61 and a labourer with 2 children. Rode over by the cavalry near the Infirmary; his right hip and left foot much hurt. 2 weeks disabled. £1 received in relief.
⁷ ditto as John.

¹ **Harper, Charles**, Pigeon-street, Ancoats-street [Manchester]: wounded badly in the hand.
¹ *repeated* with 6 Pigeon-street, Ancoats-lane: cut in the thumb and left hand bruised.
⁴ ditto as Harper, C. (male): wounded by sabre or shot.
⁶ ditto, 4 Dixon-street, Newtown: aged 20 and a weaver. Sabre-cut on the left hand and head bruised by a constable's truncheon. 2 weeks disabled. £1 received in relief.
⁷ ditto, 4 Dixon-street, Newtown.

¹ **Harper, Thomas**, 7 Prussia-street [Manchester]: slightly trampled on.
² ditto: thrown down and trampled on. A slight case. 20/– final.
⁶ ditto: aged 42 and a weaver with two children. Left arm and leg bruised by being knocked down and trampled on by the crowd. 3 weeks disabled. £1 received in relief.
⁷ ditto.

¹ **Harrison, James**, 19 Back Turner-street [Manchester]: stabbed by a Yeoman and trampled upon.

⁴ ditto as Harrison, J. (male): badly wounded by sabre or shot.
⁶ ditto of 19 Back Turner-street: aged 26. Stabbed in the side by a Yeoman and trampled on by Yeomanry Cavalry horses. 6 weeks disabled. £1 received in relief.
⁷ ditto.

---

⁴ **Harrison, N.** (male): badly wounded by truncheons of Special Constables or crushed by multitude.

---

¹ **Harrison, William**, 1 Crown-street [Manchester]: Special Constable, crushed and wounded.
² ditto with Blakeley [i.e. Blakely, now Dantzig] -street added: breast much crushed. Has not been able to work since. Skin off in some places. A man of good principles – a Special Constable. 20/- final.
⁶ ditto of Crown-street, Blakeley-street: aged 66 and a land surveyor. Knocked down and trampled on, severely hurt on the legs and thighs. Still disabled. A Special Constable. Received £1 in relief.
⁷ ditto.

Pigot's Manchester and Salford Directory, 1817, 1819: land measurer of 1 Crown-street, Blakely-street.

---

¹ **Harvey, Elizabeth**, Pendleton: dreadfully injured – saved from further violence by Mr Swift.
¹ *repeated* but as Eliza of Wright-street: severely bruised.
⁴ ditto: trampled on by cavalry – badly wounded.
⁶ ditto of Smithfield dye-works, near Pendleton: aged 24. Thrown down and trampled on, the flesh trod off her neck and face; shoulders, knees and ankle hurt severely. 7 weeks disabled. [But no relief awarded – see Isabella for reason.]
⁷ ditto as Elizabeth, Wright-street.

---

¹ **Harvey, Ellen**, Wright-street [Pendleton]: struck with a sabre.
⁴ ditto as Harvey, E. (female): trampled on by cavalry – badly wounded.
⁶ ditto of Smithfield Dye-works, near Pendleton: aged 17. Struck on the stomach by a Yeoman's sabre which cut through her stays and broke a piece of whalebone two inches wide and a quarter of an inch thick. Still unwell. Was also thrown down and trampled on. Sister of Elizabeth. [No relief mentioned- see Isabella for reason].
⁷ ditto of Wright-street.

---

¹ **Harvey, Isabella**, Wright-street [Pendleton]: struck with a sabre.
⁴ ditto: trampled on by cavalry – badly wounded.
⁶ ditto of Smithfield Dye-works, near Pendleton: aged 13. Thrown down and trampled on. When rising, received a blow from the back of a sabre on the left arm which is still bandaged and partially useless. Still unwell. Sister of Ellen and Elizabeth. The parents are respectable people who would not accept any money.
⁷ ditto of Wright-street.

Haughton, see Horton, Mary

Hays, see Heys, Mary

Hayward, see Heyward, Thomas

- ² **Dr Healy [Healey, Joseph]**, Lees, near Oldham: stabbed in the back with a sabre. Had a contusion in the back of his head. One of the prisoners which the committee noted. £10.
- ⁶ ditto but Healey, Doctor, of Lees, near Oldham: received a contusion on the back of his head and stabbed by a sabre in the back by a Yeoman. Disabled for several days. Was imprisoned with Mr Hunt. £10 received in relief.
- ⁷ ditto as Healey, Joseph.

- ¹ **Heap, James**, Oldfield-lane [Salford]: leg much bruised.
- ² ditto, 30 Hope-street, Oldfield: trampled on and much bruised. Knocked down by Holmes's horse. The next man to him was killed and his eyes forced out of his head. 20/– final.
- ⁶ ditto of 18 Hope-street, Oldfield-road: aged 37 and a dyer with 5 children. Knocked down by Holmes's horse and bruised severely on leg and body. 11 days disabled. £1 received in relief.
- ⁷ ditto.

- ¹ **Heap, John**, Richard [i.e. Richmond] -street [Salford]: sabre wound on the head. Knows the man that cut him but will not tell.
- ⁷ ditto of Richmond-street.
  Baines' Lancashire Directory, II, p. 210: gentleman of 1 Richmond-street, Cross-lane, New Windsor.

- ⁷ **Heap, Sarah**, Ring-of-Bells Entry [Deansgate, Manchester].

- ² **Hebbard [Hibbard], William**, Oldham: sabre cut on the head. A very respectable man.
- ⁶ ditto of Oldham. Sabre-cut on the top of his head. A respectable tradesman [no relief].
- ⁷ ditto but Hibbard.

- ¹ **Hepstonstall, Joseph**, Stockport: knocked down by a cavalryman who trod his great toe off. His sick-club refused to relieve him saying the meeting was unlawful.
- ⁷ ditto.

Hepwood, see Hopwood, William

- ¹ **Heys [Hays], Mary**, Rawlinson Buildings [Chorlton Row]: listed as killed (p. 87).
- ⁶ ditto, 8 Rawlinson's Buildings, Oxford-road, Manchester. Rode over by cavalry. [Died in consequence].
- ⁶ *repeated* with further details: 6 children. Knocked down and trampled on by a cavalry horse, her foot stripped of the flesh and great toenails. Was pregnant at the time and so much bruised. She continued to have fits almost daily till the 17 December when

she died. Disabled until she died. Was prematurely delivered of a seven months' child which caused her death. The husband is nearly blind. See list of killed. £5 received in relief.
⁷ ditto but Hays.

---

¹ **Heywood, Alice**, Buck [i.e. Birch], near Middleton: wrist badly cut whilst holding her bonnet near the Quakers' Meeting.
² ditto, Birch, near Middleton: a violent cut on the wrist. An interesting-looking girl. 40/– final. Manchester Committee 20/–, 20/–, 20/–.
⁵ ditto but Ann: cut on her arm (later married John Fallows).
⁶ ditto of Birch, near Middleton: aged 20. Severely wounded on the left wrist by a sabre. Arm still useless. it is feared her wrist will be always stiff. £2 received in relief. Also relief from local committee.
⁷ ditto of Birch, near Middleton.
[Samuel Dawson, giving evidence at the Redford v. Birley Trial, said that he saw, near the Quakers' meeting place 'one woman with her hand nearly cut off from the wrist'. See *Report*, p. 74.]

---

¹ **Heywood, Michael**, Four-lane-ends, Bury: wounded on the head.

---

¹ **Heywood [Haywood], Thomas**, Pendleton: bruised and crushed.
² ditto: 3 weeks in the Infirmary. Was so violently crushed the blood issued from his mouth and nose. 40/– final [pencilled in: much hurt – 40/– more].
³ ditto: fractured ribs and contusion.
⁴ ditto but Haywood, T. (male): badly wounded by truncheons of Special Constables or crushed by the multitude.
⁶ ditto as Haywood of Charlestown, Pendleton: crushed and internally injured by the crowd. Disabled for 8 weeks. Three weeks in the Infirmary. Was so dreadfully crushed the blood issued from his mouth and nose. £2 received in relief.
⁷ ditto as Heywood of Charlestown, Pendleton.

Hibbard, see Hebbard, William

---

⁶ **Hickey, Dennis**, 18 Red Bank, Scotland Bridge [Cheetham]: aged 27 and a weaver. Sabre-cut on the right elbow. Right side and hip much hurt by being trampled on. 3 weeks disabled. Knocked down by a Yeoman Cavalry horse. £1.10.0. received in relief.
⁷ ditto.

---

¹ **Hickson [Higson], Thomas**, 22 Scholes-street, Bank Top [Manchester]: slight wound in the eye.
¹ *repeated* under Higson: sabre-cut over the right eye; trampled upon and much bruised.
² ditto as Hickson, 22 Scholes-street, Bank Top: wounded in the eye and leg and much bruised. Was 7 weeks in the Infirmary. 25/–.
⁴ ditto: badly wounded by sabre or shot.
⁶ ditto as Hickson of 22 Schole-street, Bank Top: aged 58 and a weaver. Sabre-cut on the

eye and leg. Knocked down and much bruised by being trampled on by crowd. 7 weeks in the Infirmary. £1.10.0. received in relief. Relief also received from local committee.
⁷ ditto as Hickson, 22 Scholes-street, Bank Top.

⁷ **Higgins, Biddy**, 11 Leigh-street, Newton-lane [Manchester].

² **Higgins, James**, 22 Union-street, Stockport: beat and ill-used. Imprisoned 5 days. A single man. 30/– final.
⁶ ditto of 22 Union-street, Stockport: a weaver. Shoulder and elbow hurt by being beat with truncheons of the constables. 2 weeks disabled. Imprisoned five days. See imprisoned list [Statement B]: £1.10.0 received in relief. Address: 23 Union-street. Having been bailed, discharged 30 October by proclamation.

Higson, see Hickson, Thomas

¹ **Hill, Robert**, 5 Potter's Buildings, Ardwick-lane [Manchester].
² ditto: crushed in the breast and right knee. Hurt by the trampling over him.
⁶ ditto: aged 32 and a weaver. Breast and right knee hurt by being trampled on by the crowd. 2 weeks disabled. £1 received in relief.
⁷ ditto.

¹ **Hillary, Joshua**, 27 Newton-street [Manchester]: sabred and bruised.
⁴ ditto: badly wounded by sabre or shot.
⁷ ditto.
Pigot's Manchester and Salford Directory, 1821: weaver.

¹ **Hilmore [Hillmore], Sarah**, 6 Chapel-street, Bank Top [Manchester]: trampled on.
⁷ ditto but Hillmore.

⁴ **Hilton, F. (male)**: wounded by sabre or shot.

¹ **Hilton, Hannah**, Middleton: 15 years of age. Wounded on the head by a sabre.
² ditto but Ann, Little Green, near Middleton: cut on the top of her head. A young girl, a slight case. 10/– final.
⁵ ditto as Ann: cut on the head.
⁶ ditto as Ann of Little Green, Middleton: aged 17. Sabre-cut on the top of her head by a Yeoman. 2 days disabled. A slight case. 10/– received in relief.
⁷ ditto as Ann.

¹ **Hilton, Thomas**, Broken Bank [i.e. Bowker Bank], Crumpsall: stabbed in the shoulder.
⁴ ditto as Hilton, T. (male): badly wounded by sabre or shot.
⁷ ditto but Bowker Bank, Crumpsall.

² **Hilton, Samuel**, Bridge Hall, near Middleton: thrown down and trampled on by the cavalry, his leg still bad. A very stout powerful man, his finger hurt also. 30/– final.

⁶ ditto of Bridge Hall, near Middleton: aged 32 and a labourer with 1 child. Thrown down and his right leg trod on by a cavalry horse; top of middle finger of left hand trod off by horse's hoof. 3 weeks disabled. His leg still bad. £1.10.0. received in relief.
⁷ ditto.

---

² **Hindle, Joseph**, Duncan-street, Little Bolton: cut in the arm below the shoulder and tumbled in a cellar. A fortnight disabled completely and was a witness at Lancaster. 40/–.
⁶ ditto of Duncan-street, Bolton: aged 24 with 1 child. A very severe sabre-cut on the right arm just above the elbow. Several weeks disabled. £2 received in relief.
⁷ ditto.
[Gave evidence in Redford v. Birley Trial, see *Report*, pp. 55–6. He described himself as an ex-weaver. He claimed after being cut: 'To keep the blow from me, I stooped under the horses; and they cut an old man with a grey head on the head, and the blood spouted over my breast'. He came to Manchester not in a large party but with three others. On the way they overtook 6 or 7 others from Bolton. He was wounded in the right arm.]

---

¹ **Hodgin [Hodkins], James**, Bank Top [Manchester]: sabre cut on the head by a Yeomanry man.
⁴ ditto but Hodkins, J. (male): badly wounded by sabre or shot.
⁷ ditto of 22 Chapel-street, Bank Top.

---

¹ **Hodgkinson, John**, 5 Back Loom-street [Manchester]: sabred in the head.
² ditto: sabre-cut on the head. A block-cutter with a wife and two children. 20/– final.
⁶ ditto 5 Back Loom-street: a block-cutter with 2 children. Sabre-cut on the head. 1 week disabled. £1 received in relief.
⁷ ditto.

---

¹ **Hogg, Jane**, 20 Brown Cross-street [Salford]: hurt by a sabre.
⁴ ditto: badly wounded by sabre or shot.
⁶ ditto of 20 Brown Cross-street: aged 40 and wife of Joseph. Bruised in the side. Disabled 3 days. She and husband: not needy people. £1 received in relief [for both].
⁷ ditto.

---

¹ **Hogg, Joseph**, 20 Brown Cross-street [Salford]: sabred and crushed.
² ditto and Mary [but surely Jane] Hogg, 20 Brown Cross-street, New Bailey: a good deal bruised and crushed. Attended by Mr Garely. Not needy people. 20/– final.
⁴ ditto as Hogg, J. (male): badly wounded by sabre or shot.
⁶ ditto, 20 Brown Cross-street, Salford: aged 39 and a wire-drawer. Ribs much hurt by being trampled on by the crowd. Two weeks disabled.
⁷ ditto.
Pigot's Manchester and Salford Directory, 1819: shopkeeper.

1. **Holden, Jeremiah**, Rothwell-street, Bolton: wounded severely in the head.
2. ditto of 18 Rothwell-street: a severe sabre-cut on the inside of the hand. Was 8 weeks unemployed. 40/– final.
6. ditto: aged 23 and a weaver. Severe sabre-cut in the palm of the right hand. 8 weeks disabled. £2 received in relief.
7. ditto.

1. **Holt, James**, Eccles: cut on the shoulder by a Yeoman. Will swear that Dr Savage cut him.
6. ditto of Eccles: aged 28 and a tailor with 3 children. Sabre-cut on the right shoulder; right ankle hurt by a fall. 1 week disabled. £1 received in relief.
7. ditto.

7. **Holt, Robert**

4. **Home, W. (male)**: wounded by sabre or shot.

1. **Hopwood [Hepwood], William**, Stockport: rode over and sabred on the knee and various severe bruises.
2. ditto, Dow [i.e. Daw] Bank, Stockport: his right knee cut by a sabre. Knocked down and bruised. 30/– final. Manchester Committee 15/–.
6. ditto of Dow Bank, Stockport: aged 57 and a dyer with 4 children. Knocked down by a cavalry horse; right knee cut by horse's hoof, and left shoulder crushed.
7. ditto but Hepwood of Dan-bank, Stockport.

6. **Hornbuck, John**, Bridge [?Ridge] Field, Stockport [?Heaton Norris]: aged 33 and a machine maker with 4 children. Knocked down and trampled on by Yeomanry Cavalry horse, his right side much bruised. 5 days disabled. 15/– received in relief.
7. ditto.

1. **Horne [Samuel], Mr**, St Ann's Place [Manchester]: wounded in the leg and face.
7. ditto as Samuel, St Ann's Place.
   Baines' Lancashire Directory, II, p. 217: fringe-manufacturer at 65 Lever-street. *Pigot's Manchester and Salford Directory, 1817, 1819*: fringe-weaver at 16 Dale-street.

1. **Horridge, Thomas**, Hoblane [i.e. Dob-lane], Failsworth: thrown down and badly crushed.
6. ditto of Dob-lane, Failsworth: aged 42 and a weaver. Head much bruised; his breast and left side crushed; spit blood frequently for a fortnight. Still disabled. Was pitched on his head in a cellar and great numbers upon him. £3 received in relief.
7. ditto of Dob-lane.

1. **Horrocks, Margaret**, Failsworth.
6. ditto of Failsworth: aged 28. Severe sabre-cut on the left side of her head by a Yeoman

which knocked her down; her legs hurt by being trampled on by the crowd. 3 weeks disabled. £1.10.0. received in relief.
7 ditto.

---

1 **Horton [Haughton, Houghton, Oughton], Mary**, 25 Cross-street [Manchester]: cut on the head by a constable's staff whilst in the carriage.
1 *repeated* but as Houghton, 25 Cross-street, Shudehill: hurt by the constables on the head and back.
2 ditto but adds Salford: severely hurt back and head. 40/– final. [20/– more in pencil]. Manchester Committee 20/–.
6 ditto as Horton, 25 Cross-street: seven children. Beat on the head by the constables with their truncheons. 3 weeks disabled. £2 received in relief.
7 ditto but Haughton, 25 Cross-street, Shudehill.
7 *repeated* but as Oughton, Mary, 25 Cross-street.

---

1 **Howard [Howarth], Mark**, Rock-street, Bury: wounded in the arm by a bayonet.
7 ditto as Howarth, Mark, Rock-street, Bury.

---

1 **Howard, Michael**, Gorsey Clough, near Bury: wounded on the head.
7 ditto.

---

2 **Howard, Samuel**, Hollinwood: thrown down and trampled on. He fell in getting over a wall and sprained his right leg. 30/– final.
6 ditto of Hollinwood, near Oldham: aged 45 and a weaver with 6 children. Thrown down and trampled on by the crowd. Sprained his right ankle in getting over the chapel wall. Disabled 1 month. £1.10.0. received in relief.
7 ditto.

---

6 **Howard, Thomas**, Rigley [i.e. Wrigley] Head, Failsworth: aged 31 with 3 children. Legs and thighs much hurt and bruised by being trampled on by the crowd. 2 weeks disabled. Could not put on his stockings for more than a week. £1 received in relief.
7 ditto but of Wrigley Head.

---

4 **Howarth, M. (female)**: badly wounded by sabre and shot.

---

1 **Howarth, Mrs. [Sarah]**, Broad-street [i.e. Boad-street], Bank Top [Manchester]: sabred in twenty places.
2 ditto as Sarah: thrown down and trampled on, her left knee and foot hurt. A decent respectable woman. 20/– final.
6 ditto as Sarah of 9 Broad-street, Bank Top: aged 25 with 1 child. Thrown down and trampled on by the crowd; left knee and right foot hurt. 2 months disabled. Received £1 in relief.
7 ditto.

Howarth, see Howard, Mark

¹ **Howarth, William**, Walshaw-lane, near Bury: stabbed with a sabre in the back.
⁶ ditto of Tottington, near Bury: aged 20 and a weaver. Severe sabre stab on the right side, scar one and a half inches long. 5 weeks disabled. £1.5.0. received in relief.
⁷ ditto of Walshaw-lane.
[Gave evidence at Redford v. Birley Trial, see *Report*, pp. 92–3. He came to Manchester with 3 others. He stood between the hustings and the Quaker meeting house.]

¹ **Hoyle, Roger**, Oldham-road, near Boardman Square [Miles Platting, Manchester]: sabre-wound in the head.
⁷ ditto.

¹ **Hulme, Jane**, 15 Mount-street [Manchester]: trampled upon by the cavalry and seriously bruised.
⁶ ditto of 15 Old Mount-street, St Michael's: aged 31 with 1 child. Left shoulder, back and hips much bruised by being knocked down and trampled on by Yeomanry Cavalry horses. 3 weeks disabled. £1 received in relief.
⁷ ditto, 15 Mount-street.

⁷ **Hulme, John**, Mosley-street [Manchester].
[One of the Yeomanry Cavalry, unhorsed on the Field, by a flying brick-bat flung by a woman. See Bamford, *Passages*, I, p. 210. For his consequent death, see Hay to Sidmouth in Rylands English MS. 1197 (27).]

¹ **Hunt, Ann**, George-street, Salford Crescent: bruises in the body.
⁴ ditto as Hunt, A. (male): badly wounded by sabre or shot.

¹ **Hunt, Henry**, Middleton Cottage: sabre wound on the hand and about sixty blows from the constables.
⁷ ditto, with Esq. added.
[For nature of the attack, see Smith's account in *Bruton*, pp. 68–9.]

⁶ **Hurdies, William**, 22 Fawcett-street [Manchester]: aged 25 and a weaver with 1 child. Left ankle sprained and stabbed on the left side of the head by the bayonet of a soldier of the 88th Regiment. 1 week disabled. 10/– received in relief.
⁷ ditto.

² **Hurst, Isaac**, 16 Prussia-street [Manchester]: an old man, 75 years of age. Trampled on. Sometime disabled. 10/– final.
⁶ ditto of 16 Prussia-street: aged 75 and a weaver. Knocked down and trampled on by Yeomanry Cavalry horses. Several days disabled. 18/– received in relief.
⁷ ditto.

¹ **Hurst, John**, 16 Prussia-street [Manchester]: sabred in the head.
² ditto: cut on the head by a sabre. 22 years of age. 10/– final.
⁴ ditto as Hurst, J. (male): badly wounded by sabre or shot.

⁶ ditto of 16 Prussia-street: aged 22 and a weaver. Slight sabre-cut on the head by a Yeoman. Slight case. 10/– received in relief.
⁷ ditto.

---

² **Iddins, Betty**, Pendleton: thrown down and trampled on. Still unwell. 58 years of age. 40/– final.
⁶ ditto: aged 58. Knocked down in the crowd and crushed inwardly. Still disabled. £2 received in relief.
⁷ ditto.

---

³ **Jackson, Abigail**, Manchester: fractured ribs and much contused.

---

² **Jackson, Isabella**, 1 Union-street, Stockport: knocked down and trampled by horses. Hurt inwardly, still unwell. 30/– final.
⁶ ditto: aged 20. Knocked down and trampled on by the cavalry, arm and body much hurt, inwardly injured. 3 weeks disabled. Still unwell. £1.10.0. received in relief.
⁷ ditto.

---

¹ **Jackson, James**, Marshall's Yard, Duke-street [i.e. Dyche-street, Manchester]: sabred on the head.
⁷ ditto but of Dycke-street [i.e. Dyche-street].

---

¹ **Jackson, James**, Higher Ardwick: shot by the 88th Foot, who fired a volley in Port-street.
² ditto but adds Pin Mill to address: shot through the thigh by the 88th Regiment in Port-street on the evening of the 16th and still disabled. 40/– [£3 more in pencil]. Manchester Committee 40/–.
³ ditto of Ardwick: 2 shots in the thigh.
⁴ ditto as Jackson, J. (male): badly wounded by sabre or shot.
⁶ ditto of Pin Mill, Higher Ardwick: aged 22 and a carter with 2 children. Shot through the thigh by the 88th Regiment in Port-street on the evening of 16th August. Still lame. £5 received in relief. Also relief received from local committee.
⁷ ditto [*repeated*].

---

¹ **Jackson, Mary**, 43 Turner-street [Manchester]: lamed.
⁴ ditto: with 2 children and aged 31. Had her feet hurt by the fall of a wall near the hustings. Trampled on by the crowd. Disabled 1 month. Was an out-patient of the Infirmary. £1 received in relief.
⁷ ditto.

---

⁷ **Jackson, Mary**, 20 Hanover-street [Manchester].

---

² **Jackson, Nancy** [Chadderton]: her elbow broke. Was taken to the Infirmary. A weaver with 4 children, very poor. 60/– final. Manchester Committee 20/–.
³ ditto of Chadderton: broken arm, very bad.

⁴ ditto as Jackson, N. (female): trampled on by cavalry – badly wounded.
⁶ ditto of Chadderton. With 4 children. Thrown into a cellar, right arm broken above the elbow; her arm appears wasting away. Still disabled. £3 received in relief. Also relief from local committee.
⁷ ditto.

---

¹ **Jackson, Samuel**, Gravel-lane, Salford: shot in the leg – amputated.
² ditto, 4 Gravel-lane, Salford: still in the Infirmary. Shot on the knee by the 88th Regiment in Oldham-street betwixt 7 and 8 in the evening. Was going to see his aunt. Has had his leg taken off. 40/–, 20/– [£10 more pencilled in]. Manchester Committee 20/–.
³ ditto: shot in the leg, amputated.
⁴ ditto as Jackson, S. (male): badly wounded by sabre or shot.
⁶ ditto, 4 Gravel-lane, Salford: aged 21 and a dyer with 1 child. Shot in the left knee by the 88th Regiment in Oldham-street as he was walking up it betwixt seven and eight o'clock in the evening of 16 August. Carried to the Infirmary and leg afterwards amputated. Disabled for life. came out of the Infirmary when the Deputation was at Manchester. Received £15 in relief.
⁷ ditto.

---

¹ **Jacques, David**, Whittle, near Middleton: right wrist crushed and head cut.
⁶ ditto as Jaques: aged 19. Sabre-cut on his head, trampled on by the crowd and his wrist crushed. 3 weeks disabled. [No relief apart from something from local committee.]
⁷ ditto.
[Gave evidence at Redford v. Birley Trial, see *Report*, pp. 93–99. He declared himself a weaver. He claimed to have gone to Manchester with the Middleton people but was not part of the company of marchers. He stood between the hustings and the Quaker meeting house, 20 to 30 yards from the hustings.]

James, see Jones, Elizabeth

---

¹ **James, William**, with Mr Heald, painter [Manchester]: right eye injured by a sabre, leg bruised and ankle sprained.
⁷ ditto, 42 George Leigh-street.

Jaques, see Jacques, David

Jarvis, see Jervis, Mary

---

¹ **Jerron [Jerror, Jevons], William**, Back Princess-street [Manchester]: sabred in the head, face much hurt and bruised by trampling.
⁶ ditto but Jerror of 6 Back Princess-street: aged 35. Knocked down by a cavalry horse, left shoulder hurt severely. Beat on the head by the back of a sabre. Still unwell. £2 received in relief.
⁷ ditto but Jevons, 6 Back Princess-street.

¹ **Jervis [Jarvis], Mary**, 18 Longworth-street [Manchester]: crushed by the crowd and struck by a constable.
² ditto but 17 Longworth-street: trampled on and crushed dreadfully. The calf of the leg has been taken off; in consequence the doctor's bill is 4 guineas. 40/– [£5 more pencilled in]. Manchester Committee 20/–.
⁴ ditto but Jarvis: badly wounded by truncheons of the Special Constables or crushed by the multitude.
⁶ ditto as Jervis of 57 Longworth-street: 2 children. Was so dreadfully trampled on that the calf of her left leg was obliged to be taken off. Supposed lame for life. Still disabled. £7 received in relief. Relief also from local committee.

Jevons, see Jerron, William

⁴ **Jines, M. (female)**: badly trampled by cavalry.

¹ **Johnson, Ann**, Flixton: both knees dreadfully bruised.

¹ **Johnson, Edward**, 67 Henry-street [Manchester]: blow from a sabre broke 2 of his ribs.
² ditto: trod on by the cavalry and 2 ribs fractured. A weaver, 50 years of age. 20/–.
⁴ Johnson, E. (male): badly wounded by sabre or shot.
⁶ ditto of 67 Henry-street: aged 50 and a weaver. Trod on by the cavalry horses and two ribs in the right side fractured. 6 weeks disabled. £2 received in relief.
⁷ ditto.

² **Johnson, Margaret**, 24 Fawcett-street [Manchester]: twice knocked down by constables and trampled on. 20/– final.
⁶ ditto, Back of 24, Fawcett-street: aged 27 with 3 children. Knocked down, beat by constables' truncheons. 8 days disabled. £1 received in relief.
⁷ ditto as Back of 24 Fawcett-street.
Pigot's Manchester and Salford Directory, 1819: dealer in baskets and coopers' ware, Smithy-door.

¹ **Johnson, Thomas**, Queen-street [Manchester]: cut at by Meagher and much bruised in left shoulder.
[See his letter in the *Manchester Observer*, 6 Oct. 1821, p. 51 where he describes himself as a bootmaker and claims to have been one of the first to be 'cut down and trampled upon by the Manchester Yeomanry Cavalry' and then imprisoned in the New Bailey for eleven weeks.]
² ditto but adds Deansgate: knocked down and trampled on. Imprisoned from 16 August to 29 October. 60/– final. Manchester Committee 20/–.
⁶ ditto of Queen-street, Deansgate: aged 38 and a bootmaker with 2 children. Knocked down and trampled on, bruised in the body. Imprisoned 10 weeks. See imprisoned list: Statement B [no relief mentioned apart from relief from local committee]. Same list gives as address Queen-street, next door to Farmer's Arms, and states he was imprisoned for 10 weeks and 5 days.
⁷ ditto.

- [1] **Johnson, Rebecca**, Lonroyd-bridge, near Huddersfield.
- [7] ditto of Longroyd-bridge.

- [1] **Jones, Edward**, 139 Great Ancoats-street [Manchester]: shot in the thigh at New Cross.
- [2] ditto: shot through the thigh by the 88th Regiment while standing at his own door on the evening of 16 August. A desperate wound and not yet well. A respectable master butcher. £5.
- [6] ditto of 139 Great Ancoats-street: aged 45. Shot in the thigh by the 88th Regiment as he was standing at his own door on 16 August. Still disabled. A respectable man supposed lame for life. £5 received in relief.
- [7] ditto.

- [1] **Jones, Elizabeth**, 3 Brook's-court [?Brook-street], London-road [Manchester]: dreadfully crushed.
- [2] ditto: crushed and trampled on. A month disabled. 20/– final.
- [6] ditto of Brook's-court, London Road: aged 52 with 2 children. Thrown down and trampled on by the crowd. Was insensible for some time after. 1 month disabled. £1 received in relief.
- [7] ditto.

- [1] **Jones [James], Elizabeth**, 4 Back Queen-street [Manchester]: wounded in the leg.
- [2] ditto but Elizabeth James, 4 Back Queen-street, Deansgate: trampled on and much hurt by the cavalry. Was a month under the Infirmary doctors. 20/– final [20/– more in pencil].
- [4] ditto as James, E. (female): trampled on by cavalry.
- [6] ditto but James of 4 Back Queen-street: aged 50 with 1 child. Knocked down, breast crushed and right leg hurt. 2 months unwell. Was an out-patient at the Infirmary a month. £2 received in relief.
- [7] ditto.

- [1] **Jones, John**, 284 Newton-lane [Manchester]: crushed severely.
- [4] ditto as Jones, J. (male): badly wounded by truncheons of special constables or crushed by multitude.
- [7] ditto.

  Pigot's Manchester and Salford Directory, 1819: weaver of Cropper-street.

- [1] **Jones, Joseph**, Rhodes-bank, Oldham: sabred severely.
- [2] ditto: thrown down and bruised, his legs and ankle hurt, trampled and beat in the face. 40/– final.
- [4] ditto as Jones, J. (male): badly wounded by sabre or shot.
- [6] ditto of Rhodes Bank, near Oldham: aged 37 and a weaver with 7 children. Left ankle and both legs much hurt by the trampling of the crowd. Beat on the face by constables' truncheons. 3 weeks disabled. £2 received in relief.
- [7] ditto.

- [1] **Jones, Joseph**, Fleet-street [Manchester]: wounded in the thigh by Meagher, the trumpeter.
- [2] ditto, 52 Fleet-street, Deansgate: wounded by Meagher subsequent to the meeting. 20/– final. Manchester Committee 20/–.
- [6] ditto of 52 Fleet-street: iron-founder. Shot in the thigh by Meagher. 3 weeks disabled. Was in the Infirmary. Says he did not speak to Meagher. £1 received in relief. Relief also from local committee.
- [7] ditto.

- [1] **Jones, Mary**, 284 Newton-lane [Manchester]: sabred in right arm by John Burgess, Worsley.
- [2] ditto: severe cut on the arm by a sabre, disabled ever since. 67 years of age. 20/– final.
- [6] ditto: aged 67. Sabre-cut by a Yeoman on the left arm. Still disabled. Was sabred by a Yeoman 1 mile from St Petersfield on 16 Aug. £1 received in relief.
- [7] ditto of Newton-lane.

- [1] **Jones, Sarah**, 96 Silk-street [Manchester]: ill bruised in the head by Thomas Woodworth, a constable who lives in Newton-lane. [Hunt claims that she was killed, see p. 87.]
- [6] ditto of 96 Silk-street: 7 children. Severely beat on the head and much bruised by constables' truncheons. Still unwell. Says it was Wordsworth, a Special Constable. £4 received in relief. Relief also from local committee.
- [7] ditto with addition of George Leigh-street.

- [1] **Jones, Thomas**, 25 Bury's-buildings, Edgeley [near Stockport]: trampled upon by the cavalry and much bruised.
- [2] ditto: knocked down and crushed in the breast; hat cut by the Yeomen Cavalry; spits blood occasionally. 20/– final.
- [6] ditto of Edgeley: aged 27 and a weaver. Knocked down by a cavalry horse, trampled on and inwardly injured, spit blood some time. £1 received in relief.
- [7] ditto.

- [1] **Jordan, Mary**, 3 Portugal-street [Manchester]: struck by a sabre.
- [2] ditto: bruised and tumbled down but not seriously hurt. 20/– final.
- [4] ditto as Jordan, M. (female): wounded by sabre or shot.
- [6] ditto: 1 child. Thrown down and trampled on by the crowd; severely bruised on the loins. 5 weeks disabled. £1 received in relief.
- [7] ditto.

- [1] **Kay, James**, Back Canal-street, Ancoats-street [Manchester]: inwardly bruised.
- [2] ditto but of Factory-street, Ancoats: knocked down by constables and stamped on. 20/– final.
- [2] *repeated* but of Rogers Buildings, Pollard-street: knocked down by constables, trampled on, disabled near a month. 20/– final.

- [6] ditto of Factory-street: aged 44 and a weaver with one child. Knocked down by a constable and trampled on by the crowd, inwardly injured. 1 month disabled. £1 received in relief.
- [7] ditto as Back Canal-street, Ancoats-street.

- [1] **Kay, Samuel**, Tottington: sabred in the hand, arm and head.
- [6] ditto of Tottington, near Bury: aged 32 and a weaver with 2 children. Three severe sabre-cuts: one on the crown of the head, one on the left elbow and one on the palm of the hand four inches long. Also a stab on the left arm. 12 weeks disabled. £2.10.0. received in relief.
- [7] ditto.

[Gave evidence at Redford v. Birley Trial, see *Report*, pp. 91–2. He stood 40–50 yards from the hustings, near to the Quaker meeting house. He was driven up to the wall of the meeting house, among some timber, and there cut.]

- [2] **Kay, William**, Stake Hill, Middleton: trampled on by horses and inwardly injured. Disabled a month. 30/– final.
- [6] ditto of Stake Hill, near Middleton: aged 36 and a weaver with 6 children. Knocked down and trampled on by cavalry horses and inwardly injured. 1 month disabled. £1.10.0. received in relief.

- [1] **Kealing, Elizabeth**, Bond's Buildings [Cambridge-street, Chorlton Row]: leg hurt and finger broke.
- [4] ditto as Kealing, E. (female): trampled on by cavalry.

Kearsley, see Kenyon, Alice

Keenan, see Kennard, Sarah

- [6] **Kelly, John**, 10 Clowes-street, Salford: aged 33 and a weaver with 2 children. Sabre-cut over his left eye, two inches long. He fell and was trampled on by the crowd. 5 weeks disabled. Spit blood for some time. £2 received in relief.
- [7] ditto.

- [1] **Kelly, Thomas**, 126 Great Ancoats-street [Manchester]: hurt in the knee.
- [2] ditto: knocked down and his left knee hurt. Imprisoned from 16 August to 29 October. £3 final. Manchester Committee 20/–.
- [6] ditto of 126 Great Ancoats-street: aged 33 and a weaver with 4 children. Knocked down and left knee trod upon by a Yeomanry Cavalry horse, his body bruised. Imprisoned from 16 August. See imprisoned list, statement B: £3 received in relief. Relief also from local committee. Imprisoned 10 weeks and 5 days – from 16 August to proclamation of 30 October.
- [7] ditto but 126 Ancoats-lane.

¹ **Kempstone [Kempster], Rebecca**, 57 Newton-lane [Manchester]: dreadfully crushed.
² ditto but Kempster, 56 Newton-lane: ribs and foot crushed. Disabled a month. 20/–.
⁶ ditto as Kempster of 57 Newton-lane. Aged 50 and with 3 children. Ribs and foot crushed by the crowd. 1 month disabled. £1.10.0. received in relief.
⁷ ditto but Kempstone, near 57 Newton-lane.

¹ **Kennard (Keenan), Sarah**, 19 Cornwall-street [Manchester]: beat by the constables.
² ditto but Keenan and added to address is Newton-lane: beat with truncheons. 4 children. 20/– final. Manchester Committee 20/–.
⁶ ditto but Keenan: with 4 children. The skin stripped off her left arm, severely bruised by being trampled on by crowd and beat by constables' truncheons. Disabled for 1 month. Still appears to be very unwell. £1 received in relief. Also relief from local committee.
⁷ ditto as Kennard.

¹ **Kenyon [Kearsley], Alice**, 2 Spital-street [Manchester]: her ear sabred nearly off.
² ditto but Kearsley, Alice, 30 Spital-street: left ear nearly cut off. An old woman 71 years of age, disabled nearly ever since. One of the witnesses. 40/– final [£2 more in pencil].
⁴ ditto as Kenyon, A. (female): badly wounded by sabre or shot.
⁶ ditto but Kearsley, Alice of 30 Spital-street: aged 71. Wounded on the head and her ear nearly cut off by a sabre. Still unwell. £4 received in relief.
⁷ ditto as Kearsley, Alice, 2 Spittle-street.
[Alice Kearsley gave evidence at Lees' Inquest, see *Report*, pp. 182–3. Claims to have been cut by a trumpeter when 50 yards from hustings – towards the church. She presented herself as a widow, aged 71.]
Pigot's Manchester and Salford Directory, 1819: Samuel Kenyon, fustian-cutter off 30 Spital-street.

¹ **Kenyon [Kennion], Sarah**: severely wounded all over.
⁴ Ditto as Kennion, S. (female): badly wounded by sabre or shot.

² **Kenyon, Sarah**, Williamson-street, Chancery-lane [Ardwick]: bruised and crushed by the crowd. Not a very serious case. 15/– final.
⁶ ditto as Kenyon of Williamson-street, Chancery-lane: aged 32 with 2 children. Thrown down and trampled on by the crowd. 3 weeks disabled. 15/– received in relief.
⁷ ditto.

¹ **Kershaw, James**, Greenacres [Oldham]: wounded in the body.
² ditto but Greenacres Moor: thrown into a cellar and the back of his neck much hurt, his body bruised in various parts with truncheons. 26/– final.
⁶ ditto of Greenacres-moor, near Oldham: aged 42 and a spinner with 4 children. Back of his neck and body much bruised. Was thrown into a cellar. 12 days disabled. £1 received in relief.
⁷ ditto.

¹ **Kershaw, John**, Royton: collar bone broken.
² ditto: thrown down and his right collar bone broke, left thigh and leg hurt. An old man of 66. 10/– final. Manchester Committee 20/–. Rochdale Committee 15/–.
⁶ ditto of Royton: aged 66 and a weaver. Trampled on by the crowd, right collar-bone broken and his left leg and thigh hurt. 1 month disabled. 10 shillings received in relief. Relief also from local committee.
⁷ ditto.

¹ **Kershaw, Joseph**, Royton: severely bruised.
⁴ ditto as Kershaw, J. (male): badly wounded by sabre or shot.
⁷ ditto.

⁵ **Kershaw, Thomas**, of Lowerplace, Rochdale.

¹ **Kershaw, William**, Lowerplace [i.e. Lower Place], near Rochdale: trampled upon by the cavalry.
⁶ ditto: aged 70 and a weaver. Seriously injured in his breast, head bruised and the flesh stripped from his legs. 1 month disabled. Was done by the trampling of the cavalry. Still unwell. £2 received in relief.
⁷ ditto.

² **Kilner, Judith**, Eccles: a pregnant woman was much bruised and confined for a month in consequence. 40/– final [20/– more pencilled in].
⁶ ditto of King-street, Eccles: with 5 children. Thrown into a cellar with Mrs. Parkinson who was killed, and her back much hurt. 1 month disabled. Was pregnant at the time. £3 received in relief.
⁷ ditto.

¹ **Kinsey, Joseph**, Walshaw [i.e. Halshaw] Moor, near Bolton: cut under the ear by a sabre.
⁷ ditto of Halshaw Moor, near Bolton.

² **Knott [Nott], Thomas**, Charlestown, near Ashton: shoulder bruised. One week disabled. 20 years of age. A slight case. 10/– final.
⁶ ditto as Nott: aged 20 and a weaver. Shoulder bruised by constables' truncheons. A slight case. 10/– received in relief.
⁷ ditto.

² **Laing [Lang], James**, 8 Pott-street [Manchester]: his shoulder hurt and imprisoned 5 days. A slight hurt. 20/– final.
⁶ ditto: a dyer with 4 children. Shoulder hurt and five days imprisoned. See imprisoned cases under Lang [Statement B]: aged 37. After 5 days in prison, bailed, then discharged by proclamation on 30 October. £1 received in relief.
⁷ ditto as Lang.

¹ **Lancaster, Edward**, 9 Potter's Buildings [Chorlton Row]: sabred and crushed.
³ ditto of Manchester: slightly wounded.
⁴ ditto but Lancaster, E. (male): badly wounded by sabre or shot.
⁶ ditto of 9 Potter's Buildings, Oxford-road: aged 11. Sabre-cut on the back of his head; his throat trod on by a horse, and otherwise injured. Was carried to the Infirmary in an insensible state. 12 weeks disabled. His father, a widower with seven children. £2 received in relief.
⁷ ditto but near Oxford-road.

¹ **Lancaster, James**, Hollinwood [near Oldham]: sabred in the head.
⁴ ditto as Lancaster, J. (male): wounded by sabre or shot.
⁷ ditto.

¹ **Lancashire**, ———, Middleton: cut by Birley.
⁷ ditto.
[A Robert Lancashire of Middleton gave evidence at the Lees Inquest: see *Report*, pp. 566–74. He claimed to be on Peter's Field, first near the hustings, then over near the Quakers' meeting house, from 12.30 to 3–4 p.m. He saw Edward Meagher cut a woman's breast open when she stood with child in arms 10 to 12 yards from the hustings. Lancashire picked up the child when she fell. He made no mention of his own injury.]

Lang, see Laing, James

¹ **Lannifee [Lanophy, Lanniway], Edward**, 59 Thomas-street [Manchester]: crushed and carried to the Infirmary insensible.
² ditto but Lanophy of 50 Thomas-street: was in the Infirmary for some time, much bruised. A tailor. 20/– final [£2 more in pencil]. Manchester Committee 20/–.
³ ditto but Lanniway, Manchester: contusion, not dangerous. [As Lannoway when the list was printed in *Wheeler's Manchester Chronicle*, 21 August.]
⁶ ditto as Lannifee of 59 Thomas-street: several ribs displaced in his right side and seriously hurt by being trampled on by the crowd. 6 weeks disabled. Is still very unwell. Was taken to the Infirmary on 16 August. £3 received in relief. Relief also from local committee.
⁷ ditto as Lannifee.

¹ **Lappan, Bernard**, 51 Cropper-street [Manchester, near Miles Platting]: cut and trampled upon.
² ditto: knocked down by a blow on the back of his head, his loins and breast trampled on. 20/– final. Manchester Committee 20/–.
⁴ ditto but Lappan, B. (male): wounded by sabre or shot.
⁶ ditto: aged 56 and a weaver with 4 children. Knocked down by a blow from a sabre on the back of the head. Loins and breast hurt by being trampled on by the crowd. 1 month disabled. £1 received in relief.
⁷ ditto.

¹ **Largison, John**, 18 Bengal-street [Manchester]: received a ball in his right breast on 17 August.
⁷ ditto.

---

¹ **Leadbeater, John**, Cropper-street [Manchester, near Miles Platting]: cut and trampled upon.
² ditto, 44 Cropper-street: thrown down and trampled on by the crowd, left hip and shoulder and both legs hurt. A wife and 2 children. 20/– final.
⁴ ditto but Leadbeater, J. (male): wounded by truncheons of the Special Constables or crushed by the multitude.
⁶ ditto: aged 28 and a weaver with 2 children. Thrown down and trampled on. Left hip, shoulder and both legs hurt. 2 weeks disabled. £1 received in relief.
⁷ ditto.

---

¹ **Lees, Ellen**, Wood-street, Middleton.
² ditto: knocked down by the cavalry and her body much bruised. A poor washerwoman, 45 years of age with 2 children. 30/– final.
⁶ ditto of Wood-street, Middleton: aged 45 with 2 children. Knocked down by the cavalry and inwardly bruised. 2 weeks disabled. A widow. £1.10.0. received in relief.
⁷ ditto.

---

⁷ **Lees, Isaac**, Cannon-street [Manchester].
Pigot's Manchester and Salford Directory, 1819: handkerchief-manufacturer, Withington Court, Cannon-street. Home: Green-street, Ardwick.

---

¹ **Lees, James**, near Delph: two severe sabre-wounds on the head.
² ditto but Stones Wood, near Delph: 2 desperate cuts on the head, one 5 inches long, by one of the 15th [Hussars]. He was taken to the Infirmary and, after being dressed, one of the junior surgeons ordered him to a bed and put a ticket with his name on it. Dr Ransome asked him if he had enough of Manchester meetings and on his reply in the negative he was told there was no room for him. 40/– final.
³ ditto, Saddleworth: slightly wounded.
⁶ ditto of Stones Wood near Delph: aged 25 and a weaver with 2 children. A sabre-cut on the top of his head five inches long and one near the forehead by one of the 15th Hussars. 3 weeks disabled. He was taken to the Infirmary and dressed by one of the junior surgeons who put his name over the bed and ordered him to undress. Dr Ransome asked him if he had had enough of meetings. On his reply in the negative he was ordered to leave the place immediately. £2 received in relief.
⁷ ditto of Stones Wood, near Delph.

---

¹ **Lees, John**, Oldham: sabred. Killed.
⁶ ditto: sabred. A Coroner's Inquest on the body adjourned without a verdict.
[For nature of injuries, see Lees Inquest, *Report*, pp. 57, 67–8, 74, 157ff, 277ff. He is a rover [i.e. spinner] by occupation, working in his father's factory: see ibid., pp. 12–13.]

- [2] **Leigh, John**, Cheetham: cut by Birley whom he well knew. Birley, the trumpeter [i.e. Meagher] and another passed him and when Birley saw him rise he made a stroke and cut him on the left hip. A very respectable man. £3.
- [6] ditto of Cheetham: aged 27 with 1 child. Was sabred on the hip when down in the crowd. Disabled a long time. Says the trumpeter and Captain Birley passed him when down; that Birley returned and cut him. Gave evidence at the Inquest. £3 received in relief.
- [7] ditto.
  [Gave evidence at Redford v. Birley Trial, see *Report*, p. 176; and at Lees Inquest, see *Report*, pp. 562ff. At former trial, he said he stood near the Windmill Public House, 6–7 yards from the hustings; and was cut by Birley 20 yards from the Hustings as he sought to leave the ground. At latter trial he declared himself a pattern-drawer. He was within 10 yards of the hustings when cut by Birley. Then, on the corner of Windmill-street close to Deansgate, he was attacked by 3 Manchester Yeomen. To protect himself, he fell to the ground when they began to cut at him. He then went home.]

- [1] **Leigh, William**, 23 Leigh [sic] -street [Manchester]: sabred in the head.
- [2] ditto, 23 Queen-street, Deansgate: the boy was so severely cut on the head. His mother a poor woman with 4 children living in a cellar whose husband does not live with her. 40/– final. Manchester Committee 20/–.
- [4] ditto but Leigh, W. (male): badly wounded by sabre or shot.
- [6] ditto, 23 Queen-street, Deansgate: aged 19. Severe sabre-cut on the head. 2 months disabled. His mother a poor woman with four children. The boy was with Mr Pearson. £2 received in relief. Relief also from local committee.
- [7] ditto of 23 Queen-street.
  [Gave evidence at Lees Inquest, see *Report*, p. 185 where he stated 'I worked at the factory'. When wounded he was 6 yards from the hustings. He named Charlton as his attacker. He became the boy Rigg, taken to London by Hunt and exhibited with his 7 inch scalp wound. See *Peterloo Massacre*, p. 100. Also see his contrite letter from the New Bailey in 1820 when charged with going to London with Hunt: Rylands MS. 1197 (87).]

- [1] **Lingley, John**: trampled upon and his legs much bruised.
- [7] ditto of Lees.

- [4] **Little, S. (male)**: badly wounded by sabre or shot.

- [7] **Locke, Sarah**, 55 George Leigh-street [Manchester].

- [6] **Longlands, William**, 8 Chadwick's Buildings, George Leigh-street [Manchester]: aged 24 and a sand-seller. Thrown down, trampled on and internally injured. 2 weeks disabled. An out-patient of the Infirmary. £1 received in relief.
- [7] ditto.

- [1] **Ludge, Thomas**, Lancaster: sabred severely.
- [4] ditto but Ludge, T. (male): badly wounded by sabre or shot.

McCabe, see Maccobe, Ann

⁴ **McCabe, J. (male)**: badly wounded by sabre or shot.

McCabe, see Maccobe, Rose

¹ **McCabe, Owen**, Old Mount, near St Michael's [Manchester]: wounded and trampled upon and ribs broken.
² ditto, 9 Old Mount, St Michael's: a dreadful wound on the hip, trampled on. Walks on crutches ever since. A poor distressed man. 40/– [£5 to be paid at 5/– per week – pencilled in]. Manchester Committee 20/–.
⁶ ditto of 9 Old Mount-street: aged 62 and a weaver. Dreadfully hurt by the cavalry horses, his ribs crushed in on one side and out on the other. His hip still out and walks on crutches. Disabled for life. A poor distressed creature. £7 received in relief. Relief also from local committee.
⁷ ditto but MacCabe.

⁷ **McCahy, Patrick**, 22 Leigh [possibly Lees] -street, Oldham-road [Manchester].
Pigot's Manchester and Salford Directory, 1819: under McCaffery, weaver of 22 Lees-street, Oldham-road.

McCallum, see McCollum Elizabeth

³ **McCape, Owen**, near Bury: fractured ribs, not dangerous.

McClone, see McLone, Thomas

¹ **Maccobe (McCabe), Ann**, 3 Camplin's Buildings [i.e. 137 Great Ancoats-street, Manchester]: thrown down by a man who rode a roaned horse, rather light coloured on the back.
² ditto but as McCabe, 3 Camplin's Buildings: side and knee hurt and thrown into a cellar. About a month disabled. 20/– final.
⁶ ditto as McCabe, Ann, 3 Campion's Buildings: aged 17. Thrown into a cellar and much bruised in the left side and knee. 1 month disabled. £1 received in relief.
⁷ ditto as McCabe, 3 Camplin's Buildings.
Pigot's Manchester and Salford Directory, 1819: Thomas McCabe, weaver of Camplin's Buildings, Ancoats.

¹ **Maccobe (McCabe), Rose**, 3 Camplin's Buildings [Manchester]: thrown down by a man who rode a roaned horse, rather light coloured on the back [along with Ann Maccobe].
² ditto but McCabe, 3 Camplins Buildings, Ancoats: was thrown down and trampled on. Carried home by two men senseless and about a month unemployed in consequence. 20/– final.

⁶ ditto as McCabe, 3 Campion's Buildings: aged 14. Right side hurt by being trampled on. 1 month disabled. Was carried home in an insensible state. £1 received in relief.
⁷ ditto, 3 Camplin's Buildings.

¹ **McCollam [McCullum, McCollom], Duncan**, near Ancoats Hall [Manchester]: bruised in the body.
⁴ ditto but McCullum, D. (male): wounded by trampling of cavalry.
⁷ McCollom, Duncan, Ancoats-street near Ancoats Hall.

¹ **McCollom [McCallum], Elizabeth**, near Ancoats Hall [Manchester]: dreadfully bruised in the body and legs.
⁴ ditto but McCallum, E. (female): trampled on by cavalry.
⁷ ditto, Ancoats-street, near Ancoats Hall.

¹ **Macconnel [McConnell], James**, Portland-street, Newton-lane [Newtown, Manchester]: bruised and crushed severely.
² ditto but McConnell, 14 Portland-street: thrown in a cellar, his loins crushed, right leg bruised. Could not put his clothes on for a month. Has earned only 10/– since. 30/– final. Manchester Committee 20/–.
⁴ ditto as McConnell, J. (male): badly wounded by truncheons of the Special Constables or crushed by the multitude.
⁶ ditto as McConnell, 14 Portland-street: aged 50. Thrown into a cellar and his sides and loins crushed and bruised. 10 weeks disabled. Was a month before he could put on his stockings. £1.10.0. received in relief.
⁷ ditto as MacConnel, Portland-street, Newton-lane.

² **McDonald, Mary**, Union-street, Stockport: thrown down and trampled on, her left foot and right thigh much hurt.
⁶ ditto, Union-street, Stockport: with 1 child. Thrown down by a horse. Left foot and right thigh hurt by being trampled on. 3 weeks disabled. £1 received in relief.
⁷ ditto of Stockport.

² **McFadden, Samuel**, 7 Little Bridgewater-street [Manchester]: a Special Constable. Collar-bone broke, 5 weeks disabled. Attended by Dr Taylor of Oldfield-lane. Vouched by the man at the Fish Public House. 3 horses went over him. 20/– final.
⁶ ditto: left collar-bone broken and shoulder dislocated by the charge of cavalry. 3 horses went over him. 5 weeks disabled. A Special Constable at the request of his employers on the Bridgewater estate. Says all was peaceable when the cavalry charged. £1 received in relief.
⁷ ditto as MacFadden of Little Bridgwater-street.

¹ **McGairathy [Gairathy], William**, 26 Leigh-street [Manchester]: bruised in the head by a blow from a sabre, and knee out of joint by being trampled upon.
⁷ ditto as Gairathy, Back Piccadilly.

McGarth, see Macgrath, Alice

1. **Macglade [McGlead], Matthew**, 20 Fawcett-street [Manchester]: sabred in the heel.
2. ditto but McGlead, 20 Fawcett-street, Ancoats: 3 cuts on his head and his heel hurt by the tread of a horse. 20/– final.
6. ditto as McGlade, 20 Fawcett-street: aged 18 and a spinner. Three sabre cuts on his head; his heel hurt by a horse's hoof. 7 weeks disabled. £1 received in relief.
7. ditto but MacGlead.

1. **McGragh [McGrath], Sarah**, and her child four years old: both thrown down and crushed.
4. ditto as McGragh, S. (female): badly wounded by truncheons of the Special Constables or crushed by the multitude.

1. **McGragh,** ———, four-year-old child of Sarah McGragh: thrown down and crushed.

1. **Macgrath (McGarth, McGragh), Alice**, 19 Poland-street [Manchester]: bruised in the head severely.
1. *repeated* as Grath, Alice Mc, 9 Poland-street: bruised very badly.
2. ditto as McGragh, 19 Poland-street: thrown down and trampled on. Had 2 children with her. 20/– final. Manchester Committee 20/–.
4. ditto but McGarth: badly wounded by truncheons of the Special Constables or crushed by the multitude.
6. ditto as McGrath, 19 Poland-street: 3 children. Right arm hurt. Was crushed on the head and breast till the blood gushed from her nose and mouth. 1 month disabled. Had 2 children with her at the meeting. £1 received in relief. Relief also from local committee.
7. ditto, 19 Poland-street [*repeated*].

McGrath, see McGragh, Sarah

1. **Mackennagh [McKenna], Mary**, Nicholas-street [Manchester]: severely bruised on the head.
2. ditto but McKenna, 16 Nicholas Street: an interesting girl much bruised in the back part of the head by being trampled on. 40/– final [£2 more in pencil]. Manchester Committee 20/–.
6. ditto as McKenna, May, 16 Nicholas-street: aged 14. Thrown down and trampled on, the back of her head seriously hurt. 7 weeks disabled. Was a month in the fever ward of the Infirmary. £2 received in relief. Relief also from local committee.
7. ditto, with addition of Angel Meadow.

2. **McLone, Thomas**: Short-street, Bolton: thrown down and trampled on. Eye hurt. 10/– final.
6. ditto but 4 Shaw-street, Bolton: aged 26 and a weaver with 1 child. Knocked down and hurt in the eye. 2 weeks disabled. A slight case. 10/– received in relief.
7. ditto but McClone, 4 Shaw-street, Bolton Moor.

¹ **McMaghan [MacMahon], Bernard**, 30 Loom-street [Manchester]: sabred and bruised.
² ditto but 17 Loom-street: knocked down. Received a cut on the head. 20/– final.
⁶ ditto but McMahon of 30 Loom-street. Knocked down and his head cut by constables' truncheons. 10 days disabled. £1 received in relief.
⁷ ditto but MacMahon.

¹ **MacNiel [McNeil], Charles**, 1 Pigeon-street, Ancoats-street [Manchester]: trampled down and hurt on the knee.
² ditto but McNeil, 1 Pigeon-street, Ancoats: cut on the knee, knocked down by a horse and a good deal bruised. 30/– final. [*repeated*].
⁶ ditto as McNeil of 1 Pigeon-street: aged 31 and a weaver. Right knee cut by a sabre. Knocked down by a horse and his legs bruised. 6 weeks disabled. £1.10.0. received in relief.
⁷ ditto as McNeil.

¹ **Macquade, Peter**, 6 Pump-street [Manchester]: sabred in the shoulder.
² ditto but Philip McQuade: cut on the shoulder by the cavalry, his ear cut. Disabled 3 weeks. 20/– final.
⁴ ditto as McQuade, P. (**male**): badly wounded by sabre or shot.
⁶ ditto as McQuade, Peter, 6 Pump-street: aged 41 and a weaver with 1 child. Right ear and shoulder cut by a sabre. Back and sides trampled on. 3 weeks disabled. £1 received in relief.
⁷ ditto as Peter.

⁷ **McWade, Patrick**, 13 Pump-street [Manchester].
Pigot's Manchester and Salford Directory, 1819: as Pat McQuade, weaver of 13 Pump-street, Oldham-road.

Maedine, see Meadine, James

⁴ **Mahor, M.** (**male**): wounded by sabre or shot.

⁶ **Makin, James**, Hamshaw [i.e. Hempshaw] -lane, Stockport: aged 19 and a weaver. Sabre-cut under the left eye by a Yeoman. Beat by constables. 3 days disabled. Received 10/– in relief.
⁷ ditto.

Mallalieu, see Mellalieu, Betty

⁶ **Marsh, Henry** of Bolton: aged 44 and a weaver with 1 child. Knocked down by a constable. Beat on the loins and legs, his knees bruised. 2 weeks disabled. £1 received in relief.
⁷ ditto.

¹ **Marsh, Mary Ann**, near St John's [Manchester]: severely bruised.

² ditto but Swan [i.e. Span] Court, Artillery-street: collar-bone broke, knocked down and crushed, her knee hurt. 20/–.
⁶ ditto of 8 Span Court, St John's: aged 20. Knocked down, her collar-bone broken, her knee hurt severely. Bruised in the body. 1 month disabled. Her eyes were blood-shot for a month. £1 received in relief.
⁷ ditto near St John's.

---

¹ **Marsh, William**, 5 Revett's [i.e. Rivitt's] Court, Bank Top [Manchester]: sabre-cut in the head.
⁷ ditto.
Pigot's Manchester and Salford Directory, 1819: weaver of Revett's Court, London-road.

---

² **Marsh, William**, 6 Stockport Buildings [Chorlton Row]: sabre-cut on the back of the head, body crushed, a bone shattered in his left leg. 20/– final.
⁶ ditto, 6 Stockport Buildings, Chorlton: aged 57 with 6 children. Sabre-cut on the back of the head, bone in his leg splintered, and crushed in the body by being trampled on. 6 weeks disabled. He states that he had 3 children working in Birley's factory who, when he learnt of his being hurt at the meeting, discharged them. £1 received in relief.

---

⁷ **Marsland,** ———, Chadkirk [near Marple, Cheshire].

---

¹ **Martin, Mary**, Back Queen-street [Manchester]: sabred on the head.
⁴ ditto: badly wounded by sabre or shot.
⁷ ditto but 5 Cresswell's Buildings, Back Queen-street.

---

¹ **Martin, Peter**, 12 Back Queen-street [Manchester]: crushed by the trampling of the horses.
⁴ ditto: badly wounded by trampling of the cavalry.
⁷ ditto but 5 Cresswell's Buildings, Back Queen-street.

---

⁴ **Marton, S. (female)**: wounded by the truncheons of the Special Constables or crushed by the multitude.

---

¹ **Mason, James**, 22 Ledger-street [Manchester]: severely wounded by the constables on the head.
² ditto: was much trampled on and looks extremely ill and has not been able to work since. 40/–. [Repeated with addition of £2 more in pencil.]
⁶ ditto, 22 Ledger-street, Blakely-street: aged 27. Seriously injured internally by being trampled on by the crowd. Still disabled. Has an aged mother and his elder brother who is dangerously ill to support. £4 received in relief.
⁷ ditto.

---

¹ **Mason [Mayson], John**, 4 Lee [Lees or Leigh] -street, Oldham-road [Manchester]: cut in the face by a Yeoman.

- ² ditto as Mayson: cut in the face and knocked down. A month disabled. An old man. 20/– [20/– more pencilled in].
- ⁶ ditto of 1 Leigh-street: aged 66. Sabre-cut on the face, knocked down and trampled on by the crowd. 3 weeks disabled. £1 received in relief.
- ⁷ ditto as Mason.

- ² **Mason, Peter**, Chestergate, Stockport: a sabre-cut on his right arm and one on his leg. 30/– final.
- ⁶ ditto of Chestergate, Stockport: a sabre-cut on his right arm and one on the left leg. Disabled 1 month. £1.10.0. received in relief.
- ⁷ ditto.

- ¹ **Mason, William** [Manchester], in New Bailey prison: severely wounded in the head.
- ² ditto, 22 Ledger-street, Blakely-street: imprisoned 3 weeks and bruised. 60/– final. [*repeated*]
- ⁶ ditto, 22 Ledger-street: [Statement B] aged 33, labourer. Imprisoned 10 weeks and 5 days from 16 August. £3 received in relief.
- ⁷ ditto.

- ¹ **Massey, John**, 5 Pollard-street [Manchester]: sabred in the head.
- ² ditto, 5 Horton-street, Pollard-street: sabred in the head on the top. A spinner. A very decent, respectable man. 20/–.
- ⁶ ditto, 5 Horton-street: aged 29 and a spinner with 1 child. Severe sabre-cut on the top of his head. 1 month disabled. £1 received in relief.
- ⁷ ditto.

Mayson, see Mason, John

- ¹ **Meadine, James**, 16 Mason-street [Manchester]: sabred in the head.
- ⁷ ditto but Maedine.

- ² **Mellalieu [Mallalieu, Millalier], Betty**, Block-lane, Oldham: knocked down and bruised, her thigh hurt. 15/– final. Left to Mr Taylor.
- ⁴ M ———, B. (female): wounded by truncheons of the Special Constables or crushed by the multitude.
- ⁶ ditto but Millalier of Block-lane, near Oldham: aged 50. Thrown down and trampled on by the crowd. Bruised in the body and thigh. 2 weeks disabled. 15/– received in relief.
- ⁷ ditto but Mallalieu.

Mellard, John, see Millard

- ¹ **Mellor, Daniel**, Greenacres Moor [Oldham]: sabred severely.
- ² ditto but of Caverlow: a very severe cut on his left wrist. He was holding at an iron rail near the windmill when a cavalry man rode up and cut him severely. 30/– final. Manchester Committee 20/–.

- [6] ditto of Caverlow, near Oldham: aged 28 and a weaver with 1 child. Severe sabre-cut on the left wrist from a Yeoman as he held by an iron rail to keep himself from falling near the Windmill public house. 8 weeks disabled. £1.10.0. received in relief.
- [7] ditto of Greenacres Moor.

- [2] **Mellor, Elizabeth**, 10 Back Crescent, Ancoats [Manchester]: thrown down and seriously hurt. Was pregnant and has been unwell ever since. 30/– final.
- [6] ditto of 10 Back Crescent, Ancoats: aged 30 with 3 children. Thrown down by the crowd and her side seriously hurt. 2 weeks disabled. Was pregnant and has been unwell ever since. £1.10.0. received in relief.
- [7] ditto.

Pigot's Manchester and Salford Directory, 1819: Daniel Mellor, weaver of same address.

- [7] **Mellor, James**, Stockport.

- [3] **Mellor, John**, Burslem: slightly wounded.

- [1] **Mellor, Simon**, Royley, near Royton: severely cut in the thigh.
- [2] ditto: thrown down and trampled on. Breast crushed and legs bruised. 20/–.
- [6] ditto: aged 62 and a weaver with 1 child. Trampled on by the horses, legs and thighs, bruised and crushed in the breast. 3 weeks disabled. £1 received in relief.
- [7] ditto.

- [1] **Mill, Charles**, Pilkington: trampled upon and severely bruised.
- [7] ditto but Mills.

Millalier, see Mellalieu, Betty

- [1] **Millard [Mellard], John**, Burslem, Staffordshire: arm nearly cut off by a Yeoman.
- [2] ditto but Mellard: a dreadful cut in the right arm; several pieces of bone taken out. Is in Manchester now under Dr Taylor. A very respectable man, a potter. Was cut in several places and much bruised. £3.
- [6] ditto of Burslem, Staffordshire: aged 32 and a potter with 1 child. A very severe sabre-cut on the left arm; bone fractured and several pieces taken out. Is still under the care of Dr Taylor. Was beat about the head by constables. Still disabled. Received the cut as he lay on the ground from one of the Yeomen. £3 received in relief.
- [7] ditto.

- [4] **Miller, D. (male)**: wounded by sabre or shot.

- [2] **Minnis, Ann**, 32 Ancoats-street [Manchester]: thrown down and trampled on, her left leg still very bad. 5 children. 40/– final. [£2 more pencilled in].
- [6] ditto of 32 Ancoats-street: aged 34 with 5 children. Thrown down and left leg seriously hurt and trampled on. Still lame. Got her a recommendation to the Infirmary. £4 received in relief.
- [7] ditto.

⁴ **Mole, P. (male)**: badly wounded by truncheons of Special Constables or crushed by multitude.

⁴ **Monk, M. A. (female)**: trampled on by cavalry – badly wounded.

¹ **Monks, Bridget**, 35 Portland-street [Manchester]: sabred in the arm and crushed.
² ditto but Biddy, 35 Portland-street or Place: was thrown down and right shoulder dislocated. 10/– final. Manchester Committee 20/–.
⁶ ditto as Biddy, 35 Portland Place: aged 70. Sabre-cut on the left arm, right shoulder dislocated, left side and legs hurt. Still unwell. 10/– received in relief. Relief also from local committee.
⁷ ditto.

⁷ **Moon, James**, Portugal-street [Manchester].
Pigot's Manchester and Salford Directory, 1817: residing at 61 Falkner-street. Ibid., 1819: residing at 43 George-street.

² **Moon, Robert**, 61 Portugal-street [Manchester]: knocked down among the trees. Hip and leg hurt. In a very bad state of health. 20/– final.
⁶ ditto of 61 Portugal-street: aged 56. Knocked down amongst the timber. Hip and legs hurt. In an infirm state of health. £1 received in relief.
⁷ ditto.
Pigot's Manchester and Salford Directory, 1817: spinner.

⁶ **Moores, William**, 12 Back Garden-street, Shudehill [Manchester]: aged 61 and a weaver with 1 child. Stabbed with a bayonet on the right side of his back by one of the 88th Regiment. 2 weeks disabled. £1 received in relief.
⁷ ditto, 12 Garden-street, Shudehill.

⁴ **Morand, P. (male)**: badly wounded by trampling of cavalry.

¹ **Morris Patrick**, Bennet-street, Newton-lane [Manchester]: trampled upon.
⁷ ditto.

¹ **Morton (Moreton), James**, Back Lamb-street, Stockport: severe sabre cut on the head.
² ditto: a severe sabre cut on the top of the head by a Yeoman. Disabled a month. 30/– final.
⁶ ditto as Moreton of Back Lamb-street, Stockport: aged 60 and a weaver with 4 children. Sabre-cut on the crown of the head by a Yeoman. 1 month disabled. £1.10.0. received in relief.
⁷ ditto as Morton.

¹ **Morton [Moreton], Sarah**, Ancoats-street [Manchester]: sabred on the knee.
⁶ ditto but Moreton of 120 Lower Ancoats: aged 49 with 1 child. Thrown down by the pressure of the crowd, left knee hurt seriously. 1 month disabled. £1 received in relief.

⁷ ditto, 120 Ancoats-street.
Pigot's Manchester and Salford Directory, 1819: Walter Moreton, smith of Ancoats Bridge.

---

¹ **Mottershead, Eliza**, 45 Tib-street [Manchester]: severely crushed and trampled upon.
⁷ ditto but Elizabeth.

---

² **Mullin, Thomas**, 15 John-street, Pott Houses [Manchester]: knocked down and trod on, ankle dislocated. 52 years of age. 20/– final.
⁶ ditto: aged 52 and a weaver with 4 children. Right leg hurt and ankle dislocated by being trampled on by horses. 1 month disabled. £1 received in relief.
⁷ ditto but as Mullins. [Same address with addition of Ancoats-lane.]

---

⁷ **Naylor, James**, 23 Back Piccadilly [Manchester].

---

⁴ **Neale, B. (female)**: badly wounded by sabre or shot.

---

¹ **Neil [Neale], Betty**, 33 Queen-street, Deansgate [Manchester]: several limbs [ribs?] broken.
² ditto: ribs broke. Was in the Infirmary a week. 30/– [40/– more in pencil]. Manchester Committee 10/–.
⁶ ditto but Neale, Elizabeth, 33 Queen-street Deansgate: aged 31 with 2 children. Three ribs dislocated by the trampling of the cavalry. 7 weeks disabled. £3.10.0. received in relief. Relief also from local committee.
⁷ ditto.

---

¹ **Neil (O'Neil, O'Neale), Arthur**, 3 Pigeon-street, Ancoats-street [Manchester]: bruised by the constables and confined in the New Bailey.
² ditto: knocked down and bruised. Still confined in the New Bailey for want of bail. 20/–, 20/–.
⁶ ditto as O'Neil: inwardly crushed. [Died in consequence.] Was in the New Bailey till last Sessions.
⁶ *repeated* but O'Neale of 3 Pigeon-street: aged 40 and a weaver. Thrown down by the pressure of the crowd; breast bruised and internally injured. Still disabled. Is in the New Bailey, very ill. Since dead. Received £4.10.0. in relief.
⁷ ditto but O'Neil.

---

¹ **Newby [Newley], Elizabeth** [Manchester]: in the Infirmary, severely cut.
³ ditto but Newley of Manchester: contused ankle.
⁴ ditto as Newby, E. (female): badly wounded by sabre or shot.
⁷ ditto.

---

¹ **Newton, James**, 3 Canal Court, Oldfield-road [Salford]: thrown down by the crowd and trampled on; right elbow and knee hurt; bruised in several parts. 20/– final.
⁶ ditto of 3 Canal Court, Oldfield-road: aged 52 and a weaver with 1 child. Thrown down and trampled on; right elbow and knee hurt. 3 weeks disabled. £1 received in relief.
⁷ ditto, but 13 Canal-street.

¹ **Newton, John**, Bury-street, Ardwick: hurt in the left knee.
⁷ ditto.

³ **Nield, Betty**, Manchester: bruised, not dangerous.

Nott, see Thomas Knott

¹ **Nuttal, John**, Gee Cross: cut by the cavalry on the back of the head and on the right shoulder.
⁶ ditto, Gee Cross, near Stockport: aged 39 with 5 children. Knocked down by a Yeoman with the back of his sabre; head severely hurt and trod on by the horses. 2 weeks disabled. £1 received in relief.
⁷ ditto.

⁷ **Ogden, Betty**, Smallshaw Green, near Ashton.

¹ **Ogden, Joseph**, 29 George Leigh-street [Manchester]: stabbed with a bayonet.
² ditto: several cuts and a bayonet wound by one of the 88th Regiment. The bayonet broke or got loose and he knocked him down with the butt-end. 20/– final. Manchester Committee 20/–.
⁴ ditto as Ogden, J. (male): badly wounded by sabre or shot.
⁶ ditto of 29 George Leigh-street: stabbed on the head by a bayonet of one of the 88th; several other wounds. 6 weeks disabled. When struck with the bayonet, it broke or got loose and he was knocked down by the butt-end. £1 received in relief.
⁷ ditto.
Pigot's Manchester and Salford Directory, 1819: weaver of 8 Loom-street.

¹ **Ogden, William**, Wood-street [Manchester]: sabred on the eye and head.
² ditto of 26 Wood-street: cut on the eye and back of the head much bruised. 76 years of age. The individual alluded to by Canning. 40/– [£2 more in pencil].
⁴ ditto as Ogden, W. (male): badly wounded by sabre or shot.
⁶ ditto of 26 Wood-street: aged 76 and a printer with 3 children. Sabre-cut on the head and a thrust from a sabre in the eye. Was much bruised by constables' truncheons. Still disabled. The person who was confined in Horsemonger-lane, of Canning notoriety. £4 received in relief.
⁷ ditto.

⁶ **Oldham, Thomas**, Crow-alley, Unsworth [near Whitefield]: aged 18 and a weaver. Left ankle dislocated by being trampled on by the crowd. 1 week disabled. 15/– received in relief.
⁷ ditto, Crow-alley, near Unsworth.

² **Ollerenshaw, John**, Petty Car, Stockport: a sabre cut on his forehead and otherwise bruised. 20/– final.

⁶ ditto of Petty Car, Stockport: a hatter with 2 children. Sabre-cut on the forehead by a Yeoman. 1 week disabled. £1 received in relief.
⁷ ditto.

⁶ **O'Neale, Betty**, 23 Rigby's Buildings [Salford]: aged 79. Thrown down and trampled on in the crowd; shoulders, arms and chest hurt and internally injured. 10 weeks disabled. Was taken from the ground in an insensible state but was afraid to apply to the Infirmary, expecting to be sent to the New Bailey. £2 received in relief.
⁷ ditto as O'Neil, 23 Rigby's Buildings, Oldfield-lane.

O'Neale see Neil, Arthur

O'Neil, see Neil, Arthur

² **O'Neil [O'Neale], Catherine**, 34 Shakespeare-street [Manchester]: thrown down and trampled on. Parts with blood ever since. 10/–.
⁶ ditto but O'Neale, 4 Back Mather-street: aged 66. Trampled on by the crowd. 1 week disabled. A slight case. 10/– received in relief.
⁷ ditto, 4 Back Mather-street.

⁷ **O'Neil, John**, 40 Hone-street, Oldfield-lane [Salford].

² **O'Neil, Mary**, 27 Dean-street [Manchester]: thrown into a cellar and good deal bruised. 10/– final.
⁶ ditto of 27 Dean-street: aged 40. Thrown into a cellar and body bruised. 2 weeks unwell. Case rather slight. 10/– received in relief.
⁷ ditto with addition of Ancoats-lane.

¹ **Orm (Orme), Mary**, Camp-street [Manchester]: leg bruised and hip disjointed.
² ditto but Orme of 18 Camp-street, Deansgate: thrown down and much trampled on; still very lame. An old woman. Thinks her hip is out. 40/– [£2 more pencilled in]. Manchester Committee 10/–.
⁶ ditto but Orme of 18 Camp-street: aged 68. Her hip put out, left leg hurt by being thrown down and trampled on by the crowd. Still disabled. £4 received in relief. Relief also from local committee.
⁷ ditto.
Pigot's Manchester and Salford Directory, 1819: Roger Orme, baker of same address.

Oughton, see Mary Horton

¹ **Owen, William**, 12 Baker-street [Manchester]: trampled upon by the cavalry.
⁴ ditto as Owen, W. (male): badly wounded by trampling of cavalry.

² **Owen, William**, Silk-street [Manchester]: thrown down by the crowd and his leg hurt. Spinner.

⁶ ditto: aged 21 and a spinner with 1 child. Thrown down by the crowd and leg hurt. 3 weeks disabled. £1 received in relief.
⁷ ditto.

⁶ **Oxley, Catherine**, 55 George Leigh-street [Manchester]: aged 30 with 5 children. Thrown down and trampled on; right side hurt, head bruised so as to occasion deafness. Still unwell. Was pregnant at the time of the meeting. £2 received in relief.
⁷ ditto.

Parkinson, see Partington, Martha

¹ **Parkinson [Partington], Charles**, Birch, near Middleton: severely cut on the arm by a Yeoman.
⁵ ditto but Partington.
⁶ ditto of Birch, near Middleton: aged 19. Stabbed by a sabre on the left arm just above the elbow, a very bad wound, the bone being hurt; his body bruised by being trampled on by the crowd. Disabled 1 month. £1.10.0. received in relief.
⁷ ditto.

² **Parkinson, Frederick**, Bolton: thrown down by the crowd and right knee crushed. A good deal hurt. 40/– final.
⁶ ditto of Bolton: aged 40 and a weaver with 4 children. Thrown down by the crowd and his right knee hurt. 2 weeks disabled. £2 received in relief.
⁷ ditto.

¹ **Parr, James**, Garret-lane [Manchester]: trampled upon.
⁴ ditto as Parr, J. (male): badly wounded by trampling of cavalry.

² **Parr, James**, Bolton: crushed in a dreadful manner inwardly. Certified by Mr Brandreth of Bolton. 20/– final.
⁶ ditto: a weaver with 5 children. Trampled on by the crowd and injured internally. 1 week disabled. £1 received in relief.
⁷ ditto.

¹ **Parry, Bridget**, 1 Golding [i.e. Goulden] -street, Newton-lane [Manchester]: wounded and bruised.
⁷ ditto.

⁷ **Partington, George**, Tyldesley.

¹ **Partington [Parkinson], Martha**, Eccles: crushed to death in a cellar-hole.
² ditto but Parkinson: was thrown into a cellar and killed. Left 2 children. Gave the husband £5 final.
⁶ ditto as Partington: thrown into a cellar. Killed on the spot.
⁶ *repeated* as Parkinson of King-street, Eccles: aged 38 with 2 children. Thrown into a cellar and was killed. Paid the husband £5.

[Coroner's Inquest on 18 August, see *Wheeler's Manchester Chronicle*, 21 August: a woman from Barton-upon-Irwell killed at the top of Bridge-street by pressure of the mob. Also see Rylands MS. 1197(26, p. 8): died in a cellar at the top of Bridge-street, a long way from place of meeting.]

7 **Partington, Moses**, Back Lime-street [Miles Platting, Manchester].
Pigot's Manchester and Salford Directory, 1819; weaver.

7 **Pearson, Charles**, Barton-upon-Irwell.

2 **Peel, Ann**, 22 Thomas-street [Manchester]: beat by constables and disabled by hurts for some time. Was a long time insensible. 20/–. Manchester Committee 10/–.
6 ditto of Thomas-street: aged 28 with 1 child. Severely beat about the head by constables. 1 week insensible. Still complains of her head. £1 received in relief. Relief also from local committee.
7 ditto, 22 Thomas-street.

2 **Perrin [Penin], Catherine** [Manchester].
4 ditto but Penin: wounded by truncheons of the Special Constables or crushed by the multitude.
7 ditto as Perrin, 13 Pollard-street.
Pigot's Manchester and Salford Directory, 1819: Maurice Perrin, roller-coverer of Roger's Row, Pollard-street.

1 **Petty, Mr**, St Ann's Square [Manchester]: a constable, trampled upon.
4 ditto as Petty, ——— (male): badly wounded by trampling of cavalry.
7 ditto.

Phurlis, see Thewles, James

1 **Piccup [Picrop], Ellen**, 48 Port-street [Manchester]: shoulder broken.
4 but Picrop, E. (male): badly wounded by truncheons of the Special Constables or crushed by the multitude.
7 ditto as Piccup.

6 **Pickering, John**, 44 Bolton Moor: aged 49 with 10 children. Left arm and thigh hurt and bruised in the body. 2 weeks disabled. £1 received in relief.
7 ditto.

2 **Pimblet, John**, Little Lee, near Northwich: stabbed with a bayonet through the underside of the left arm above the elbow which went through the flesh part and pinned it to his side, the point penetrating to some depth. This man may probably be heard of at his mother's, Alice Halkins as above, he being single and obliged to get work as he can. 20/– final.

⁶ ditto: aged 38 and a labourer. Had his left arm pinned to his body by a bayonet which went through the fleshy part underside. 3 weeks disabled. £1 received in relief.
⁷ ditto.

---

¹ **Pollitt [Pollett, Powlett], Stephen**, 28 Duke-street [Manchester]: sabred on the head.
² ditto, 1 Dimity-street, Newtown: cut through his hat. Unable to work for a fortnight. Begged the Yeomanry to let him pass. One of them cursed him and struck at him. 20/– final.
⁴ ditto as Powlett, S. (male): badly wounded by sabre or shot. [Repeated as Pollett, S.]
⁶ ditto of 1 Dimity-street, Newtown: aged 32 and a weaver with 2 children. Severe sabre-cut on the top of his head. 2 weeks disabled. Begged of the Yeomanry to let him pass; one of them cursed him and struck him. £1 received in relief.
⁷ ditto, 1 Dimity-street, Newtown.

---

¹ **Pollitt, Thomas**: sabre-wound on the forehead.
⁷ ditto.

---

⁶ **Pomfret, Margaret** [Royton]: aged 19. Breast much hurt; was taken off the ground in an insensible state. 3 weeks disabled. £1 received in relief.
⁷ ditto of Royton.

Powlett, see Pollitt, Stephen

---

¹ **Prestwick [Preswick, Prestwich], Joshua**, Droylsden Castle: sabred very severely.
² ditto but Joseph Prestwich: 2 fingers cut and one of his knees hurt. Knocked down by a constable. 6 children. 32 years of age. 20/– final.
⁴ ditto but Preswick, J. (male): badly wounded by sabre or shot.
⁶ ditto but Prestwich, Joseph of Taunton, near Ashton: aged 32 with 6 children. Severe sabre-cut on his fingers, his knee hurt. Sometime disabled. £1 received in relief.
⁷ ditto as Joshua Prestwich of Droylesden Castle.
[Gave evidence at Redford v. Birley Trial, see *Report*, pp. 60–7. He presented himself as Joseph Prestwich, a weaver from Droysden near Fairfield. He came to Manchester on the day not in a large party but with 6 or 7 others from Droysden, having been told 'it would be a grand sight'. He claimed to have been slightly wounded by a slashing sabre on the finger as he withdrew his hand. The same person also gave evidence at the Lees Inquest, see *Report*, pp. 536–40. He claimed to have seen three Manchester Yeomen – Redford, Oliver and Samuel Harrison – cutting at the crowd close to the hustings. He saw young Oliver cut 3 people and Harrison cut a woman in the breast.]
Leigh's Lancashire General Directory, 1818–20: weaver living near George and Dragon, Old-street.

---

¹ **Prince, John**, 20 Copperas-street [Manchester]: crushed and trampled upon.
² ditto but 7 Tib-street: shoemaker. Knocked down and trampled on. Disabled 3 weeks. Leg hurt. 20/– final.
⁴ ditto as Prince, J. (male): badly wounded by trampling of cavalry.

- 6 ditto of 7 Tib-street: aged 29, a shoemaker with 1 child. Knocked down by a cavalry horse; left leg and breast hurt. 3 weeks. £1 received in relief.
- 7 ditto but 20 Copperas-street.

- 1 **Punlott, John**, 43 Silver-street [Manchester]: sabred and stabbed.
- 7 ditto.

- 2 **Quin, William**, Pot Houses no. 12 [Manchester].
- 7 ditto, 12 Pot Houses, Ancoats-lane.

Radcliffe, see Ratcliffe, Robert

- 2 **Rafftray, John**, Lees: severe sabre-cut on the left side of the head. A young man and tailor. Certified by Dr Earnshaw. 20/– final.
- 6 ditto but Raftery of Lees, near Oldham: aged 17 and a tailor. Severe sabre-cut on the left side of his head by a Yeoman. A month disabled. £1 received in relief.
- 7 ditto.

Raftery, see Rafftray, John

- 1 **Ramsbottom, Alice**, Blackford Bridge, near Bury: cut in the foot by a cavalryman.
- 6 ditto of Barlow Fold, near Bury: aged 50 with 9 children. Knocked down by a Yeoman Cavalry horse which trod on her feet; the left foot still very bad. Still lame. £2.2.0. received in relief.
- 7 ditto.

- 1 **Ratcliffe, [Elizabeth]**, wife of Robert, Stockport: thrown into a cellar and much bruised.
- 2 ditto with Elizabeth added: thrown into a cellar, her ankle and foot crushed. Was in the Infirmary 5 weeks. 20/–.
- 6 ditto of Heaton Norris: ankle and foot much crushed by falling in the cellar. 5 weeks disabled. Wife of Robert. Was five weeks in the Infirmary. £1 received in relief. Relief also from local committee.
- 7 ditto of Heaton Norris, Stockport.

- 4 **Ratcliffe, F. (male)**: badly wounded by trampling of cavalry.

- 1 **Ratcliffe [as Radcliffe], Robert**, Heaton Norris, Stockport: crushed.
- 2 ditto as Ratcliffe: thrown into a cellar and much bruised. Was 3 days at the Infirmary. A carpenter. 20/– final. Manchester Committee 40/–.
- 3 ditto as Ratcliffe of Stockport: bruised leg.
- 6 ditto as Ratcliffe of Heaton Norris: aged 47 with 2 children. Thrown into a cellar and body bruised. 3 weeks disabled. Was two days in the Infirmary. £1 received in relief. Relief also from local committee.
- 7 ditto.

6 **Ravey, Mary**, 333 Newton-lane [Manchester]: aged 36 with 4 children. Right arm bruised by being trampled on by the crowd. 2 days disabled. 10/– received in relief.
7 ditto.

---

1 **Redford, Thomas**, Middleton: sabred on the shoulder severely.
2 ditto, Wood-street, Middleton: shoulder blade very badly cut. Disabled 5 weeks. 30/– final. Manchester Committee 20/–.
4 ditto as Redford, T. (male): badly wounded by sabre or shot.
5 ditto. Also see Bamford, *Passages*, I, pp. 214–15: 'I found Redford's mother bathing his wound with warm milk and water ... It was a clean gash of about six inches in length and quite through the shoulder blade ... She asked who did it? and Tom mentioned a person; he said he knew him well (as did the mother) ... The wound having been linted and bound with sticking plaster, Tom put on his clothes, the slash in his coat having been sewed and the blood sponged off by a young woman'.
6 ditto of Middleton: aged 32 with 3 children. Severe sabre-cut on the right shoulder blade. 5 weeks disabled. Carried the Middleton flag. Says he was cut by young Oliver (Swan with Two Necks). £1.10.0. received in relief. Relief also from local committee.
7 ditto.
[In 1822 he brought an action against Birley and other Yeomanry Cavalry. See *Report on Redford v. Birley Trial*. For examination of his injuries, see pp. 195–7. For his part in commanding the drilling of reformers prior to Peterloo and his selection to carry the flag, see p. 213. At the trial he was described as a journeyman hatter, see p. 276, living in a Middleton cellar, see p. 96. According to Bamford (p. 210): 'Thomas Redford who carried the green banner held it aloft until the staff was cut in his hand and his shoulder was divided by the sabre of one of the Manchester Cavalry'.]

---

1 **Reeves, Robert**, 11 Pump-street [Manchester]: thrown down and much bruised.
2 ditto: thrown down and bruised. His wife ill. 2 weeks disabled, a very slight case. 10/– final.
6 ditto: aged 43 and a weaver. Thrown down and trampled on; bruised in the body. 2 weeks disabled. £1 received in relief.
7 ditto.

---

1 **Renshaw, William**, 23 Major-street [Manchester]: bruised in the arm and head.
2 ditto: bone in the arm broke. A poor man, a weaver, 45 years of age, a poor creature 20/– [20/– more in pencil].
4 ditto as Renshaw, W. (male): badly wounded by truncheons of Special Constables or crushed by multitude.
6 ditto: aged 65, a weaver with 2 children. Right hand and arm hurt by being trampled on. 6 weeks disabled. £2 received in relief.
7 ditto but Under 23 Major-street.

---

4 **Reynolds, E. (female)**: trampled on by cavalry – badly wounded.

---

1 **Reynolds, Hannah**, 9 Southern-street [Manchester]: ankle dislocated.

⁶ ditto: nailer. Wounded in the leg by Meagher who shot him from his window on 2 October. 5 weeks disabled. Was in the Infirmary. £2 received in relief.
⁷ ditto.

---

¹ **Robinson, Joseph**, Thomas-street, Stockport: forced down by the crowd and injured in the ankle.
⁶ ditto: aged 60 with 2 children. Trampled on by the crowd; right side and breast much hurt; spit blood for several days. 3 weeks disabled. £1.10.0. received in relief.
⁷ ditto.

---

¹ **Robinson, William**, White Cross Bank [Salford]: bruised.
³ Robinson, William: contusion on head. [In publication of list in *Wheeler's Manchester Chronicle*, 21 August, he is described as of Salford.
⁴ ditto as Robinson, W. (male): badly wounded by trampling of cavalry.
Pigot's Manchester and Salford Directory, 1819: shoemaker of 14 Wood-street, Salford.
Baines' Lancashire Directory, II, p. 256: shoemaker of 3 Spaw-street, Salford.

---

¹ **Roper, Catharine**, 14 German-street [Manchester]: trampled down by the cavalry and bruised.
² ditto but Kitty: leg bruised and trampled on. Still unwell. 20/– final. Manchester Committee 20/–.
⁶ ditto but Catherine of 3 German-street: aged 22. Right leg and ankle much hurt by a horse trampling on her when down. 2 months disabled. Still lame. £1 received in relief. Relief also from local committee.
⁷ ditto, 14 German-street, Newton-lane.
Pigot's Manchester and Salford Directory, 1819: William Ropert, whitesmith of 3 German-street.

---

¹ **Routledge, John**, Bellhouse's timber-yard [Chorlton Row]: a constable. Trampled upon by the cavalry and nearly killed.
² ditto but of Chorlton Row: a Special Constable. Was thrown down and trampled on in a dreadful manner at the charge up to the hustings. He lay insensible till the following Saturday and although attended by 5 doctors had his shoulder out for 6 weeks and is still disabled. Dr Taylor of Oldfield-lane set his shoulder and attends him now.
⁶ ditto of Chorlton Row. Thrown down and trampled on in a dreadful manner on the charge of the Yeomanry up to the hustings. Had his shoulder dislocated six weeks before it was discovered. Still disabled. A Special Constable. Was carried home in an insensible state and remained so till the following Saturday. Had his shoulder set at last by Dr Taylor who still attends him. A respectable man, a master mason. [No relief stated].
⁷ ditto [but no address].
Baines' Lancashire Directory, II, p. 257: stone and marble mason, resident of 5 Brook-street, Chorlton Row. *Pigot's Manchester and Salford Directory, 1817, 1819*: stone-mason of 9 Sackville-street.

¹ **Royle, Ann**, 6 Gravel-lane [Salford]: arms broken.
⁷ ditto.

¹ **Royle, Esther**, 5 Hanover-street [Manchester]: trampled upon and much bruised.
² ditto: thrown down and trampled on. A widow with 7 children. 20/–.
⁶ ditto: with 7 children. Thrown down and trampled on by the crowd, body bruised. 5 weeks disabled. £1 received in relief.
⁷ ditto.

⁴ **Sandforth, J. (male)**: wounded by sabre or shot.

⁶ **Sandiford, Jonathan**, Queen-street, Salford: aged 40 and a weaver with 2 children. Trampled on and right shoulder dislocated, thumb of his right hand broke, his leg cut against some steps. 5 weeks disabled. Unable to weave since but works on the roads for the parish for 3/6 per week. £2 received in relief.
⁷ ditto, 4 Withington Buildings, Queen-street, Salford.

¹ **Sands, Bernard**, 16 Pott-street [Manchester]: legs bruised and struck by the constables.
² ditto: trampled on and bruised. Hurt by straining his leg in getting over a wall. 20/– final.
⁶ ditto: aged 24 with 1 child. Body bruised by being trampled on by the crowd. Sprained his right leg in getting over a wall. 2 weeks disabled. £1 received in relief.
⁷ ditto.
Pigot's Manchester and Salford Directory, 1817: John Sands, weaver of same address.

¹ **Sands, Ellen**, 11 Portugal-street [Manchester]: hurt by a blow to the shoulder.
² ditto but 21 Portugal-street: thrown down and trampled on, a good deal bruised.
⁶ ditto as 21 Portugal-street: beaten in different parts of the body by the constables. 3 days disabled. [No relief stated.]

² **Scholes, Ann**, Block-lane, Oldham: thrown down and trampled on. Beat about the head with truncheons. 15/– final. Was left to Mr Taylor to enquire.
⁶ ditto of Block-lane, near Oldham: aged 36 with 3 children. Trampled on by the crowd and beat on the head by the constables. 2 weeks disabled. 15/– received in relief.
⁷ ditto.

¹ **Scholes, Samuel**, 2 Back Blackley [i.e. Blakely] -street [Manchester]: wounded in the right leg.
⁷ ditto.

² **Schofield, William**, 16 Old Mount [-street], St Michael's [Manchester]: cut on the temple, his hat cut. Saw both cuts. An elderly respectable man confined about 8 days. 40/– final.

⁶ ditto of 16 Old Mount-street: aged 63 and a weaver. Sabre-cut on his temples and one on the arm. 2 weeks disabled. £2 received in relief.
⁷ ditto, near St Michael's.

---

⁴ **Scolfield, G. (male)**: badly wounded by sabre or shot.

---

² **Scholfield, James**, Greenacres Moor [Oldham]: severe sabre-cut over the left eye about two inches long. Certified by Mr Taylor. 20/– final.
⁶ ditto of Greenacres Moor, near Oldham: aged 32 and a weaver with 2 children. Severe sabre-cut above the right eye, two inches long. 2 weeks disabled. £1 received in relief.
⁷ ditto.

---

² **Scholfield [Scolfield], John**, George-street, Oldham: head beat by truncheons. Was taken to the Infirmary senseless. 3 weeks disabled. 30/– final.
³ but Scolfield: slightly wounded – cured.
⁶ ditto as Schofield of George-street, Oldham: aged 29 with 2 children. Thrown down and trampled on by the crowd. Beat on the head by constables. 3 weeks disabled. Was taken to the Infirmary in an insensible state. £1.10.0. received in relief.
⁷ ditto.

---

² **Scott, Ann**, 5 Liverpool-road [Manchester]: a constable of the name of Ashworth kicked and bruised her a great deal. She was then taken into custody and kept 9 weeks. 60/– final.
⁶ ditto: beat and kicked by a constable, nine weeks imprisoned. See imprisoned cases. Statement B: imprisoned 9 weeks, then bailed. Discharged by proclamation, 30 October. [No relief.]
⁷ ditto.

---

² **Seal [Ceal], John**, Hurst Brook, near Ashton: knocked down and trampled on, his legs and body much bruised. 74 years of age. 40/– final.
⁶ ditto of Hurst Brook, near Ashton: aged 74 and a weaver. Knocked down and his legs and body much bruised. 1 month disabled. £2 received in relief.
⁷ ditto but Ceal of Osbrook. [Repeated as Seal.]

---

² **Seal [Ceal], Robert**, Hurst, near Ashton: knocked down by the Trumpeter and his knee hurt. Disabled a fortnight. 20/– final.
⁶ ditto of Hurst Brook, near Ashton: aged 43 and a weaver with 7 children. Knocked down and knee trampled on by crowd. 2 weeks disabled. £1 received in relief.
⁷ ditto but Ceal of Osbrook. [Repeated as Seal.]

---

¹ **Seed, Benjamin**, Temple-street, Chorlton [Row]: thigh broken and ankle cut.
² ditto but 7 John-street, Chorlton Row: this young man was thrown into a cellar with Mrs Partington. His thigh was broke, his ankle much cut by being thrust in at a window. A very genteel young man. Was 2 months in the Infirmary. 60/– [40/– more in pencil]. Manchester Committee 30/–, 30/–, to receive 10/– per week.

³ ditto of Manchester: fractured thigh.
⁶ ditto of 7 John-street, Ardwick: aged 24 with 2 children. Thrown into the cellar where Mrs Parkinson was killed. Had his thigh broken, his ankle much cut in being thrust in at a window. This young man appears in a declining state of health. Was 2 months in the Infirmary. £5 received in relief. Relief also from local committee.
⁷ ditto of Temple-street.
Pigot's Manchester and Salford Directory, 1819: spinner of Butterworth Court, Little Ormond-street. Ibid., 1824: spinner of Taylor's Place, Greek-street, Chorlton Row.

⁶ **Sellers, Betty**, 77 Hanover-street [Manchester]: aged 35 with 1 child. Beat on the head by constables, her lip cut. 1 week disabled. Says Owen the pawnbroker was one of them. £1 received in relief.

⁷ **Sellers, Mary**, 2 Silver-street [Manchester].

¹ **Settle, Samuel**, 4 Dimity-street, Newtown [Manchester]: wounded in the arm and leg.
² ditto: thrown down and trampled on, his left leg much hurt and ankle dislocated, right arm bruised. 20/– final.
⁶ ditto: aged 52 and a weaver. Ankle dislocated, left leg and right arm bruised, trampled on by cavalry horses. 3 weeks disabled. £1 received in relief.
⁷ ditto.

⁴ **Settle, T. (male)**: badly wounded by sabre or shot.
⁷ ditto as Thomas.

⁷ **Shaw, John**, Tottington.

¹ **Shawcross, Thomas**, Little Moor, Stockport: trampled upon and much bruised.
² ditto: thrown down and trampled on, right leg much hurt by a cavalry horse. 30/– final.
⁶ ditto: 53 and a hatter with 4 children. Thrown down and trod on by a horse, right leg much hurt. 5 weeks disabled. £1.10.0. received in relief.
⁷ ditto.

⁷ **Shelmerdine, Robert**, 6 Richmond Row, Pendleton.

² **Shields, John**, 15 Fetter-lane, Minshull-street [Manchester]: his hat was knocked off by a constable. Stooping to pick it up, a cavalry man made a back-handed cut at him which took a piece out of his head. 20/–.
² *repeated* with more detail: cut by a back-handed stroke from a Yeoman as he was picking up his hat which a Constable had knocked off. The sword took a piece the size of a half crown clean off his head. 20/– final.
⁴ ditto as Shields, J. (male): badly wounded by sabre or shot.
⁶ ditto of 15 Fetter-lane: aged 57 with 2 children. A weaver. Sabre-cut on the head.

2 weeks disabled. His hat was knocked off by a constable and whilst stooping to pick it up a yeoman cut him with back-handed blow. £1 received in relief.
⁷ ditto.

Sixsmith, see Smith, Wright

² **Slater, James**, Chestergate, Stockport: cut in the chin. A respectable man, a book-keeper. Was in the chapel yard attempting to get into a small outhouse. Found it full. 4 of the cavalry chased him round the trees and cut his hat to tatters. 20/– final.
⁶ ditto: aged 40 and a weaver with 6 children. Sabre-cut on his chin. Was in the Chapel yard and attempted to run into a small outhouse but found it full. Four of the Yeomanry chased him round the trees and cut his hat to tatters. £1 received in relief.
⁷ ditto.

¹ **Slater, William**, Ripponden: shoulder much bruised by the constables.
⁷ ditto.

¹ **Smith, Mr.**, Lockhouse, Failsworth: arm broken, leg much bruised and hurt in various other parts.
⁷ ditto, with addition of 'near Dob-lane'.

⁶ **Smith, James**, Eccles: aged 34 and a weaver with 3 children. Had his toe-nails torn off by being trampled on. Right side of his head and body bruised. 3 weeks disabled. £1.10.0. received in relief.
⁴ ditto as Smith, J. (male): wounded by trampling of cavalry.
⁷ ditto of Pitso Moor, Eccles.

¹ **Smith, James**, Gravelhole [i.e. Gravel Hole], near Middleton: severely wounded and bruised.
¹ *repeated*, with addition of 'Thornham' and 'sabred on the right hip and left leg and much bruised'.
² ditto but Gravelhole, near Royton: a sabre cut on the hip which he partly escaped by falling. Legs hurt. 40/– final. Has had from the Manchester Committee and Rochdale Committee £3.
⁵ ditto: bruised in the right leg and arm and badly cut on the hip.
⁶ ditto of Gravelhole, near Royton: aged 33 with 7 children. Sabre-cut on the right hip. Both legs hurt by being trampled on. 10 weeks disabled. 10/– received in relief. Relief also from local committee.
⁷ ditto of Gravelhole, Thornham.

⁷ **Smith, Jane**, 6 Ash-street, Boardman's Square [Miles Platting, Manchester].

¹ **Smith, Mary**, Failsworth: arm broken and otherwise much bruised.
⁴ ditto as Smith, M. (female): trampled on by cavalry – badly wounded.

⁶ ditto of Lockhouse, Failsworth: aged 46. Had her left arm broken, her left leg dreadfully hurt, a large lump has risen on her throat in consequence of its being trod upon. Still disabled. Is still in a bad state of health and will probably not recover. £2 received in relief. Relief also from local committee.

⁷ ditto of Dob-lane, Failsworth.

---

¹ **Smith [Sixsmith], Wright**, Stockport: trampled upon by the cavalry, and beat by the constables, left insensible on the field; taken to the Infirmary gates and from thence in a coach to Stockport.

² ditto but Sixsmith, Hamshaw-lane, Stockport: severely bruised on the head and body and the cap of his shoulder knocked off by a sword. A wife and 7 children. 40/– final. Manchester Committee 30/–.

⁶ ditto as Sixsmith of Hamshaw [i.e. Hempshaw] -lane Stockport: aged 12 [42?] and a weaver with 7 children. The cap of his shoulder knocked off by a sabre. Head and body bruised. 5 weeks disabled. £2 received in relief.

⁷ ditto as Smith of Stockport. [Repeated as Sixsmith].

---

¹ **Smithies, John**, Wood-street, Middleton.

² ditto: bruised and disabled near a fortnight. A weaver with 4 children. 20/– final.

⁶ ditto: aged 55 and a weaver with 4 children. Right arm bruised by a blow from the butt end of a musket. 2 weeks disabled. £1 received in relief.

⁷ ditto.

---

⁴ **Smithers, J. (male)**: badly wounded by sabre or shot.

---

¹ **Smithson, John**, Leeds.

⁷ ditto.

---

¹ **Southern, Richard**, 15 Mather-street [Manchester]: his hat cut by a sabre and wounded in the leg by the horses.

⁷ ditto.

---

¹ **Spencer, Ambrose**, 74 Newton-lane [Manchester]: trampled upon, hurt in the belly and back.

² ditto: thrown down and trampled on and a stab or cut near his eye. An old man of 75. 20/– final.

⁶ ditto: aged 75 and a weaver. Cut in the eye, thrown down and trampled on. 2 weeks disabled. £1 received in relief.

⁷ ditto.

---

¹ **Stafford, Charles**, third cellar in Boardman's Buildings, Canal-street [Manchester]: wounded.

² ditto, Boardman's Buildings, New Islington: thrown down and trampled on, his leg and heel much hurt. A single man. 25/– final.

⁶ ditto of 3 Boardman's Buildings: aged 21 and a stripper. Thrown down and trampled on. Left leg and right heel much hurt. 3 weeks disabled. £1.5.0. received in relief.
⁷ ditto.

---

² **Stafford, Samuel**, Charlestown, near Ashton: knocked down by a blow from a constable. Thumb cut. 10/- final.
⁶ ditto: a weaver. Knocked down by a blow on the shoulder and trampled on. His thumb cut. Disabled 1 week. 10/- received in relief.
⁷ ditto.

---

² **Stafford, William**, Charlestown, near Ashton: knocked down, his ankle hurt and trampled. A slight case. 10/- final.
⁶ ditto: knocked down and trampled on by crowd. Ankle hurt and body bruised. 10/- received in relief.
⁷ ditto.

---

¹ **Stanfield, John**, Taunton, near Ashton: knocked down and much crushed by the cavalry.
² ditto: thrown down and trampled on by Meagher, the trumpeter's horse. A wife and one child. 25 years of age. 20/- final.
⁶ ditto: thrown down and trampled on, body bruised and leg hurt. Disabled 1 week. £1 received in relief.
⁷ ditto.

---

⁴ **Statters, R. (male)**: badly wounded by sabre or shot.

---

⁴ **Steel, J. (male)**: wounded by truncheons of Special Constables or crushed by the multitude.

---

⁴ **Steel, R. (male)**: wounded by truncheons of Special Constables or crushed by multitude.

Stewart, see Stuart

---

⁶ **Stoddart, William**, Tollbar-street, Stockport: aged 46 and chair-mender. Thrown down, right leg and thigh hurt and body bruised. 2 weeks disabled. £1 received in relief.
⁷ ditto.

---

⁷ **Stoddart, William**, Lane End, near Newcastle.

---

¹ **Street, James**, Little Moss, near Ashton: sabred on the left side.
² ditto: thrown down and trampled on by the cavalry. 70 years of age, a weaver. 20/- final.
⁶ ditto of Little Moss, near Ashton: aged 70. Thrown down and trampled on, body bruised. £1 received in relief.
⁷ ditto.

² **Stuart [Stewart], William**, 51 Portugal-street [Manchester]: much trampled on. Very bad side and leg. A wound on his head. 40/– [£2 more pencilled in], Manchester Committee 20/–.
⁴ ditto but Stewart, W. (male): badly wounded by sabre or shot.
⁶ ditto as Stewart: aged 52 with 5 children. Sabre-cut on the head and three ribs dislocated. Had his legs badly trampled on. 2 months disabled. Was taken off the field for dead. A bad case. £4 received in relief. Relief also from local committee.
⁷ ditto as Stewart, 59 Portugal-street.

¹ **Taylor, Ann**, Little Moss [Ashton]: trampled upon by the cavalry.
² ditto, Little Moss, near Ashton: trampled on and her thigh hurt. A weaver. 2 months disabled. 50 years of age. 40/– final.
⁴ ditto as Taylor, A. (female): trampled on by cavalry – seriously wounded.
⁶ ditto: aged 50. Knocked down and trampled on, severely crushed in the body and thigh. 3 months disabled. £2 received in relief.
⁷ ditto.

¹ **Taylor, Daniel**, Haughton near Ashton: a severe sabre-wound on the head.
⁷ ditto.

¹ **Taylor, George**, 30 Church-street [Manchester]: wounded in the back.
² ditto: struck on the left shoulder by a ball from the 88th Regiment about 7 o'clock in Oldham-street. 20/– final.
⁴ ditto as Taylor, G. (male): wounded by sabre or shot.
⁶ ditto: aged 27 and a shoemaker with one child. Shot in the left shoulder by the 88th Reg. in Oldham-street. 2 weeks disabled. £1 received in relief.
⁷ ditto but under 30 Church-street.

² **Taylor, James**, Royton: trampled on by the cavalry, his right leg and thigh hurt. 3 weeks disabled. 20/– final.
⁶ ditto of Royton: weaver. Trampled on by a cavalry horse, right leg and thigh hurt. 3 weeks disabled. £1 received in relief.
⁷ ditto.

⁶ **Taylor, John**, 9 Eltoft-street [i.e. Elltoft-street, off Byron-street], Campfield [Manchester]: aged 37 and a cork-cutter with 1 child. Sabre-cut on the left side of his forehead. Breast and sides hurt by being trampled on. 2 weeks disabled. £1 received in relief.
⁷ ditto but 9 or 10 Eltoft-street, near Haymarket.

¹ **Taylor, John**, Withy Grove [Manchester]: wounded and bruised in the body.
⁴ ditto as Taylor, J. (male): wounded by sabre or shot.

⁶ **Taylor, Jonathan**, High Knowles [Knowl], near Lees: aged 29 and a weaver with 2 children. Sabre-cut on his nose and upper lip by a Yeoman, the toenails of his right foot trod off by a cavalry horse. 3 weeks disabled. £1.10.0. received in relief.
⁷ ditto of Higher Knowles, near Lees.

1. **Taylor, Sarah**, 13 Mather-street [Manchester]: cut on the head and very much bruised in other parts of the body. Was under the hustings and saw a man [i.e. John Ashton] killed who carried the black flag. F.n. 'the man who carried the Black Flag died on the 18th'.
2. ditto: cut on the head and bruised by one of the 15th [Hussars]. A queer customer. 20/–. Manchester Committee 20/–.
6. ditto of 33 Mather-street: aged 26. Sabre-cut on the head by one of the 15th Regiment. 3 weeks disabled. £1 received in relief.
7. ditto, 13 Mather-street, Ancoats-lane.

1. **Taylor, Thomas**, West-street, Oldham: wounded in the forehead.
2. ditto: knocked down and his forehead cut. Elbow much bruised by horses trampling. 15/– final.
4. ditto as Taylor, T. (male): badly wounded by trampling of cavalry.
6. ditto: aged 24 and a weaver with 2 children. Forehead cut and right elbow bruised by the trampling of cavalry horses. 2 weeks disabled. 15/– received in relief.
7. ditto.

1. **Taylor, William**, Boardman-lane, near Middleton: sabred severely.
2. ditto: a severe cut on the head. A wife and 2 children. Disabled a month. 40/– final. Manchester Committee 20/–.
3. ditto of Middleton: sabre-wound on head.
4. ditto as Taylor, W. (male): badly wounded by sabre or shot.
5. ditto: badly cut on the head and was for a considerable time a patient in the Infirmary.
6. ditto of Boardman-lane, near Middleton: aged 23 and a weaver with 2 children. Severe sabre-cut on the right side of the head. 5 weeks disabled. Was a week in the Infirmary. £2 received in relief.
7. ditto.
[Also see Baker, John.]

7. **Taylor, William**, Scotland Brook, Ashton-under-Lyne.

4. **Teasdale, J. (male)**: badly wounded by trampling of cavalry.

1. **Teeling, Betty**, Taylor's Buildings, near Peter Marshall's factory [Chorlton Row].
6. ditto of 16 Taylor's Buildings: aged 44 and a widow. Thrown into a cellar. Two fingers on the right hand broken and trampled on. 3 weeks disabled. £1 received in relief.
7. ditto but 16 Taylor's Buildings, near Peter Marsland's factory.

1. **Teesdale, Thomas**, Windsor [Salford]: badly wounded.
7. ditto.

1. **Thewles [Phurlis, Thulas, Thurlis], James**, Strinesfield, Saddleworth: severely trodden on the legs.
2. ditto but Phurlis, Staines-fold, Saddleworth: got the calf of his right leg trod from the bone. Unable to follow his employment 6 weeks. Certified by Dr Earnshaw. 40/– final.

⁶ ditto but Thulas, James, Stainesfold, Saddleworth: aged 35 and a weaver with 4 children. Right leg so dreadfully trampled on that the flesh was severed from the bone. 6 weeks disabled. £2 received in relief.

⁷ ditto but Thurlis of Strinesfold, Saddleworth.

---

¹ **Thompson [Thomson], John**, Miles Platting [Manchester]: sabred and much hurt.

² ditto: fingers badly cut. A decent looking man cut by the Manchester Yeomen Cavalry. 40/– final. Manchester Committee 20/–, 10/–.

⁴ ditto as Thompson, J. (male): wounded by sabre or shot.

⁶ ditto as Thomson of Miles Platting: aged 46 and a weaver. Severe sabre-cut on the right hand. 10 weeks disabled. Dr Basnett has some doubts whether he will have the proper use of his fingers again. £2 received in relief.

⁷ ditto.

---

¹ **Thompson, Thomas**, Cross Keys, Bolton: sabre-wound in the foot.
Pigot's Manchester and Salford Directory, 1824: straw-hat manufacturer, New Market Place.

---

¹ **Thompson, Thomas**, Bolton Moor: wounded in the eye.

⁷ ditto.

Pigot's Manchester and Salford Directory, 1821: cotton spinner of Edgeworth.

---

² **Thompson, William**, Middle-street, Moor-lane [Bolton]: thrown down and trampled on, stabbed in the right eye with a sabre. 20/– final.

⁶ ditto of Middle-street, Bolton: aged 24 and a weaver with 1 child. Stabbed in the right eye with the point of a sabre and trampled on. 2 weeks disabled. £1 received in relief.

⁷ ditto.

Thorley, see Thornley, William

---

⁴ **Thornbury, J. (male)**: wounded by trampling of cavalry.

---

¹ **Thornbury, Richard**, Irlams-o'-th'-Height: bruised and mangled severely.

² ditto: trampled on and hurt in his private parts. Was carried off the field. 20/–.

⁶ ditto: aged 22 and a labourer. Knocked down by the cavalry, body badly bruised. 5 weeks disabled. His eyes were so swelled he was nearly blind some time. £2 received in relief.

⁷ ditto.

---

¹ **Thornley [Thorley, Thorneley], William**, Droylsden: sabred in the head.

² ditto as Thorley of Droylesden Castle: a cut on the head, knocked down and trampled on. A single man about 30 years of age. 20/– final.

⁴ ditto as Thornley, W. (male): badly wounded by sabre or shot.

⁶ ditto as Thorneley of Droylsden Castle: sabre-cut on the head, trampled on and bruised. £1 received in relief.

⁷ ditto as Thornley.

¹ **Thorpe, Susannah**, 36 Primrose-street [Manchester]: bruised severely.
² ditto but Thorp: thrown down and internally bruised. Still disabled. A poor woman whose husband travels with small articles. 20/– [£2 more pencilled in].
⁴ ditto as Thorpe, S. (female): badly wounded by truncheons of the Special Constables or crushed by the multitude.
⁶ ditto: thrown down and trampled on, internally bruised. Still unwell. £3 received in relief.
⁷ ditto but 30 Primrose-street.
Pigot's Manchester and Salford Directory, 1819: Peter Thorpe, pedlar of 36 Primrose-street.

Thulas, see Thewles, James

¹ **Tilford, Andrew**, Campfield [Manchester]: dreadfully trampled upon and bruised.
⁷ ditto.
Pigot's Manchester and Salford Directory, 1817: victualler at the Roe Buck. *Baines' Lancashire Directory*, II, p. 273: the Roebuck, 3 Ashton-street, St John's.

⁷ **Tillotson, John**, Barn Brook Bridge, Bury.

¹ **Tinkler, Peter**, 26 Ancoats-street [Manchester]: wounded in the back and foot.
² ditto: thrown down and trampled on by the cavalry, his right foot was much hurt and is not yet well. A poor man. 20/– final. Manchester Committee 10/–.
⁶ ditto: aged 38 with two children. Knocked down and right foot trampled on and bruised by a cavalry horse. 3 weeks disabled. £1 received in relief. Relief also from local committee.
⁷ ditto.

¹ **Tinsley, Catherine**, 3 Little Pitt-street, Port-street [Manchester]: knocked down and trampled upon.
² ditto: thrown down and trampled on by the cavalry. Was seriously hurt. 30/– final.
⁶ ditto of 3 Little Pitt-street: with 2 children. Thrown down and trampled on, right knee hurt seriously. 2 weeks disabled. £1.10.0. received in relief.
⁷ ditto.

¹ **Tole, Patrick**, 42 Matthew [i.e. Mather] -street [Manchester]: dreadfully crushed in the body.
² ditto but 42 Mather-street, Ancoats: breast very bad and still under medical care. A very poor man. Very grateful. 40/– final [40/– pencilled in].
² *repeated* with addition of 'still under medical care, his breast crushed and a very poor man. 40/– final'.
⁶ ditto, 42 Mather-street: aged 46 and a weaver with 1 child. Thrown down and trampled on by crowd, internally injured. Still unwell. Still an out-patient of the Infirmary. £4 received in relief.
⁷ ditto, 42 Mather-street.

¹ **Tomlinson, James**, near Tinker's Gardens [Manchester]: trampled upon by the horses.
⁷ ditto.

² **Tomlinson, James**, Coldhurst-lane, Oldham: severe sabre-cut on the top of the head. A single man, a hatter. 15/– final. Left to Mr Taylor.
⁶ ditto: aged 23. Severe sabre-cut on the top of his head. Disabled for sometime. 15/– received in relief.
⁷ ditto.

⁶ **Tomlinson, John**, Pole-lane End, Failsworth: aged 38 and a weaver with 5 children. Knocked down and hip bruised by a cavalry horse. 5 days disabled. 15/– received in relief.
⁷ ditto.

¹ **Tomlinson, William**, Bullock Smithy [near Stockport]: sabre wound on the head and hand.
² ditto: sabre-cut in his face and right hand. His breeches were also cut. Disabled 5 weeks. 30/– final.
⁶ ditto of Bullocks Smithy: aged 24 and a cotton-printer with 2 children. Sabre-cut on the face and one on the right hand. 5 weeks disabled. [No relief stated.]
⁷ ditto.

² **Tonge [Tong], Thomas**, Church-street, Bolton: foot much crushed and cut with a sword as he was falling over some timber. Has not been able to work since. 60/– [£2 more pencilled in].
⁶ ditto but Tong of Church-street, Bolton: aged 24 and a labourer. Received a cut on the left foot as he fell over some timber and was severely crushed and trampled on. Still disabled. £4.15.0. received in relief.
⁷ ditto.

¹ **Travis John**, Taunton, near Ashton: wounded in the head.
² ditto: cut in the back of the head, a fortnight totally disabled. 47 years of age with a wife and 8 children. 40/– final.
⁴ ditto as Travis, J. (male): wounded by sabre or shot.
⁶ ditto of Taunton: aged 47 and a weaver with 8 children. Sabre-cut on the back part of his head. 3 weeks disabled. £2 received in relief.
⁷ ditto.

⁷ **Troy, William**, 4 Pump-street, Newton-lane [Manchester].

¹ **Trueman Sally**, Cornwall-street [Manchester].
⁷ ditto, 19 Cornwall-street.

¹ **Turner, David**, Birch, near Middleton: sabre-cut in the head.
⁵ ditto.

1. **Turner, Mary**, 35 Hanover-street [Manchester]: very badly bruised.
2. ditto: had her thumb put out and was trampled on by the cavalry. 20/– final.
6. ditto: with 2 children. Knocked down and trampled on by the cavalry. Thumb put out and body bruised. 2 weeks disabled. £1 received in relief.

---

1. **Tweedale, Thomas**, 5 Oak-street [off Hope-street], Oldfield-road [Salford]: cut on the back and left arm and had his right thigh broke.
7. ditto. [Repeated with '5 Back-street [?Back Oak-street], Oldfield-road'].

---

4. **Vekalfield, W. (male)**: badly wounded by sabre or shot.

Wallwork, Ann, see Walworth

---

1. **Walkden, James**, 74 Loom-street [Manchester]: stabbed in the back and bruised. Saw a Yeoman fire into a house.
2. ditto: shoulder bruised and struck by a horse. Ill-treated by the constables. 20/– final. Manchester Committee 20/–. The above person saw one of the Yeomen fire into a house.
6. ditto: with 2 children. Horse struck him down with his forefeet by a blow on the breast, his shoulder bruised also. Disabled for some time. An out-patient of the Infirmary. Saw one of the Yeomen fire into a house. Received £1 in relief.
7. ditto.

Walker, Ellen, see Evans, Ellen

---

1. **Walker, John**, Charlestown, near Ashton: leg much bruised.
2. ditto: leg trod on and thrown down. 50 years of age. Disabled ever since. 40/– final.
6. ditto: aged 50 and with 13 children. Knocked down and trampled on; his leg much hurt. 3 weeks disabled. £2 received in relief.
7. ditto.

---

1. **Walker, Peter**, Clayton Mill [Manchester]: sabred on the head.
4. ditto as Walker, P. (male): badly wounded by sabre or shot.
6. ditto of Clayton Mills: aged 60 and a labourer with 4 children. Sabre-cut on the head, which knocked him down when he was trampled on by the crowd. 3 weeks disabled. £1.10.0. received in relief.
7. ditto of Clayton Mills.

---

1. **Walker, Samuel**, Ashton: trampled upon.
2. ditto, Hurst, Ashton: trampled on, his ankle much hurt. A wife and 5 children. 20/– final.
4. ditto: wounded by truncheons of Special Constables or crushed by multitude.
6. ditto of Hurst, near Ashton: aged 52 and a weaver with 5 children. Trampled on and bruised in the body. Disabled for some time. £1 received in relief.
7. ditto of Charlestown, near Ashton.

⁴ **Wall, A.** (female): wounded by truncheons of the Special Constables or crushed by the multitude.

Walton, see Wolton, Charles

¹ **Walton, Mary**, Brick-croft, Rochdale: thrown down and trampled upon by the cavalry.
⁷ ditto.

⁴ **Walton, R. (male)**: badly wounded by trampling of cavalry.

¹ **Walworth [Wallwork, Wallworth], Ann**, Chancery-lane [Harper's Buildings, see ⁶ suggesting Chorlton Row]: bruised in the shoulder.
² ditto as Wallwork: thrown down and leg and thigh hurt. Manchester Committee 20/–.
⁴ ditto as Wallworth, A. (female): wounded badly by truncheons of Special Constables or crushed by the multitude.
⁶ ditto as Wallwork of Harper's Buildings [Chorlton Row], Chancery-lane: aged 50. Thrown down; right leg and thigh hurt. [no relief stated] Relief from local committee.
⁷ ditto as Wallwork, Chancery-lane.

⁷ **Warburton, Alice**, 6 Pump-street, Cropper-street [Manchester, near Miles Platting].

¹ **Warburton, Peter**, Bradshaw-street [Manchester]: seven times cut in the head.
² ditto, 7 Bradshaw-street, Shudehill: 7 bayonet and sabre wounds on the head and different parts of the body. Was in the 16th Dragoons and discharged twelve months. Confirmed by the neighbours. Was pinned against the wall and struck at. 40/– final.
⁴ ditto as Warburton, P. (male): badly wounded by sabre or shot.
⁶ ditto: aged 24 and a labourer. 7 bayonet and sabre-wounds on his head and different parts of his body by the 88th Regiment and 15th Hussars. 2 months disabled. Has been in the 16th Regiment of Dragoons. £2 received in relief.
⁷ ditto.

Ware, see Weir, James

¹ **Waring [Wareing], Elizabeth**, 17 Allum-street [Manchester]: sabred in the head and struck by a constable.
² ditto: knocked down by a constable, her head very bad. 5 weeks disabled. Trampled on. Lost her basket of fruit. One child. 20/– final.
⁴ ditto as Waring, E. (female): badly wounded by sabre or shot.
⁶ ditto as Wareing of 17 Allum-street: aged 32 with 1 child. Sabre-cut on the top of the head and much bruised. 5 weeks disabled. £1 received in relief.
⁷ ditto as Waring.

² **Washington, Charles**, 2 Back Blakely-street [Manchester]: wounded in the leg by the horse of one of the 15th Hussars who were cutting at the people in the Quakers' Chapel yard. A respectable man. 25/– final.

⁴ ditto as Washington, C. (male): wounded by truncheons of the Special Constables or crushed by the multitude.
⁶ ditto of 2 Back Blakeley-street: weaver. Hurt in the leg by one of the horses of the 15th Hussars, about six of whom he saw in the Chapel yard. 3 weeks disabled. £1 received in relief.
⁷ ditto.

---

⁶ **Webb, Isaac**, Lancashire Hall [i.e. Hill], Stockport: aged 23 and a spinner with 1 child. Knocked down and so much crushed that his eyes were blood-shot for a fortnight. 1 week disabled. 15/– received in relief.
⁷ ditto of Coulson's Row, Lancashire Hill, Stockport.

---

¹ **Webster, Daniel**, 11 Rigby's Buildings [Salford]: crushed in the body.
⁶ ditto but David, 11 Rigby's Buildings, Oldfield Road: aged 44 and a weaver with 5 children. Seriously injured by being crushed against the wall behind the hustings. 6 weeks disabled. £2 received in relief.
⁷ ditto but David, 11 Rigby's Buildings, top of Oldfield-road.

---

¹ **Webster, Thomas**, 11 Swan's Court, Canal-street [Salford]: disabled by a constable's bludgeon.
² ditto but Canal-street, Oldfield-road: knocked down by constables, his head much bruised. This young man's face on the right side was so much hurt that he has not been able to eat on that side since his head was swelled. 15/– final.
⁴ ditto as Webster, T. (male): badly wounded by truncheons of Special Constables or crushed by multitude.
⁶ ditto of Canal-street: aged 25 and a shoemaker with 1 child. Knocked down by a constable's truncheon; right side of his face so much bruised that he has not been able to eat on that side since. 1 week disabled. 15/– received in relief.
⁷ ditto.

---

¹ **Weir [Ware], James**, 11 Gun-street [Manchester]: bruised and trampled upon.
² ditto as Ware: thrown down and trampled on, his loins much bruised. A weaver and a poor man. Wife and child. 20/– final.
⁴ ditto as Weir, J. (male): badly wounded by trampling of cavalry.
⁶ ditto as Ware, 11 Gun-street: aged 36 and a weaver with 1 child. Trampled on and his loins much hurt by the cavalry. 3 weeks disabled. £1 received in relief.
⁷ ditto as Weir.

---

⁵ **Weir, James** of Gravel-hole in Thornham. [In Middleton party.]

---

² **Welch, Peter**, 56 Crapper-street [i.e. Cropper], Oldham-road [Manchester, near Miles Platting]: cut by Meagher. 22 years of age. Much bruised, 3 weeks disabled. 20/– final.
⁶ ditto of 56 Cropper-street: aged 22 and a weaver. Sabre-cut on his left wrist by Meagher. Trampled on and bruised. 3 weeks disabled. £1 received in relief.

- 1 **Whalley, Samuel**, 14 Silk-street [Manchester]: crushed and struck by cavalry, breast and back crushed.
- 4 ditto as Whalley, S. (male): badly wounded by sabre or shot.
- 6 ditto: a spinner. Trampled on by crowd and his breast and back crushed. 1 month disabled. £1 received in relief.
- 7 ditto.

- 1 **Wheeler, Ann**, 25 Spital-street, Newton-lane [Manchester]: breast and arm bruised by the constables.
- 2 ditto: beat by constables and her breast and arms much hurt. Married and has 2 children. 20/– final.
- 6 ditto of 25 Spital-street: aged 28 with 2 children. Beat and bruised by constables and trampled on by crowd. 3 weeks disabled. £1 received in relief.
- 7 ditto.

Whitaker, see Whittaker

- 1 **Whitby, Silas**, 1 Jackson's Buildings, James-street, near Oldfield-lane [Salford]: sabred in the shoulder and hand.
- 2 ditto but 1 James-street, Oldfield: cut on the shoulder and back of the hand. A dyer, a young man. 20/– final.
- 6 ditto of 1 James-street, Jackson's Buildings: aged 18 and a dyer. Severe sabre-cut on his right shoulder and one on his hand. 1 week disabled. Received £1 in relief.
- 7 ditto.

- 1 **White, Andrew**, 6 Sycamore-street [Manchester, near Miles Platting]: bruised very much.
- 4 ditto as White, A. (male): badly wounded by truncheons of Special Constables or crushed by multitude.

- 1 **Whitehead, Daniel [David]**, 9 Potter's Buildings, Chorlton Row: much crushed.
- 2 ditto as David: thrown down and trod on by horses, left arm much hurt. A month disabled. 20/– final.
- 6 ditto as Daniel: aged 56 and a weaver with 5 children. Left arm bruised by being trampled on by the cavalry. 1 month disabled. £1 received in relief.
- 7 ditto as Daniel.

- 1 **Whitehead, Daniel**, Woodbrook, Saddleworth: trampled upon and much bruised.
- 2 ditto: sabre-cut on his left arm. Was down and trampled on and for some time insensible. A weaver with 9 children. 40/– final.
- 6 ditto of Woodbrook, Saddleworth: aged 40 and with 9 children. Severe sabre-cut on the left shoulder, which knocked him down, and was much trampled on. 3 weeks disabled. Was carried off the ground in an insensible state. £2 received in relief.

- 1 **Whitehead, Henry**, Hurst, near Ashton: sabred very severely in the head, back and leg.

² ditto: horse sprung on him at the charge. Knocked down and bruised him. A cotton twister. 60 years of age. 20/– final.
⁶ ditto: aged 60. Horse sprung on him at the charge of cavalry and was knocked down and bruised. 2 weeks disabled. £1 received in relief.
⁷ ditto.

---

¹ **Whitehead, Martha**, Charlestown: her hand very ill crushed, completely disabled.
² ditto of Charlestown, Ashton: was hurt by the breaking of the railing, 3 weeks. Could not dress and undress. Fell into a cellar. Has one child. About 30 years of age. 20/– final.
⁶ ditto of Charlestown, near Ashton: aged 30 with 1 child. Fell into a cellar by the breaking of the rails. Was so much hurt she could not put on her clothes for three weeks. 3 weeks disabled. £1 relief received.
⁷ ditto.

---

⁶ **Whitnall, Sarah**, 11 Span Court, Artillery-street [Manchester]: aged 30 with 1 child. Internally injured by the pressure of the crowd. Both legs severely hurt. 3 weeks disabled. £1.10.0. received in relief.
⁷ ditto with addition of 'near St John's'.

---

¹ **Whittaker, Elias**, Failsworth.
⁶ ditto of Back-lane, Failsworth: aged 17. Left leg bruised by a cavalry horse treading on him. 1 week disabled. 10/– received in relief.
⁷ ditto.

---

¹ **Whittaker [Whitaker], Martha**, 28 Leigh-street [Manchester]: bruised and three ribs broken.
² ditto as Whitaker, 28 Leigh-street, Ancoats: crushed by the people, two ribs broken. Severely bruised and disabled ever since. 40/– [40/– more in pencil]. Manchester Committee 20/–, 10/–.
³ ditto as Whitaker of Manchester: very much bruised.
⁴ ditto as Whittaker, M. (female): trampled on by cavalry.
⁶ ditto as Whitaker of 28 Leigh-street: aged 45. Three ribs broken and inwardly crushed by being trampled on by crowd. Still disabled. £4 received in relief. Relief also from local committee.
⁷ ditto as Whitaker.
Pigot's Manchester and Salford Directory, 1819: weaver of 28 Lees-street, Great Ancoats Street.

---

¹ **Whittaker [Whitaker], Richard**, 12 Pot-street [Manchester]: trampled upon by the cavalry. Ribs and head crushed.
² ditto as Whitaker, 12 Pott-street: thrown down and bruised. Knocked over a piece of timber. 5 weeks disabled. A very respectable man. 40/– final. [Repeated with addition of 'trampled on'].
⁴ ditto as Whittaker, R. (male): wounded by sabre or shot.

⁶ ditto as Whitaker of 12 Pott-street: aged 47 and a weaver with 7 children. Thrown down over the timber and right leg hurt severely. 5 weeks disabled. £2 received in relief.
⁷ ditto as Whitaker, 12 Pot-street, Ancoats-lane.

---

¹ **Whitten, Johnson**, 17 Lees-street, Brown's Field [off Great Ancoats-street, Manchester]: cut in the leg and much bruised.
⁷ ditto.

---

² **Whitworth, James**, Ashton: knocked down and vomited blood. A poor weaver with 4 children. 20/– final.
⁶ ditto: a weaver with 4 children. Body trampled on and spat blood some days. Disabled for some time. Received £1 in relief.
⁷ ditto.

---

¹ **Whitworth, Joshua**, Hyde: killed by a shot.
³ ditto as Whitworth, J. (male): shot in the head, since dead.
⁶ ditto but Joseph: shot. [Dead in consequence].
⁶ *repeated* as Joseph of Hyde, near Stockport: aged 19. Killed by a musket-ball in Ancoat's-street on the evening of 16 August. Died at the Infirmary on following Friday. [An Inquest was held stating he was shot at New Cross. See *Manchester Massacre*, p. 29.] For his father, an old man of 70 principally supported by his son: £4 received in relief.
⁷ ditto.

---

⁷ **Wild, John**, Charlestown, Ashton.

---

¹ **Wilde [Wild], Mary**, Charlestown, near Ashton: severely bruised in the back and breast.
² ditto: knocked down and trampled on, breast and back hurt. A single woman 30 years of age. Fortnight disabled. 20/– final.
⁶ ditto but Wild of Charlestown: aged 30. Knocked down, breast and back crushed. Spat blood a fortnight. 2 weeks disabled. £1 received in relief.
⁷ ditto as Wild.

---

¹ **Wilde, Richard**, 9 Coope [i.e. Coop] -street [Manchester]: sabred in the head.
² ditto of 9 Coop-street, Swan-street: a boy cut in Oldham-street on the back of the head severely. The mother a widow with 4 children, one of which is deaf and dumb but going to the Asylum. 20/– [20/– more in pencil].
⁶ ditto: aged 14. Sabre-cut on the back of his head in Oldham-street by a Yeoman. 2 weeks disabled. His mother, a widow with 4 children, one of whom is deaf and dumb. £2 received in relief.
⁷ ditto, 9 Coope-street.

---

¹ **Williams, Edward**, Cropper-street [Manchester, near Miles Platting]: cut with a sabre.
⁷ ditto.
Pigot's Manchester and Salford Directory, 1819: batter of 17 Cropper-street.

- 4 **Willington, J. (male)**: badly wounded by sabre or shot.

- 1 **Wilmot [Wilmore], Sarah**, 6 Little Chapel-street, Bank Top [Manchester]: trampled upon by the people and by a horse.
- 4 ditto but Wilmore, S. (male): trampled on by cavalry. Badly wounded.
- 7 ditto as Wilmot.

Winn, see Wynne, John

Winn, see Wynne, William

- 1 **Withington, John**, 15 Ancoats-lane [Manchester]: sabred on the head.
- 7 ditto.

- 1 **Wolton, Mr**, Salford: severe contusions on the ear.
- 7 ditto but Walton, Charles of Worsley.

- 1 **Wood, David**, 18 Woolley [i.e. Worsley] -street, Bank Top [Manchester]: sabred on the head.
- 2 ditto, 18 Worseley-street, Bank Top: cut on the left arm and right knee. Was some time insensible under the people. 9 children under 15 years of age. 40/– final.
- 4 ditto as Wood, D. (male): wounded by sabre or shot.
- 6 ditto of 16 Worseley-street, Bank Top: aged 19 [39?] and a carder. Sabre-cut on the right knee. Fell into a cellar and was much bruised. 2 weeks disabled. £1 received in reward.
- 7 ditto of Wowley-street, Bank Top.

- 1 **Wood, Ellen**, 3 Portugal-street [Manchester]: bruised and trampled on.
- 2 ditto: thrown down and trampled on. A good deal bruised. 20/– [£2 more in pencil].
- 4 ditto as Wood, E. (female): badly wounded by truncheons of the Special Constables or crushed by the multitude.
- 6 ditto: aged 23 with 1 child. Knocked down and trampled on and bruised in the loins. Still poorly. Pregnant at the time. Since delivered of a child which is blind, the doctor says in consequence of her injuries. Received £3 in relief.
- 7 ditto.

Wood, see Woods, Oliver

- 1 **Wood, Peter**, 6 Blackley [i.e. Blakely] -street [Manchester]: trampled upon by the cavalry.
- 1 *repeated* with addition of 'sabre cut in the arm'.
- 2 ditto of Blakley-street: wounded in the right elbow by a sabre. His hat much cut. An old artillery man and expects a pension. 20/– final. Manchester Committee 30/–.
- 6 ditto, 17 Blakeley-street: aged 32 and a tailor. Sabred on the right arm just above the elbow. 5 weeks disabled. Was ten years in the Artillery. Says he was cut by Shelmerdine. £1 received in relief. Relief also from local committee.
- 7 ditto, 6 Blakely-street [*repeated*].

⁴ **Wood, R. (male)**: badly wounded by sabre or shot.

¹ **Woods [Wood], Oliver**, Middle-street, Bolton Moor: leg wounded by the cavalry.
² ditto: trampled on by horses. Thrown repeatedly. A fortnight disabled. 25/– final.
⁶ ditto as Wood of Bolton: aged 27 with 2 children. Thrown down repeatedly, right leg trampled on. 2 weeks disabled. £1.5.0. received in relief.
⁷ ditto as Woods.

² **Woolstonecroft [Woolstencraft], James**, Lees Hall, near Oldham: sabre-cut on the head. One above the left elbow and his breast bruised. An old man. 20/– final.
⁶ ditto but Woolstencraft of Lee's Hall, Oldham: aged 62 and a weaver with 10 children. A sabre-cut on his head and one on his left elbow. Breast crushed. 3 weeks disabled. £1 received in relief.
⁷ ditto as Woolstonecroft.

¹ **Worral [Worrall], Elizabeth**, 33 John-street, Salford: shoulder put out.
² ditto: shoulder put out and bruised. A single woman. Mother in decent circumstances. 20/– final.
⁴ ditto as Worral, E. (female): trampled on by cavalry.
⁶ ditto as Worrall: aged 28. Left shoulder dislocated by being thrown down and trampled on. 1 month disabled. £1 received in relief.
⁷ ditto.
Pigot's Manchester and Salford Directory, 1819: Charles Worrall, brick-setter at same address.

¹ **Wright, Mr**, a reporter from London: wounded on the shoulder and on the arm by a sabre.
⁷ ditto.

¹ **Wrigley, John**, Warrington: trampled upon by the cavalry.
² ditto: crushed by the crowd. So seriously hurt that he has been disabled 10 weeks. His wife attended and it was certified by some of the Manchester Committee. £3 final.
³ ditto: fractured ribs, much bruised. [According to *Wheeler's Manchester Chronicle*, 21 August, he was taken to Infirmary on Monday/Tuesday.]
⁶ ditto of Warrington. Knocked down and dangerously crushed in the body by the crowd. 10 weeks disabled. £3.5.0. received in relief.
⁷ ditto, 6 Fennel-street, Warrington.

¹ **Wrigley, Joseph**, Quick, Saddleworth: trampled upon by the horses. Was with John Lees of Oldham when he was wounded.
² ditto: knocked down and trampled on. Was injured internally, a month unable to work. Certified by Dr Earnshaw. This man knew James [i.e. John] Lees and saw him cut. 40/– final.
⁶ ditto: aged 36 and with 5 children. Knocked down and seriously injured internally.

1 month disabled. Dr Evans has certified this to be a very dangerous case. £2 received in relief.
⁷ ditto as Joshua.
[see *Report*, Lees Inquest, pp. 38–44, which shows that he fell off the hustings, and had his hat cut by a Yeoman. On the day he had with him the handle of an old umbrella to serve as a walking stick.]

---

¹ **Wroe, Edward**, Pendlebury: wounded in the leg and trampled on by the cavalry.
⁷ ditto.

---

¹ **Wynne [Winn], John**, Royle-street, Stockport: wounded in the breast and legs.
¹ *repeated* with addition of 'trampled upon and bruised'.
² ditto: right leg cut, knocked down and much bruised. An old man of 75 years. A tailor. 30/– final. Manchester Committee 30/–.
⁴ ditto as Winn, J. (male): 75 years. Badly wounded by sabre or shot.
⁶ ditto as Winn of Royle-street, Stockport: aged 75 and a tailor. Knocked down, right leg and arms dreadfully cut and bruised. 5 weeks disabled. £1.10.0. received in relief.
⁷ ditto.

---

¹ **Wynne [Winn], William**, Stockport: trampled upon and leg wounded.
² ditto, Rosemary-lane, Stockport: thrown down and trampled on left leg. Much hurt by the horses. 31/–.
⁶ ditto as Winn, William, Rosemary-lane, Stockport: aged 69. Left leg hurt by a horse treading upon it. 5 weeks disabled. £1.11.0. received in relief.
⁷ ditto.

Index

As the casualty lists are arranged alphabetically, this index is confined to chapter I.

Allcard, Samuel, casualty 52–3
Ancoats, Manchester 18, 25, 50, 54
Ardwick, parish of Manchester 19, 22
aristocracy *see* gentlemen
artillery 3
    see also firearms; Royal Horse Artillery
Ashton, John, casualty 26, 34, 40, 45, 47
Ashton-under-Lyne, Lancashire 1–2, 10–11, 13–14, 17, 19, 22–3, 38, 49, 50
Ashworth, John, casualty 12, 44, 47, 52

Bamford, Samuel, reformer 8, 11, 28–9
Bank Top, Manchester 18
banners *see* flags
Bardsley, Ann, casualty 32, 41
Barlow, Hannah, casualty 33
Barnes, William, casualty 53
barracks, Manchester 50, 52
Barrett, James, casualty 41
Barron, Thomas, casualty 34
Barton-upon-Irwell, Lancashire 19, 45
Batsan, William, casualty 54–5
bayoneting 2, 3, 31–2, 45, 47, 53–5
Bee, Malcolm and Walter, historians 5, 13, 24–5, 32, 47–9, 55
Bell, John, casualty 29
benefit societies 11–12
Berry, James, casualty 34
Billinge, William, casualty 56
Billington, Thomas, casualty 34
Birley, Hugh, commander in Manchester Yeomanry 12
Birmingham 16, 55
Black, John, casualty 34

Blackburn, Lancashire 19, 23, 38
Blackley, parish of Manchester 8, 19, 22
Blakely Street (now Dantzig Street) 15
blanketeers' meeting (10 March 1817) 37
Bolton, Lancashire 1–2, 19, 22
Bond, Elizabeth, casualty 33
Bootle Street, Manchester 49–50
Boulter, John, casualty 34, 54
Boston, near Ashton 23
Bradshaw, William, casualty 44–5
Brazenose Street, Manchester 50
Bridge Street, Manchester 44
Brierley, John, casualty 41
Brierly, Joseph, eye-witness 11
Brookes, John, casualty 54
Brookes, Joseph, casualty 54
Brown, Thomas, casualty 41, 52
Buckley, Thomas, casualty 45, 47, 54
Bullock's Smithy, near Stockport 23
Burnley, Lancashire 19
Burslem, Staffordshire 23
Bury, Lancashire 1–2, 11, 13, 15, 17, 19, 22–3, 40, 50
Butterworth, William, casualty 56

Campbell, Robert, casualty 12, 44–5
caps of liberty 1–2, 5, 26, 34, 37, 40
Carbett, Robert, casualty 29
Carlile, Richard, radical journalist and publisher 24, 31, 38
Cartwright, John, reformer xi
cavalry 2, 10, 12, 15, 30–7, 40–1, 44–7, 49–50, 52–3, 55
    see also Hussars; Manchester and Salford Yeomanry Cavalry;

Cheshire Yeomanry Cavalry
censuses 22, 29, 48
Chadderton, Lancashire 1, 11, 19, 45
Chadkirk, near Stockport 23
Chambers, Elizabeth, casualty 33
Chapman, James, casualty 12
Charlestown, near Ashton 23
Cheadle, Cheshire 2
Cheetham, parish of Manchester 19, 22
Cheshire Yeomanry Cavalry 50, 52–3
Chesworth, James, casualty 12, 52
children, 13, 36
    see also William Farren; William Fildes
Chiswall, James, casualty 34
Chorlton Row see Chorlton-upon-Medlock
Chorlton-upon-Medlock, parish of
    Manchester 19, 22, 28
Church Street, Manchester 9
Clark, Thomas, casualty 41
Clarke, Jonathan, casualty 12
clergy 1, 26, 38
Coates, John, casualty 34
Cobbett, William, reformer, x
Coil, Dennis, casualty 29
Collinge, Ann, casualty 8
Collyhurst, parish of Manchester 28
compensation see relief
constables 2, 30–1, 40, 45–7
    see also Special Constables
Cooper Street, Manchester 44
corn laws 25–6
Crompton, James, casualty 45–7
Crompton, Lancashire 10–11
Cropper Street, Manchester 18
crowd, the 1–2, 6–7, 12–13, 18, 31, 33–4,
    36–7, 39–41, 43–4, 46, 48–9, 53–4
Crumpsall, parish of Manchester 19, 22

Dantzig Street see Blakely Street
Darbyshire, Robert, casualty 12, 52
Darwin, Lancashire 19
Dawson, Edmund, casualty 26, 40, 45, 47
Dawson, William, casualty 26, 40, 45, 47
Deansgate, Manchester 13, 15–16, 18, 47
deaths 9–10, 44–6

Delph, Saddleworth 12
Dickinson Street, Manchester 50, 54
Dimity Street, Manchester 29
dismissal from work 11–12
Dixon Street, Manchester 29
Downes, Margaret, casualty 32, 45, 47
Droylesden, near Ashton 19, 23
Dukinfield, parish of Stockport 19, 23
dyers 25

Eccles, Lancashire 19, 22
Edgeley, near Stockport 23
Edwards, John, casualty 34
88th Foot 50, 53–5
elderly casualties 35–6
Elliott, John, casualty 36
Entwisle, Roger, eye-witness 11, 17
Entwistle, William, casualty 34
Evans, Ellen, casualty 8
Evans, Mary, casualty 54
Evans, William, casualty 12, 44–5, 52

factory workers, factories 25, 40
Failsworth, Lancashire 1, 11, 19, 22
Farren, Elizabeth, casualty 32–3, 56
Farren, William, casualty 3
Fell, John, eye-witness 53
female reform societies, female reformers
    1–2, 5, 24, 33
Fildes, Mary, casualty 1–2, 5, 33, 40
Fildes, William, casualty 44–5, 47
firearms 3, 31, 33–4, 44–5, 47, 54, 56
Flag Row, Manchester 29
flags 1–2, 5, 19, 26–7, 29, 33–4, 37, 40
Flixton, Lancashire 19
Foster, John, casualty 34, 47
France 35, 38
Friends' Meeting House 15, 41, 47, 49,
    53–5
Froggatt, Henry, casualty 12, 52

Gaunt, Elizabeth, casualty 33, 56
Gee-cross, near Stockport 23
gentlemen, gentility 1, 26, 37–8, 56
George Leigh Street 18, 54

INDEX

The Globe 7
Goodwin, John, casualty 54
Goodwin, Margaret, casualty 33, 56
Gorton, parish of Manchester 19
Graves, Frederick, casualty 34
Graves, Sarah, casualty 41
Great Ancoats Street, Manchester 18, 28, 39
Greaves, James, casualty 53
Green, James, casualty 56

Hall, Ann, casualty 33
Hall, Daniel, casualty 41
Hall, Robert, eye-witness 18
Hall, R.W. of Metropolitan and Central Relief Committee 9
Hardman, John, casualty 54
Hargreaves, John, casualty 47
Harper, Charles, casualty 29
Harrison, William, casualty 12
Harrison, William, eye-witness 11
Harvey, Ellen, casualty 32
Harvey, Isabella, casualty 36, 41
Haslam, James, journalist 26
hatters 25
Haughton Green, near Ashton 23
Hay, Rev. William, Salford magistrate 6, 18
Heath, James, eye-witness 11
Heaton Norris, parish of Manchester 19, 22
Henry Hunt's Addresses to Radical Reformers 8
Heptonstall, Joseph, casualty 12
Heys, Mary, casualty 45–7
Heywood, Alice, casualty 32
Hibbert, John, eye-witness 11
Higgins, James, casualty 34
Horton, Mary, casualty 33
Howard, Mark, casualty 54
Howarth, Sarah, casualty 32
Huddersfield, Yorkshire 23
Hulme, parish of Manchester 19, 22, 45, 50
Hulton, William, chief magistrate 6, 8, 11, 44

Hunt, Henry, reformer x–xi, 1, 8, 15–16, 25–6, 28, 30, 37–9, 49, 54–6
Hurdies, William, casualty 54
Hurst, near Ashton 23
Hussars 43, 50, 52–3, 55
hustings (speakers' platform) 2, 13–15
Hyde, parish of Stockport 23

imprisonment 9, 11–12, 46, 53, 56
   see also New Bailey Prison
infantry 2, 34, 53–5
Irish casualties 28–9, 40
Irish town, Manchester *see* Newtown
Irlams o' th' Height, Lancashire 19

Jackson, Samuel, casualty 48, 56
Jackson's Row, Manchester 47
Jerron, William, casualty 41
Jervis, Mary, casualty 33, 56
Jolliffe, Sir William 43, 50, 53
Jones, Edward, casualty 48
Jones, Joseph, casualty 34
Jones, Mary, casualty 32, 47
Jones, Sarah, casualty 33, 45–7
Jones, Thomas, casualty 41
Johnson, Joseph, reformer 28

Kay, Samuel, casualty 34
Keenan, Sarah, casualty 33
Kelly, Thomas, casualty 56
Kenyon, Alice, casualty 56
Kershaw, Thomas, casualty 8
Kidd, Alan, historian 44

labourers 25
Lancaster, Edward, casualty 36
Lancaster 19
Leeds, Yorkshire 23, 55
Lees, James, casualty 12, 34, 53
Lees, John, casualty 45, 47
Lees, Lancashire 10
Leigh, John, casualty 56
Leigh, William, casualty 56
Leigh, Lancashire 23, 38
Levenshulme, parish of Manchester 19

Little Moor, near Stockport 23
Littlemoss, near Ashton 23
Liverpool 2, 23, 55
Liverpool Mercury 18
London 16, 55
Loom Street, Manchester 18
Lower Mosley Street 50

McCabe, Owen, casualty 56
Macclesfield, Cheshire 23, 38
Maccobe, Rose, casualty 36
Macconnel, James, casualty 29
McFadden, Samuel, casualty 12, 52
Macglade, Matthew, casualty 34
Mackennagh, Mary, casualty 36
McMaghan, Bernard, casualty 34
magistrates of Manchester and Salford 2, 6, 31, 33, 35, 37, 39, 44, 46, 52
  see also Hay; Hulton
Manchester, manorial borough of
  casualties 10, 15–16, 18–19, 22, 45–6
  Irish residents of 28–9
  loyalism in 38–40
  population of 48
  powerloom threat 25
  presence on field 15–18, 50
  reformers in 5, 16, 37–8
  rioting in 39–40
Manchester Courier 6
Manchester Female Reform Society 1–2, 40
Manchester Infirmary 2, 6, 12, 56
Manchester Observer 2, 6, 7–8, 10, 39–40
Manchester Relief Committee 8–9, 11–12, 16
Manchester and Salford Yeomanry Cavalry 12, 32–3, 41, 50, 52–3, 55
manufacturers 32, 38, 50
Marsh, William, casualty 12
Metropolitan and Central Relief Committee 8–10, 11
  see also relief of victims
Middleton, Lancashire 1, 8, 11, 13–17, 19, 22–3, 40, 50
Miles Platting, Manchester 18–19

Millard John, casualty 56
Miller Street, Manchester 15
Mills, J., eye-witness 11
monarchy, attitudes to 26, 38
Monks, Bridget, casualty 32
Moores, William, casualty 54
Moorhouse, James, reformer 11
Morris, William, eye-witness 11
Morton, Sarah, casualty 32
Mosley Street, Manchester 13, 16
  see also Lower Mosley Street
Mossley, Lancashire 10
Mount Street, Manchester 5, 13, 15, 48–9, 52–3
muskets 34, 54
  see also firearms
Mutrie, Robert, eye-witness 13, 17–18

Neil, Arthur, casualty 45–6, 48, 56
New Bailey Prison, Salford 46
  see also imprisonment
New Cross, Manchester 18, 25, 28, 39–40, 44, 46, 53
Newcastle-under-Lyne, Staffordshire 23
Newton Lane *see* Oldham Road
Newtown, Manchester 18, 19, 28–9
Northwich, Cheshire 23
Norwich, Norfolk 55
Nuttel, John, casualty 41

Ogden, Joseph, casualty 54
Oldham, Lancashire 1, 7, 10, 11, 13–14, 16–17, 19, 22–3, 38, 45–6, 49, 50
Oldham Road (Newton Lane), Manchester 39, 45–6
Oldham Street, Manchester 47
O'Neale, Betty, casualty 12
Owen, Edward, eye-witness 18

parliamentary reform, reformers 1–2, 6, 16, 19, 23, 25–9, 37–9, 41, 48, 56
Partington, Martha, casualty 44–5, 48, 56
Pearson, Charles, reformer 6–7
Peel, Ann, casualty 33

INDEX

Pendlebury, Lancashire 19
Pendleton, Lancashire 12, 19, 22
Peter Street, Manchester 13, 48–9
Peterloo Massacre, journal 7, 41–2
petitioning 37
Petty, Mr, casualty 12, 52
Piccadilly, Manchester 13, 16, 18, 47
Pimblet, John, casualty 54
police 5, 31, 35, 37, 44–5, 47
   see also constables; Special Constables
Pollitt, Stephen, casualty 41
Portland Street, Newtown in Manchester 29
powerlooms 25
Prentice, Archibald, reformer 9, 10
Prestwich, Lancashire 19
processions, incoming 11, 13–19, 28, 37
professional men 32, 50
publicans 32, 39, 50
Pump Street, Manchester 18

Quaker Meeting House *see* Friends' Meeting House
Quick, Yorkshire *see* Saddleworth

Radical Reform 16, 38
   see also Hunt
Railton, John, eye-witness 52, 54
Rayner, Joshua of Metropolitan and Central Relief Committee 9
Read, Donald, historian 10, 42–4
Red Bank, Manchester 28
Reddish, parish of Manchester 12, 19
Redford, Thomas, casualty 34, 40
reform societies *see* parliamentary reform
relief of victims 8–9, 12, 55–6
revolution, fears of 2, 32, 38–9
Reynolds, Patrick, casualty 29, 47
Rhodes, John, casualty 45, 47, 56
Richardson, James, casualty 47
Ripponden, Yorkshire 23
Rochdale, Lancashire 1, 8, 10–11, 14–17, 19, 22, 38, 50
Rochdale Relief Committee 8, 10
Rothwell, Thomas, eye-witness 11

Routledge, John, casualty 12, 52
Royal Horse Artillery 50
Royton, Lancashire 1, 10–11, 13, 19, 22
Rusholme, parish of Manchester 19, 22

sabres, use of 2–3, 6–7, 9–10, 12, 31–2, 34, 36, 40–1, 44–5, 47, 50, 52–4, 56
Saddleworth, Lancashire and Yorkshire 1, 10–11, 19, 22–3, 26–7, 40, 45, 48
St John's Church, Manchester 20, 51, 54
St Michael's Church, Manchester 15, 18, 21, 28, 54
'Saint Patrick's Day in the Morning' 29
St Peter's Field, Manchester 1, 15–16, 19, 28–9, 37–8, 47–9, 53–4
Salford, Lancashire 1, 12, 19, 22, 28, 39, 48
Salford Infirmary 6
Scholes, Ann, casualty 33
Scholfield, John, casualty 34
Scotland Bridge, Manchester 28
Scott, Ann, casualty 31, 56
Scottish casualties 28
Seed, Benjamin, casualty 56
Service, G.W. of Metropolitan and Central Relief Committee 9
Settle, Samuel, casualty 29
Shelley, Percy Bysshe, reformer xii
Sherwin, William, radical journalist and publisher 38
Shields, John, casualty 41
shoemakers 25
shopkeepers of Manchester 32, 38, 39, 50
Shudehill, Manchester 13, 16, 18
Shuttleworth, John, eye-witness 18
Sidmouth, Lord, Home Secretary 6
Slater, James, casualty 41
Smallshaw Green, near Ashton 23
Smedley cottage 28
Smith, John, Liverpool journalist 18
Smithies, John, casualty 54
South Street, Manchester 49
Southern Richard, casualty 41
Special Constables 12, 33–4, 39, 44–7, 50, 52

Spenceans 38
spinners 28, 40
The Star 2
sticks, walking 37, 49
Stockport, Cheshire 1–2, 11–14, 17, 19, 22–3, 28, 38, 49, 50
Stretford, parish of Manchester 19
Style Street, Manchester 54
Swan Street, Manchester 16, 39

tailors 25
Taunton, near Ashton 23
taxation, complaint against 25–6
Taylor, John Edward, reformer 9, 11–12
Taylor, Sarah, casualty 53
textile industry 23
    see also spinners; weavers; powerlooms
Thelwall, William, eye-witness 18
31st Foot 50–1
Thompson, E.P., historian 25, 28
The Times 6
top hats, attacks on 37, 40–41
trades unions 25
Travis, Joseph, eye-witness 11
truncheons, use of 2–3, 31–4, 45, 47
Trevelyan, G.M., historian 4, 5
Tyldesley, Lancashire 19

Unsworth, Lancashire 19

Vauxhall Gardens (now Queens Park, near Smedley) 28

Wade, John, reformer 42, 49

Wain, James, casualty 8
Walker, Ellen *see* Evans, Ellen
walking sticks *see* sticks
Walmsley, Robert, historian 44
Warburton, Peter, casualty 34, 53–4
Warrington, Cheshire 23
Washington, Charles, casualty 53
weavers, handloom 25–9, 37, 40
Webster, Thomas, casualty 34
Weir, James, casualty 8
Welsh casualties 28
Wheeler's Manchester Chronicle 6
Whitefield, Lancashire 19, 45
Whitfield, Captain 53
Whitworth, Joshua, casualty 44–5, 56
Wigan, Lancashire 23
Wilde, Richard, casualty 36, 47
Windmill Street, Manchester 5, 13, 15, 47–50, 52
Wolseley, Sir Charles, reformer xi, 6–7
women 1–2, 5, 7, 9, 10, 13, 16, 24–5, 30–5, 37, 40, 55–6
Wood, Peter, casualty 41
Woodworth, Thomas, Special Constable 45–6
Worsley, Lancashire 19
Wrigley, Joss, veteran of Peterloo 26–7
Wroe, James, radical journalist 5, 7–8, 10, 16, 41–2, 52
Yeomanry Cavalry *see* Cheshire Yeomanry Cavalry; Manchester and Salford Yeomanry Cavalry
youth casualties 35–6